Detroit Monographs in Musicology/Studies in Music, No. 43

Editors
J. Bunker Clark† and Susan Parisi
University of Kansas and University of Illinois

NEGOTIATING ETHNIC BOUNDARIES

Polish American Music in Detroit

by
Paula Savaglio

HARMONIE PARK PRESS
Warren, Michigan   2004

Cover:
"Polka Dance"
Courtesy of *Illustrated London News*, 23 March 1844, 84

Copyright © 2004 by Harmonie Park Press

Printed and bound in the United States of America
Published by
Harmonie Park Press
23630 Pinewood
Warren, Michigan 48091

Publications Director, Elaine J. Gorzelski
Editors, J. Bunker Clark† and Susan Parisi
Cover design, Mitchell Groters and Nathan Turner
Book design and Typographer, Colleen McRorie

Library of Congress Cataloging-in-Publication Data

Savaglio, Paula, 1961-
  Negotiating ethnic boundaries : Polish American music in Detroit / by Paula Savaglio.
    p. cm. — (Detroit monographs in musicology/Studies in music ; no. 43)
  Includes bibliographical references (p.) and index.
  Contents: Jostling for a place in the crowd : pre- and post-war Polish-American settlements—The Polish church, the sum of all its members : music and identity in the church—We brought what we could, we'll keep what's good : cultural clubs and secular choirs, Polish or English?—Lutnia : the story of one choir—You wanna dance, or something? : the polka in the mainstream and the ethnic market—We'll have a little swing with that polka : dance bands from the 1920s to the 1950s—So what'll it be (rock, country, or Polish?) : dance bands since the 1950s—United we stand : the establishment of a polka industry—I'm not with him : music and identity.
  ISBN 0-89990-126-3
  1. Polish Americans—Michigan—Detroit—Music—History and criticism. 2. Polish American musicians—Michigan—Detroit. I. Title: Polish American music in Detroit. II. Title. III. Series.

ML3560.P65S28 2004
780$'$.89$'$9185073—dc22

2004054058

To my family and friends
for all of the music

Contents

List of Illustrations ix
List of Music Examples xi
Preface xiii

1   Introduction 3

2   Jostling for a Place in the Crowd 13
Pre- and Post-War Polish-American Settlements

3   The Polish Church: The Sum of All Its Members 25
Music and Identity in the Church

4   We Brought What We Could. We'll Keep What's Good. 39
Cultural Clubs and Secular Choirs: Polish or English?

5   Lutnia 57
The Story of One Choir

6   You Wanna Dance, or Something? 71
The Polka in the Mainstream and the Ethnic Market

7   We'll Have a Little Swing with that Polka 81
Dance Bands from the 1920s to the 1950s

8   So What'll It Be? (Rock, Country, or Polish?) 107
Dance Bands since the 1950s

9	United We Stand	121
	The Establishment of a Polka Industry	
10	I'm Not with Him	131
	Music and Identity	
	Bibliography	145
	Books and Journal Articles	145
	Articles in Newspapers and Magazines	155
	Internet Sources	157
	Discography	157
	Index	159

Illustrations

Figures

1.1	A street in Hamtramck	*facing* 6
1.2	Mural of Polish Folk Dancers in John Paul II Square, Hamtramck	*facing* 7
3.1	St. Florian Church, Hamtramck	*facing* 30
3.2	Sweetest Heart of Mary, Detroit	*facing* 31
3.3	Sweetest Heart of Mary, pulpit	*facing* 31
4.1	Polish American Congress storefront, Hamtramck	*facing* 42
4.2	Polish Legion of American Veterans Post 10	*facing* 42
4.3	Members of the Club Filarets	*facing* 43
4.4	Suburban Polonia of Sterling Heights	*facing* 43
5.1	Lutnia Chorus during its heyday	56
6.1	"Polka Dance"	73
7.1	Bill Schwartz, Syl, Ted, and Frank Wienclaw	*facing* 98
8.1	Part Books of Polish dance band music	106
9.1	Senate Cafe, Hamtramck	120

Table

6.1	Polkas Recorded and Designated for a Particular Ethnic Group	78

Music Examples

Examples

3.1	Serdeczna Matko	34
3.2	Witaj Pani	34
3.3	Zawitaj, Królowo	35
3.4	Kiedy ranne wstają zorza	35
3.5	Wysławiajmy Chrysta Pana	36
3.6	Matko Pocieszenia	36
4.1	"Kukułeczka," from the library of the Polonaise Chorale	53
4.2	Excerpt from "Marsz kosynierow" by J. Stefani, arranged by Karol Hofman	54
7.1	The mazurka	82
7.2	The sister of the mazukra, the mazur	82
7.3	The oberek	83
7.4	The krakowiak	83
7.5	The sztajerek	84
7.6	The polka, subtitled goralska	84
7.7	Transcription no. 1, "Bachelor's Polka"	91
7.8	Transcription no. 2, "Kochanka"	92
7.9	Transcription no. 3, "Uncle"	92-93
7.10	Transcription no. 4, "Trzymajmy Się Polka"	93-94

Preface

In the course of conducting fieldwork we might spend years amassing all sorts of data; we continually make decisions about which facts or observations are most pertinent to the topic at hand, and which may be set aside. Usually, in the process, we stumble upon a number of key ideas or concepts. And, while we may be fortunate enough immediately to recognize the significance of a particular idea, there are times, I am sure, when we toss that very idea impatiently aside in our single-minded pursuit of our original plan. When I began researching Polish-American music, I determinedly turned my back on all styles of music that didn't seem to "fit"—styles that originated somewhere outside of the ethnic group. Clearly, I thought, some music required a closer look, while other pieces fell outside the realm of Polish music. The polka band playing Creedence Clearwater Revival's "Proud Mary," the Polish choir's holiday performance of "White Christmas," the inclusion of Irish jigs in my grandfather's Polish fiddle repertory—these were all anomalies to be ignored.

I don't recall when exactly I began to broaden my definition of Polish-American music, but sometime in the midst of conversing with the musicians themselves, I realized the significance of a *mixture* of genres to the musicians' livelihood, and to the lives of their audience. Irish reels, mariachi trumpets, "God Bless America," Mozart, and country-western songs are in fact integral to Polish-American choral and polka band repertories. From the moment this concept became clear to me, it was the mixture itself that consumed my interest. This book is essentially an analysis of the interrelationships of musical styles and repertories and the roles they play in the negotiation of Polish-American identity.

Researching this project has been quite an adventure, made most enjoyable by the people whom I met along the way. Without exception, the many, many people I approached for interviews welcomed me openly, and answered my questions thoughtfully and directly. I would especially like to thank in this regard long-time family friends Walter and Lucy Kaperzinski, as well as Frank and Shirley Leja, Lottie Kustra, Barbara Gronet Bialek, Walt Dana, Rick Szmatula, Virginia Janek, "Polka" Joe Marcissuk, Chris Wolak, Ken Pitlak, Marshall "Big Daddy" Lackowski, and Fr. Stan Ulman. To Eddie Siwiec, who has shown eternal graciousness in answering my many questions, and to Ted Koltowicz, who willingly shared with me his honest appraisals of the dance band business, I offer deepest thanks. I feel fortunate to have witnessed the great camaraderie of the Wienclaw brothers, Frank, Ted, and Syl, who recounted for me numerous family stories and musical anecdotes. These men, as well as Keith Habratowski, Johnny Zelasko, and Paul Fudalla, extraordinary musicians all of them, were patient and generous teachers.

Likewise, I am indebted to the choral groups of the Detroit area—Bronisław Siarkowski and Ewa Siarkowska-Depa and the Polonaise Chorale, and Walter Budweil and his Club Filarets. To a person, they welcomed me kindly and made me feel at home. The women of the Lutnia choir, Toni Colasanti, Pani Ewa Pencak, Barbara VanHulle, Joan Hickey, Jean Nash, Rosemary McCormick, and Joann Nawrocki were generous in sharing their stories with me. I am so very grateful to Barbara VanHulle for her invitation that I spend some time with the choir as a conductor. I will always feel privileged for having been part of their circle. All of the analyses and interpretations of the information I collected during interviews are of course my own. Any peculiarities or errors therein are mine as well.

Some ideas presented in this book I first worked out in articles published in the journal *Ethnomusicology* and in *Polish American Studies*, the journal of the Polish American Historical Association. I thank the editors here for permission to reprint statements quoted from interview materials.

I would also like to express my gratitude to Frank Gladney for his suggestions regarding my translations of Polish songs, to the late J. Bunker Clark for his gentle humor and careful editing of my manuscript, to Elaine Gorzelski for her guidance and support throughout the publishing process, to Susan Parisi for her painstaking work in the final stages of editing, and to Colleen McRorie for her promptness and professionalism in typesetting these pages. To Bruno Nettl I am indebted for his steadfast support of this project, and even more for his wisdom and the kindness he has shown me over these many years. Finally, I must thank the members of my family, without whom this book would not be. From their example and from their faith I take strength.

PAULA SAVAGLIO

Royal Oak
June 2004

NEGOTIATING ETHNIC BOUNDARIES

Polish American Music in Detroit

1

Introduction

I opened the door of a building that housed the headquarters of one of Detroit's Polish-American organizations. As I stepped over the threshold, a woman swept out of one of the offices, stood barring my further entry and said "You cannot come in here unless you are at least one-quarter Polish." I answered quickly "Half. My mother is Polish, my father Italian." Even as I answered I wondered at the strangeness of her criterion and my response. We were talking in precise terms—in the sense people might talk about a container of cream or half-and-half—as if, were we to open my veins at that moment we would have found my blood comprised of half Italian and half Polish corpuscles. But ethnicity is a more slippery than precise notion. The criteria that define it are many and various, and may range from place of birth (or national origin) to religion, or even from physical characteristics, to economic class or educational background. They offer the means by which one individual may ascribe ethnicity to another, or define himself or herself as belonging to a particular group. Depending upon the motivations of the persons involved, ethnicity may be defined in any number of ways—it is like a game, the rules of which keep changing. During our very brief interchange, the doorkeeper at the Polish-American organization had laid down her challenge in terms of national (political) heritage, and I had immediately agreed to those terms. She just as easily might have stipulated "You cannot come in unless you can speak Polish (or play a Chopin etude)," and in my eagerness to gain admittance I would have attempted to produce either of these as surely as I had my half-and-half ancestry. That she might have required some familiarity with Polish music on my part would not have been wholly unimaginable. Music plays a central role in the delineation of ethnic identity in the United States. We regularly associate musical criteria—sound, singing style, language, or repertory—with the parameters of national origin, class, or educational background.

What are the musical criteria that delineate Polish-American ethnicity? The question demands practical and concrete answers; it raises an issue with which Polish-American musicians grapple on a daily basis. For more than a century now, Polish-American musicians have found themselves in the peculiar position of serving a diverse audience. They have provided the ethnic community with music it would recognize as its own, and they have played for a more general audience (constituted also, in part, of Polish-Americans) in churches, concert halls, and dance halls. The musicians have walked a line of continual musical negotiation—at times they have borrowed more heavily from American mainstream styles—styles that receive the bulk of the music media's attention. And at other times, they have traded primarily in music from the old country, the texts, tunes, and life-cycle rituals of which refer to another time and another place.

This book is about the Polish-American musicians' negotiations in ethnicity. How do they define themselves and their audience in terms of a shared national heritage? Do they refer to a shared American past—the old Polish neighborhood, the parish church, labor issues, the Depression, two world wars, big band music, rock and roll—or do they refer to Poland? And if they choose Poland, which Poland might that be? There are a number of historical pictures with which one might identify. There is Renaissance Poland—one of the grand states of Europe between the fourteenth and sixteenth centuries, a powerful nation where courtly processional dances were in vogue. There is also modern, post-Communist Poland—a country struggling to increase its economic power, and whose youth enjoy listening to European and American rock music. A third picture of Poland is that of a foreign European country to which U.S. professionals and blue-collar laborers travel to discover their "roots." From these, many identities are fashioned, and music acts as a reference point. A musical ensemble reveals much about its political stance, about its self-definition, or its visions for the future, its very concept of *who* its members are, through its choices of repertory, the celebrations in which it takes part, the language in which it communicates, even its choice of dress. This musical self-identification is an on-going dynamic process, and as will be seen in successive chapters, leaves much room for disagreement as groups approach their identity from a number of different vantage points.

This study explores the topic of ethnic identity and music by focusing specifically on the musical ensembles of Polish-Americans in Detroit and more generally situating these within a larger national picture. The community in the metropolitan area is quite large, numbering over a half million, and offers a rich musical life comprised of dance bands, Catholic church music (congregational and choral), and secular choral groups. Each of its ensemble types has a place within community life, in religious worship, weddings, picnics, parades, weekend dances, and public exhibitions. Whatever their various responsibilities, all ensembles function to delineate Polish-American identity.

Central to this study is the idea of boundaries developed by Frederic Barth in 1969 and explained in an article entitled "Ethnic Groups and Boundaries" (in Barth 1981). He began his discussion with a critical analysis of a definition of ethnic groups offered by Raoul Narroll (1964). Barth did not contest the elements of Narroll's list of characteristics—biological self-perpetuation, sharing of fundamental cultural values, production of a field of communication and interaction, and identification of self and identification by others—but rather their implied emphasis:

Introduction

> Most critically, it allows us to assume that boundary maintenance is unproblematic and follows from the isolation which the itemized characteristics imply: racial difference, cultural difference, social separation and language barriers, spontaneous and organized enmity. This also limits the range of factors that we use to explain cultural diversity: we are led to imagine each group developing its cultural and social form in relative isolation [Barth 1981, 200].

For Barth, and for our purposes here,

> The critical factor then becomes . . . the characteristic of self-ascription and ascription by others. A categorical ascription is an ethnic ascription when it classifies a person in terms of his basic, most general identity, presumptively determined by his origin and background. To the extent that actors use ethnic identities to categorize themselves and others for purposes of interaction, they form ethnic groups in this organization sense [ibid., 203].

Both components of Barth's "critical factor" play a role in the identity of the Polish ethnic group in Detroit. "Self-ascription" by Polish-Americans is demonstrated through their membership in nationally based organizations such as the Polish American Congress, the Polish National Alliance, and the Polish Singers' Alliance of America. Although the agendas of these organizations vary, from influencing national policy to perpetuating Polish art, all are examples of Abner Cohen's (1974, 66) "formal organizations": groups that develop mechanisms or activities

> that are aimed at the solution of a number of basic operational problems: the problem of distinctiveness, of communication, decision-making, authority, ideology and discipline. [The organization is] arranged rationally on bureaucratic lines and its aims are specifically known.

Self-ascription also plays a role in what Cohen has termed "informal organizations," which have the same problems of distinctiveness, communication, and ideology as the formal organizations, but may be more loosely associated. Cohen offers the ethnic group itself as an example of such a group.

"Ascription by others" has been demonstrated when the media has characterized Hamtramck, an island city within the city of Detroit, as a Polish enclave. People of Polish descent constitute less than half the population of the city, but the area is often singled out by the media as a Polish area because of the great number of Poles who settled there between

1930 and 1980.[1] The national government, for instance, ascribed Polish ethnicity to the small city in April 1989 when President George Bush traveled there to outline the intended United States policy toward Poland (*Detroit News*, 17 April 1989). The Polish-American community of Detroit, Hamtramck, and the suburbs thus has been identified by others as a subgroup of the larger Detroit community, and it has identified itself as such with regard to organizational membership. It is a microcosm of the national Polish-American community with its local chapters of such groups as the Polish American Congress and the Polish Singers' Alliance of America.

In this book, I am extending Barth's explanation of boundaries between ethnic groups—understanding the term "boundary" to mean a line of separation between groups that is maintained through constant re-negotiation and interaction—to refer on another level to boundaries and distinctions *within* the one group. The occurrence of factions, or at least differentiated groups within a community, was noted by Anthony Cohen (1985, 20):

> The "commonality" which is found in community need not be uniformity. It does not clone behavior or ideas. It is a commonality of forms (ways of behaving) whose content (meanings) may vary considerably among its members. The triumph of community is to so contain this variety that its inherent discordance does not subvert the apparent coherence which is expressed by its boundaries.

Ascription by others and self-ascription—key elements in a discussion of intergroup boundaries—play a role in the maintenance of intra-group boundaries as well. A community faction may define intra-group boundaries in order to distinguish itself from the rest of the ethnic community, and thereby distance itself from stereotypes ascribed to the community *as a whole* by an outside group.

The rubric "Polish-American" in itself enforces an outsider's sense of commonality on a group of common national descent. And while there is not a lack of coherence in the community, its membership is not uniform. Non-uniformity in the Polish-American community has been especially evident where disapproval has been voiced by one faction over the failure of another to act properly with respect to their ascribed ethnicity. Not surprisingly, disagreements and factionalism have surfaced regularly in the political arena throughout the twentieth century—regarding American-European diplomatic relations as well as domestic issues (see Allen 2000 and Ubriaco 1994). But they have surfaced also—permeated, in fact, the community's musical life. Music is a vital part of Polish-American

---

[1] The ascription has not gone unchallenged. In 1980 the press's reference to the area south of Hamtramck as "Poletown" was cause for complaint by the many non-Poles living there during a much-publicized battle between the citizens and the General Motors Corporation (see Wylie 1989, 65). The battle concerned GM's attempt to build an automated factory on 465 acres of land, occupied at that time by some 4,200 residents. The car company won its case in court through argument of "eminent domain" and the residents were forced to abandon their property.

Fig. 1.1. A street in Hamtramck

Fig 1.2. Mural of Polish Folk Dancers in John Paul II Square, Hamtramck

prayer, celebration, and mourning; an established repertory of songs and instrumental pieces is elemental to rites of burial, marriage, religious services, and various holidays. Music defines the event. Thus, the issue of a music's appropriateness in any given situation—the values and characteristics it ascribes to an event (and to the event's participants)—is one that receives much attention within the community itself and poses questions for the student of ethnicity as well.

The non-uniformity, varied constituency, and boundaries of Polish ethnicity in the United States are expressed through a mosaic of musical styles. Subgroups within the ethnic group associate musical style with a variety of in-group distinctions and accord them relative value, such that identification with one or another musical style might imply identification with a range of stereotyped attributes, including political orientation and class. A musical style's capacity to function symbolically renders it useful for the definition and redefinition of boundaries between Polish-Americans and non-Polish-Americans, and for marking distinctions within the ethnic group. The polka, in particular, has played a major role in the musical self-definition of Polish-Americans since the 1970s. Highly visible in the community's musical life, it has been ascribed various, and even contradictory, meanings. It is the primary focus of the latter part of this study because it holds a particularly ambiguous position in the community, as it is of non-Polish origin, and is both popularly celebrated, and in certain contexts, publicly denigrated. This ambiguity has yielded the polka to a greater density of meaning than has been ascribed to the other musical genres.

*   *   *   *

Only since 1980 have musicologists begun to explore the dynamics of musical pluralism among various ethnic communities in the United States. A thesis written by Philip Bohlman (1980), for example, describes the wide range of musical genres produced by German-Americans in north central Wisconsin. In 1985 Manuel Peña wrote a study of the Texas-Mexican *conjunto*, in which he suggested that two distinct ensemble types in Tex-Mex society represent two opposed ideologies in the modern culture.

Although sociological studies of Polish-Americans are relatively numerous, musical ethnographies of Polish communities in the United States are rare; only three book-length studies devoted to Polish-American music were published between 1950 and 1990. Each of these offers a descriptive analysis of only a single aspect of the Polish-American repertory. The music of Polish-Americans, specifically, first received attention from scholars in the early 1950s. Helen Goranowski (1951) and, later, Harriet Pawlowska (1961) noted the diverse cultural makeup of the community in Detroit. Each chose to focus, however, on a single musical genre—folk song—in order to demonstrate hypotheses of acculturation and cultural retention. Their work followed a trend established earlier in sociological and anthropological ethnographies that focused on Polish-American communities in order to demonstrate various stages of acculturation. In the classic comparative study *The Polish Peasant in Europe and America* (1918-20), authors William I. Thomas and Florian Znaniecki compared the values and attitudes of peasants in Poland with the system of values exhibited by early Polish immigrants in the United States. Some thirty years later (1949), Peter Ostafin published an article, "The Polish Peasant in Transition: A Study of Group Integration as a Function of Symbioses and Common Definitions," in which he contrasted the stages of acculturation between urban and rural Polish communities. In 1955 the sociologist Arthur Evans Wood examined Polish acculturation within the confines of a single city—*Hamtramck Then and Now: A Sociological Study of a Polish American Community*. Pawlowska (1981) and Goranowski (1951) offered musical counterparts to these sociological studies, and their works remain important documents of Polish folk song repertory in Detroit.[2]

A third book-length musical study by Janice Kleeman reveals the strong influence of both of these earlier works. Kleeman's doctoral dissertation (1982) is a well-documented musical history in which she traces the changing styles of the Polish-American polka since its introduction to the United States in the nineteenth century. Except for pointing out differences between urban- and rural-based styles, however, she does not comment on division among Polish-Americans regarding the genre as a whole. One exception to this earlier trend in the musicological literature is Charles Keil's article "Class and Ethnicity in Polish America" (1979). He summarizes the musical differences within the Polish-American community as a class-based dichotomy. A provocative, but unfortunately brief piece, this article sparked my interest in the pluralistic aspect of Polish-American music, and laid the groundwork for my current thinking on the subject. (I will return to a discussion of this article in chapter 10.)

Two significant book-length studies published after 1990, *Polka Happiness* (1992) by Keil, Keil, and Blau—and Greene's 1992 *A Passion for Polka* of the same year—do not focus so much on a single ethnic group as they do on the broader social and commercial aspects of European-American dance music. The Keils and Blau concentrated instead on the polka's dynamism as a unifying form of leisure in the old European neighborhoods of Buffalo, Chicago, and Milwaukee. Greene amassed evidence of the ethnic musician's influence on the mass media in the United States. Greene's book, especially, demonstrates the significance of "old-time" dance music to a multiplicity of ethnic groups.[3]

*   *   *   *

---

[2] Social anthropological ethnographies since the 1970s have tended to approach the Polish-American community in terms of its diverse composition. See, for example, Paul Wrobel's *Our Way* (1979), and Stanislaus Blejwas's "Old and New Polonias: Tensions within an Ethnic Community" (1981).

[3] We must await a book-length study of Polish choral music in the United States. The Polish history scholar Stanislaus Blejwas completed a manuscript prior to his untimely death in the fall of 2001. It has not yet been published.

Introduction 9

My interpretations, organizational descriptions and analysis of Polish-American music reflect research I conducted for the most part in the 1990s and early 2000s in Detroit and substantiated through comparison with musicological and sociological studies carried out in Chicago, Detroit, and New York. The community in Detroit is rather widely dispersed. However there are geographical centers of musical activity and it was in these that I began research. My fieldwork included observation and participation at ethnic festivals, polka parties, parades, and religious services. I attended festivals in three distinct geographical areas: the downtown, the suburbs, and a mission established for new immigrants in 1979. Through my selection I hoped to avoid the possibility of drawing general conclusions for one area and inferring the same for all areas. I also joined a large cultural organization that met monthly, and attended fundraisers and picnics sponsored by this and smaller organizations. While the observation of highly formal meetings of the cultural club provided an insight into the club's goals and operational procedures, the annual picnics it sponsored afforded greater opportunity for meeting and talking with individual members.

The majority of the musicians with whom I spoke are third- and fourth-generation descendants of Poles who settled in the industrial centers of the United States between 1880 and 1920. A smaller number are post-war émigrés. Together they may be described by profession or occupation as clerks in department stores, salesmen, engineers, secretaries, electricians, machinists, workers in factories and chemical plants, cooks, organists, and members of the Roman Catholic clergy. Blue collar and white collar alike, they value owning their own home, and whether they live with parents, or are parents themselves, almost all are situated within a family setting.

My direct involvement with dance bands included attending their various playing engagements. These ranged in formality from a black-tie dinner at a Knights of Columbus Hall, to the after-parade festivities held in the streets of Hamtramck, to Friday night gigs in a small bar. I was already familiar with the dance band repertory. I had heard it at countless weddings as a child, and I had been taught to play some of the older folk melodies by my grandfather who had been a fiddler in a rural band. But I was not as familiar with stylistic characteristics of urban Chicago and Detroit sounds. One band extended to me an invitation to attend rehearsals that were held in the basement of a band member's house. These rehearsals were quite instructive as they allowed me the opportunity to watch and listen as the musicians discussed matters of style and arrangement.

My work with choral groups followed a path of ever-increasing involvement. I had begun by merely observing rehearsals of each of the three choirs downtown. I then joined one of the choirs and continued to observe rehearsals of the other two. Two years after I had completed the bulk of the choral research, I received a phone call from a member of one of the choirs. She told me that the group was looking for a new director. I needed the work (they were offering twenty-five dollars for every rehearsal and concert), and more significantly I felt I owed it to the group because they had received me quite graciously when I had approached them as a stranger a few years earlier. Of the four jobs I was working during the next two years, conducting this choir soon became one of the most enjoyable. It was a great relief to me to participate in the musical life of the Polish-American community without feeling a responsibility to ask questions. The years I spent with them did not alter the information I had originally gathered concerning choral repertory and self-representation, but it did enhance my understanding of the role the choirs play in the social life of the community.[4]

Materials I gathered from interviews became an essential part of this study. The largely undocumented history of the music rests in the memories of the people who lived, danced, grieved, and prayed to its accompaniment. The telling of this story would be sparse indeed without the voices of the musicians, radio disc jockeys, and event organizers who granted me formal interviews. The interviews took place in some cases in the homes of those interviewed, and in other instances, in the person's place of work, or a restaurant. I taped the majority of the interviews, except in the few cases where the person with whom I spoke requested I not use a recorder, and in those cases where distance or the wishes of the person involved dictated that we speak over the phone. Men are more heavily represented in the material concerning the fields of church music and dance bands, while women provided most of the information concerning choral singing and festival planning. This balance reflects the roles of leadership held by men and women in these spheres of musical activity. In addition to the scheduled, and thus perhaps more formal interviews, I had plenty of opportunities to converse with fellow audience and church members, members of the Polish American Congress, store clerks, and choir members.

As significant to a community-based study were news items and articles that appeared in the *Detroit News*, the *Hamtramck Citizen*, and the *Dziennik Polski* (*Polish Daily*), as well as a collection of early radio memorabilia at the Burton Historical Collection in the Detroit Public Library. My analysis of older dance music is based on my listening to early recordings, veteran band musicians' descriptions of the music, and the information provided by Richard Spottswood in his compilation of ethnic series recordings made prior to 1943 (its contents are more thoroughly discussed in chapter 6). My descriptions of early Polish folkways and customs in chapter 6 were drawn not only from interviews I had conducted, but also from field reports held at the Wayne State University Folklore Archives, a collection established by Emelyn Gardner and Thelma James in 1939. This collection consists of more than 170 papers and reel-to-reel recordings. At least seventy-five percent of these deal with foodways and forms of verbal lore. However, thirty-nine parts of the collection deal specifically with music or traditions in which music plays a role.

---

[4] I have not covered Gorale organizations because none exist in Detroit. There are individuals of Gorale descent living in the area, but they do not form a large population, and choose to participate in more general Polish-American organizations. The Gorale—people sometimes referred to as Polish highlanders—represent a distinctive culture originating in the foothills of the Tatras in southern Poland. The Gorale descendants living in the United States have formed cultural centers in Chicago, Arizona, New York, and New Jersey. There is also a large Highlander community in Canada. Timothy Cooley (1998 and 2000) and Louise Wrazen (1991) have published studies on these groups in the United States and Canada, respectively.

Introduction

*   *   *   *

The following chapter (2) lays the groundwork for the subsequent discussion of the Polish-American community's music. It begins with a history of the Polish immigrant and identifies and describes two major periods of Polish immigration to the United States. I point out basic economic, motivational, and educational differences between members of each of the two periods and explore issues of intra-ethnic conflict and cooperation. From there I switch my emphasis to Polish-American interaction with neighboring nationality groups.

Chapter 3 focuses on Polish-American identity in the Catholic church and the group's decisions concerning its self-representation. Polish-language hymns, English translations of Polish hymns, church choirs, and polka Masses play varying and—at times—conflicting roles in delineating the Polish character of a congregation.

Chapter 4 presents three Detroit-based secular choirs as examples of ensembles that express a dualistic allegiance—first to the United States and secondly to Poland. In secular arts clubs and choirs, the choice of language—Polish or English—occupies a central role in the decisions the group makes regarding organizational procedures, the public performance of songs, and interaction with outsiders. On a less theoretical level, this chapter offers a description of choral rehearsals and performances and examines the sung repertory.

I intend the fifth chapter to serve as a subchapter of the fourth. It presents a detailed history of one choir, Lutnia, in order to illustrate some of the more general concepts laid out in the previous chapter. This chapter, like chapters 7 and 8, incorporates a good amount of material from my interviews with musicians.

In chapter 6 I look specifically at the polka on the international stage. From its beginnings in Prague, I trace its performances in nineteenth-century American theaters. The genre's prominence on "ethnic-series" recordings and its popularity among ethnic groups and in the musical mainstream of the 1930s make up the bulk of this chapter.

Chapter 7 is an introduction to Detroit's Polish-American dance bands of the 1930s and 40s. Using musical transcriptions culled from representative recordings, a comparison is drawn between Detroit's musical counterparts in Chicago and the eastern United States. This chapter presents the personal histories of four musicians, their methods of learning, rehearsing, and performing music, and discusses the ways in which they have balanced various American and Polish elements in their careers.

The eighth chapter is a chronological continuation of the seventh. In it, parallels are drawn between young musicians in Detroit—their careers and repertories—and the veteran musicians introduced previously. Following this is a discussion of Polish folk tunes and American rock and country music influences on modern Polish dance bands. Again, the question is pondered, in this case from the vantage point of the younger musicians: to what extent can a Polish-American dance band borrow from contemporary American pop music styles without losing its Polish identity? What role do the Polish language and old-country tunes play in the self-representation of the younger bands?

Chapter 9 is a description of the rather recent establishment of an entire industry—recordings, radio, internet sites, and press—all dedicated to the promotion of German, Slovenian, Czech, and Polish polkas and waltzes. The polka press makes explicit the controversies surrounding the influence of the mainstream on European-American dance genres.

The final chapter, offers examples of specific ways in which Polish-Americans have used music, particularly the polka, to negotiate their identity vis-à-vis American mainstream value systems and politics and to mark the distinctions of class and background within their own community.

For at least seventy years Polish-American musicians have fashioned dualistic careers for themselves, playing both within and outside of their community. In order to serve the musical demands of a varied clientele, they pieced together a number of repertories and styles from an assortment of old-European and American pop music elements. In the following pages, I argue that the careful balancing of these elements has been a significant constant in Polish-American musical life of the twentieth century. Any group of musicians striving to provide the ethnic community with the music it perceives to be its own, while remaining viable as professionals in the larger urban area, must struggle with the issue of self representation. Secular and religious choral groups and dance bands regularly make decisions concerning language (Polish or English texts?), repertory, and style (should they reject or accept influence from the American mainstream?); with every decision made, the ensemble re-negotiates its dual (American and Polish) identity.

Going back to the brief narrative with which I began this introduction, if Polish-American ethnicity is merely a matter of national heritage—the political boundaries of one's ancestry—as was suggested by the doorkeeper, then there is little more to say on the topic. But if indeed ethnicity is closer to what Barth suggested, a fluid process by which a group of people continually realigns itself musically, politically, historically, and socially within the United States, it makes for a fascinating study of a community, which when it is undertaken reveals a great deal about the pluralistic organization of America's music.

2

Jostling for a Place in the Crowd

Pre- and Post-War Polish-American Settlements

In 1936 the International Board of the United Auto Workers appointed the Polish-speaking Stanley Nowak to organize second-generation Polish-American workers. Through biweekly speeches on Polish-language radio and at open-air meetings in the Polish neighborhoods, Nowak appealed to the Polish-American worker whose thinking, he once stated, "was very much the same as the thinking of other industrial workers."[1] Nowak's assignment with the UAW points up the dualistic dynamic that constituted the identity of second-generation Polish-Americans in the first half of the twentieth century—a dynamic that is still resounding in the lives of their descendants. Speaking Polish at home, worshipping in Polish-language churches, the sons and daughters of Polish immigrants belonged to two worlds—worlds separated by language (one Polish, the other English), but worlds inextricably bound to each other through family ties, social obligations, and economic need. The musical life of Detroit's Polish-Americans has reflected the tensions of that generation—and the tensions of the generations that have followed it.

Polish-American communities situated in a metropolitan area such as Chicago or Detroit where more than a dozen different nationality groups interact, are continually renegotiating their cultural boundaries. Although they assimilate musical ideas from surrounding groups— often consciously, at other times, perhaps unintentionally—they maintain lines of demarcation by which they may continue to circumscribe and differentiate themselves. Issues of Polish ethnic identity, however, are charged as intensely by internal dynamics as they are affected by external influences, for the rubric "Polish-American" enforces an outsider's sense of commonality on a group of people who do not address issues of politics, religion, or music uniformly. While they do share a common national descent, the Polish ethnic community

---

[1] Institution of Labor and Industrial Relations, "Unionism in the Automobile Industry Project Interview" (1960), 3. Nowak leaned toward the political left. A pro-Soviet socialist, he was an editor of the Polish Communist weekly, *Głos Ludowy* (*Peoples Voice*).

in the United States in fact derives from at least three massive movements of people out of Poland over the course of one hundred years.

A descriptive scheme of Polish *immigration* that is particularly relevant to modern Polish-American musical life in the urban midwest is one that divides the influx of Poles into two periods. The first occurred between the 1870s and the onset of World War II, and corresponds to the first large-scale *emigration* of Poles from Europe. The second period, referred to as the "new" or "post-War" immigration, actually encompasses two separate instances of Polish mass emigration following the end of World War II.[2] The ethnic communities resulting from each of the two periods are termed the Old Polonia and the New Polonia. (The Latin term "Polonia" refers to any community of Poles living outside of Poland.) Members of the two Polonias differ in their political orientation, educational background, use of the Polish language, and number of generations in this country.

The tremendous movement of people out of Poland—some three million—between 1870 and 1920 resulted from events that had transpired a century earlier. Feudal Poland had been one of the most powerful political entities in Europe in the fifteenth and sixteenth centuries. Internal dissension and a system of decentralized power, however, had considerably weakened the state by the eighteenth century, leaving it vulnerable to encroachment by powerful neighbors. In three successive moves, the first of which occurred in 1772, Russia, Prussia, and Austria annexed areas of Poland to their individual domains. The Polish landed gentry's attempts at reform in the late eighteenth century, aimed at strengthening and unifying what remained of Poland, proved ineffective in staving off the final two partitions. By 1795, Poland ceased to exist as an independent political state on the map of Europe. It would not reemerge until after the First World War.

Government policies differed in each of the three partitioned areas, but all policies in the long run doomed the predominantly rural populations of former Poland to a level of poverty that would eventually force the issue of emigration. In the Prussian-governed section of former Poland known as Poznania, the government instituted a policy of reform calling for the emancipation of Polish serfs from the land. This policy of 1807 led to a surplus of labor—people skilled in agriculture, but without any land to work (Kieniewicz 1969, 58). By 1880 these landless agricultural workers constituted eighty percent of the rural populations of Poznan and Pomerania (Bukowczyk 1987, 6). Not only did they struggle against economic hardship, but they also suffered under certain cultural constraints imposed by the Prussian government. In 1870 Otto von Bismarck, in an attempt to unify and Prussianize the then century-old acquisition of Poznania, initiated a program of *Kulturkampf*. This "cultural

---

[2] Haiman (1939) and, later, Gros (1976) devised much more elaborate divisional schemes in order to explain the variety of Polish migrations to this country. These schemes not only take into account immigration movements of the eighteenth century, but also analyze in great detail the variety of motives of twentieth-century Polish immigrants. While these schemes are interesting with regard to the sociological analysis of the ethnic group, their minute divisions do not find musical correlation, and thus do not contribute greatly to an understanding of the Polish ethnic group's musical life in the United States.

imed at colonizing the western part of former Poland with
the only acceptable language in schools and churches. The
ania, together with the devastating economic effects of the
uraged the mass emigration of non-Prussians from that area.
sia "freed" its Polish serfs, Austria emancipated the peasants
ever, prevented the eviction of agricultural laborers from the
asants with certain land use rights, and allowed for partitioned
tter how small the plot in question. This last resulted in the
ls which barely supported those who farmed them. By 1900,
alicia were landless, while another forty-eight percent found
of five or fewer acres (ibid., 8). Ultimately, Austria's policies
eady existing divisions among the social and economic strata.
's initial attempts to discourage people from leaving the country,
is typhus and cholera epidemics, made for an insufferable
tual emigration of one million people prior to 1914.
ormer Poland, known as the Congress Kingdom, was financially
or Poznania during the nineteenth century. The more heavily
position to offer to its landless peasants work in steel, iron,
dvantageous situation did not continue after the onset of the
The war effected a reduction in eastern trade and rendered
the current level of Russian production unnecessary. The economy plunged. Polish workers reacted to the ensuing economic depression with labor strikes, to which the Russian government responded by moving centers of production out of the Congress Kingdom and into Russia proper (ibid., 10). Approximately 1.3 million people eventually emigrated—the majority Roman Catholic Poles, but including also ethnic-religious minorities: Jews and Protestant Ukrainians, Ruthenians, Byelorussians, and Kashubians.

The millions who left the Congress Kingdom, Poznania, and Galicia did not head for the rural areas of Texas, Michigan, and Wisconsin, where earlier Polish immigrants had settled. Discouraged on the one hand by the high price of land, and drawn on the other by the economic opportunities advertised by industries, the newcomers flocked to the heavily industrialized centers of New York, Cleveland, Pittsburgh, Chicago, Detroit, and the Pennsylvania mining fields. They and their descendants came to constitute the Old Polonia.

Those Poles who immigrated to Detroit established two enclaves in the city, east and west of Detroit's main, northwest-southeast thoroughfare—Woodward Avenue. These neighborhoods in Detroit characteristically grew outward from a centrally located church. The majority of the immigrants were Roman Catholic, and parish life provided a basis for socializing as well as for religious expression. The church's physical centrality was a manifestation of its significance in the lives of its parishioners, as it provided an area for civic meetings and social functions, and served as sacred space for the celebration of the sacraments and rituals marking the life cycle: baptisms, marriages, and funerals. (Even at the beginning of the twenty-first century, it is not uncommon for Polish-Americans to identify the area of Detroit or the suburbs in which they live by referring to the parish to which they belong.)

Almost immediately following their organization into parishes, Polish immigrants formed mutual aid societies that provided the immigrant with small loans and insurance benefits. While mutual aid societies such as those associated with Polish churches remained local, others such as the Polish National Alliance and the Polish Roman Catholic Union were national in scope and could exercise some political muscle, in some cases aligning their agendas with organizations in Poland. Communication among the various organizations, as well as within cities, was enhanced through newspapers. Polish-American communities across the eastern and midwestern United States established a Polish-language press. Some newspapers fared well over the decades, especially those backed by the national mutual aid and political alliances. Many others folded—in some cases within a year of their founding.

In Detroit at least forty different newspapers served the Polish-American reading public at different times since the nineteenth century. The earliest known was *Narodowe Gazeta* (*National Gazette*), a weekly Anarchist paper published from 1884 until 1885. Other papers, affiliated with a particular parish church, or a particular political view, or offering items of local interest or gossip, had a greater life span. The longest-lived Polish paper in Detroit is the *Dziennik Polski* (*Polish Daily*), which has been in existence since 1904. It began as a Polish-language weekly, but spawned an English-language edition, *Detroit American*, as early as 1905.[3] Polish-Americans who held views similar to those espoused by the Communist Party were served by the long-enduring *Głos Ludowy* (*People's Voice*), which began publication in 1909 and continued until the early 1990s. Socialist newspapers also found an audience among Poles, the majority of whom belonged to Detroit's working class. The Polish-language *Głos Robotniczy* (*Voice of the Workers*) during World War I, and later, the *Trybuna Robotnicza* (*Workers' Tribune*) were two that lasted longer than a year. The *Gazeta Handlowa* (*Business Gazette*) was a monthly publication begun in 1914. With the exception of the *Detroit American*, all of these newspapers were printed in Polish.[4] If we take the Polish-language newspaper as our standard of measure for a well-settled community, the old Polonia was firmly established by 1890. Its members had set up a communication network of newspapers and radio, and they had organized themselves into social clubs, mutual aid societies, and a system of parishes.

---

[3] The English edition seems to have lasted until the late 1960s. Currently, the *Polish Daily* exists as a single, bilingual publication—half of it carries news items, ads, and editorials in Polish, and half in English. The two languages feature different articles (although may cover the same topics) and are not merely translations from one language to the other.

[4] For a listing of forty Polish newspapers known to have been published in Detroit since the nineteenth century, see Hathaway 1978. Father Piotr Taras in *Polonia w Detroit* (1989) offers a list of sixty-three titles of newspapers available to the Polish reading public in Detroit since 1916. His list includes papers published in other cities that were sold also in Detroit, such as *Nowy Dziennik* of New York, *Gwiazda Polarna* from Stevens Point, Wisconsin, *Sokol Polska* from Pittsburgh and, from Chicago, *Zgoda*, *Głos Polek*, and *Narod Polski*.

Every one of these institutions, sooner or later, had to tackle the question of their hyphenated identity, or as it was often phrased, "Are we Poles first or Americans first?" Pressure from without to Americanize or assimilate was echoed by pressures from within the group. The general sentiment among Polish-Americans, especially as the second generation came of age, was that the community owed its first allegiance to the United States. Moreover, many immigrants ascribed to the belief that the only way to survive in the new country was to learn its language and adopt its values. *Dziennik Polski* began publishing an English-language version of the paper as the *Polish Daily* as early as 1905. Polish-language radio, from its inception, featured popular American tunes with English vocals. Polish-American enthusiasm for American (English-language) news and song texts was tempered, however, by the immigrants' fears of forgetting their first language, losing their old system of values, and, ultimately and most terrifying, losing their children to a new and strange world.

The Polish churches in Detroit, while confronting the question of their identity, dealt with issues that went well beyond that of language usage. In Poland, Poles had been accorded some say over church finances, and the choice of a pastor. In the United States, Polish immigrants often found themselves in conflict with a largely Irish and German hierarchy. It was their struggle for some degree of control, and not theological differences, that led to ruptures within the church body. In one extreme case at the turn of the century, disagreements between the laity and church authority led to a break in the Catholic Polish-American churches and the establishment of the Polish National Church in the United States.[5]

While the Polish-American laity struggled to establish a workable relationship with the Catholic church hierarchy, they also had to confront issues of their status vis-à-vis other nationality groups in the church, the workplace, and the neighborhood. Numbering almost fourteen thousand in Detroit at the turn of the century, Poles constituted only fifteen percent of the foreign-born population (Hyde 1980, 13). The Polish enclaves or ghettos that could be measured out in city blocks and identified by the name of a centrally located Catholic church, coexisted with numerous other, equally well identified ethnic neighborhoods—Irish, African, German, Italian, and East European Jewish areas of the city.[6]

These ethnic enclaves or ghettos, culturally distinct as they were, were not completely segregated one from the other. Stanley Mackun (1964), a sociologist who researched patterns of Polish settlement in Detroit, demonstrated that varying degrees of ethnic integration existed even within areas that were primarily Polish. He made good use of Polk's City Directories, and compared his findings with census tract statistics, mapping patterns of Polish settlement.

---

[5] For a discussion that deals specifically with the traditional balance of authority within the Polish-American church, see Orzell 1979.

[6] David Katzman in his study of African-American neighborhoods in nineteenth-century Detroit noted that as early as the 1880s Detroit residents identified certain streets and areas of the city with specific ethnic groups: the east side with Irish-Americans, the St. Antoine area with African-Americans, Gratiot with German-Americans, Hastings with Polish and Russian Jews, Paradise Valley with Italian-Americans, and Hamtramck (an island city within the city limits of Detroit) with Polish-Americans.

Mackun marked zones within and on the peripheries of Polish neighborhoods as either solid (constituted of over forty percent Polish surnames), transitional (between 10 and 39.9 percent Polish surnames), or fringe (less than 9.9 percent). David Katzman (1973), a scholar who conducted research in Detroit almost a decade after Mackun's dissertation was completed, echoed Mackun's findings; Katzman, whose work focused on African-Americans in Detroit during the 1870s and 80s described a similarly integrated African-American settlement which was "scattered among" foreign-born whites. Detroit's various ethnic groups not only worked in the same factories, but in some instances also socialized in the same neighborhoods and worshipped in the same churches.

The dynamics of interaction among Detroit's ethnic groups were not constant but changed with respect to varying residential and institutional patterns.[7] For example, inter-ethnic boundaries were established early on between the Germans and Poles in the churches of Detroit. Because the first great influx of Poles followed chronologically closely upon that of the Germans, Poles settled initially into already-formed German neighborhoods and attended German parish churches. Ultimately, their communities would monopolize the areas as German-Americans abandoned them for the suburbs. In 1870, a German immigrant neighborhood in Detroit began building a new Catholic church. Their plans called for a separate seating section for the Poles, from whom they wished to keep their distance. The Polish immigrants, propelled to action by German attempts to segregate the church, responded by building their own church, St. Albertus in 1872 (Stanczyk 1955).

Ten years after its founding, St. Albertus became the site of a strenuous battle that pitted a Polish priest against the German bishop, and Polish parishioners against each other. In 1882 an anonymous group of churchgoers, presumably from within the parish itself, accused their pastor, Dominic Hippolytus Kolasinski of mismanagement of church funds and sexual misconduct, and filed charges with Bishop Casper Borgess of the Archdiocese of Detroit. Kolasinski asked the German-American bishop for a chance to defend himself to those who had accused him, but was denied permission and sent away. Before leaving St. Albertus Church, he delivered an impassioned speech to his parishioners, "in which he presented himself as a victim of traditional Prussian oppression and persecution" (Skendzel 1979, 7).

Kolasinski's parish was divided, for and against him. In the eyes of some Polish-Americans, he had committed a grave error in mismanaging church funds. They had sacrificed time and money building a church and expected to take part in administrative decisions and to have knowledge, if not control, over where and how church monies were distributed.

In December 1885, two days after parishioners had listened to Kolasinki's speech, they began rioting. The Polish pastor who had been appointed to replace Kolasinski required

---

[7] The various positions taken by the Polonia of Detroit (and Chicago) with regard to neighboring communities have been well documented and analyzed in the areas of church, housing, and the labor-related issues of unionization, race, class, and militancy. See, for example, Skendzel (1979), Parot (1972), Leggett (1968), Meier and Elliott (1979), and Moore (1978).

a police escort to enter the church. Three days later the church was officially closed (not to reopen until June 1887). Thousands of St. Albertus members, angered that the church hierarchy would dare to close their church without their consent, marched to Bishop Borgess's residence on Christmas day. The bishop escaped by way of a back door, and celebrated mass at a neighboring German church. That afternoon the crowd, still milling about in the streets, stormed places of business owned by those Poles who supported Kolasinski's replacement. Incidences relating to the Kolasinski case continued to occur for almost eight more years.

The Kolasinski case is an extreme example of intra-church conflict. Immigrant Poles sought to gain control more often through requests than through riots. They petitioned the hierarchy for permission to build their own churches and requested that Polish-speaking priests, familiar with Polish devotional liturgies, be assigned to their congregations. The Detroit hierarchy's response to the immigrants' petitions was tempered by its belief that acquiescence to such requests would encourage separatism among different immigrant groups and thereby threaten the unity of the Church in the United States. In this belief, the American Catholic hierarchy echoed nationally held views that the assimilation and Americanization of immigrants were necessary to the survival of the country itself. On the other hand, the Church did not want to risk the loss of members through its failure to provide immigrants with a spiritual haven. In their efforts to maintain and increase church membership, the hierarchy did respond favorably to certain petitions. Thus in 1885, when two Polish priests, Joseph Dąbrowski and Leopold Moczygęba, requested permission to establish a seminary for the training of Polish-American priests, their proposal found support with Pope Leo XIII and received official approval from Bishop Borgess. (Dombrowski's and Moczygęba's petition ultimately resulted in the founding of the Saints Cyril and Methodius Seminary in Detroit.)

As Poles moved into the once-German parishes and churches, they similarly replaced the German immigrants at lower entry-level positions at factories, when those workers moved to semi-skilled jobs in the same plant. Of the some 48,000 Polish immigrants in Detroit, sixty-seven percent were semi-skilled and unskilled laborers (Wylie 1989, 2; Oestreicher 1989, 34). Approximately ten percent managed to accumulate capital and open small businesses, including bakeries, butcher shops, funeral homes, and taverns. Some of these early businesses advertised a common ancestry with their customers through use of the Polish symbol of the white eagle in their trademarks, as did for example the White Eagle Cigar Factory of 1889 and the White Eagle Brewing Company established in 1890 (Serafino 1983, 10). A much smaller group of immigrants worked as brokers, accountants, electricians, engineers, lawyers, and physicians.

By the turn of the century six of every ten workers in Detroit were born outside of the United States (Oestreicher 1989, 3). There was much opportunity for tension and resentment among the various ethnic groups that competed for unskilled and semi-skilled work. African-Americans found themselves forced down economically while the white newcomers had a better if not always good chance for some economic improvement. Immigrants who came to the industrial worlds of Detroit, Chicago, or Pittsburgh ignorant of their standing with regard to older, more established ethnic groups, shed their ignorance quickly. Sooner or later they were baptized in the fires of strike politics. When workers staged a strike (for better hours, job safety, the right to unionize, or a better wage), management typically attempted to offset any loss of production by hiring recently arrived immigrants to replace the strikers. Companies would try to enlist Polish immigrants, for example, as scabs to replace striking German workers. Management shrewdly exacerbated tensions between ethnic groups—their aim not simply to bust a strike, but also to ensure divisiveness within a potentially strong working class.

How successful was management in realizing the latter aim? There exist enough examples of both ethnic unity and ethnic divisiveness in the workforce between 1900 and 1940 that labor and ethnic historians can argue either side of the question. Were immigrant workers able to see beyond their national differences and unite as *workers*? Certainly, yes. John Bukowczyk (1987, 79) offered a list of eight "epic strikes" in the Midwest from 1900 to 1919 in which Polish men and women instigated workers' revolts, and acted in cooperation with Italians, African-Americans, Jews, Slovaks, and Hungarians. He argued that the Polish ethnics' militancy continued well into the following decades, describing second-generation Poles as having "a greater stake than their parents in America's factories." Armed with "the savvy of second-generation industrial workers," and having "the legal right to organize guaranteed them by the National Labor Relations Act of 1935 . . . the sons and daughters of immigrants had created modern American industrial unionism." Bukowczyk's findings for the Polish midwest find corroboration in the work of the historian Dick Hoerder (1986). Hoerder published a compilation of essays that together suggested a revision of the earlier "fragmentation paradigm" of immigration. Using examples from Anglo and Slavic, and Jewish and Italian labor solidarity, the contributing authors demonstrated that differences in immigrant background did not necessarily preclude unification in class struggles. John C. Leggett (1968) narrowed the focus of the question specifically to Detroit, where, he contended a working-class consciousness was alive and well. He noted that there were conflicts between European and African ethnic workers, but demonstrated that workers were involved in the struggle to varying degrees, and these degrees of militancy were directly related to the cultural heritage and past employment experiences of the various groups. Gilbert W. Moore (1978), a labor historian, has argued otherwise. Shifting his attention to the 1930s, he pointed out areas of tension between African-Americans, Southern whites, and European ethnic groups that doomed a class-based workers' movement to failure. Significantly, all of these historians concur that labor-management struggles in the industrial centers of Detroit, New York, and Chicago have involved some measure of struggle among the workers themselves. Perhaps that is what makes the *success* of the "epic strikes" all the more glorious.[8]

---

[8] To Bukowczyk's list of eight may be added the sit-down strike of 1937 that took place at the Dodge Main plant in Polish Hamtramck. More than ten thousand workers, of diverse ethnic backgrounds, with the support of their

Members of the old Polonia were well divided over issues of politics and religion. Still, the majority were Roman Catholic, urban-dwelling and certainly, by the second generation, already well entrenched in American life. A significant portion of the working class, they constituted a large percentage of American Catholics, and they carried enough political clout that politicians from the local wards all the way up to President Franklin D. Roosevelt paid some attention to their concerns (see Ubriaco 1994). Just at that point when the second and third generations looked upon themselves as Americans of Polish descent, when they had forgotten some Polish words and were more concerned with domestic issues in the United States than they were with foreign affairs, a new group of Poles—well educated and knowledgeable concerning the affairs of Europe—arrived on American soil. The question of identity had posed a challenge to Polish-Americans before the Second World War. The question would only increase in complexity when the old Polonia came face to face with the new.

During the eight years following the invasion by Nazi Germany in 1939, Poland lost over a quarter of its population. Though the war in Poland officially ended with the capitulation of the Nazis and the Soviet "liberation" in 1945, the Polish underground army continued fighting against the Soviets into 1948 (Davies 1984, 81). Many who managed to escape mass murders and to survive Soviet deportations sought refuge in the United States.

Thirty years later, another large group of some 350,000 emigrated from Poland following the dissolution of the trade union Solidarity and the imposition of martial law. The formation of Solidarity followed upon a history of economic crises and labor strikes in Poland. Norman Davies, a Polish history scholar, argued that First Secretary Gomulka's policies between 1956 and 1970 both led to greater political experimentation in the country and worsened an already poor economic situation there, as Gomulka permitted an independent Catholic Church, a semblance of political pluralism, and dissolved collective farming on the greater portion of arable acreage. While the Polish government had returned eighty percent of cultivated land to private ownership, it competed against these farmers with heavy investment in the publicly held land (ibid., 13). Price hikes and a scarcity of food sparked a series of strikes, the first two occurring in 1968 and 1970 during Gomulka's term, and then in 1976 and 1979 while Gierek was serving as First Secretary.

In July 1979 the government once again raised food prices, touching off localized strikes around the country. In August, hoping to quell the increasing discontent among Polish workers, the Party offered some concessions to the laborers at the Lenin Shipyards in Gdansk. In a move unexpected by Gierek's advisors, shipyard workers refused the settlement offered them, choosing to support fellow workers on strike elsewhere in the country. Their refusal marked the beginning of a movement that eventually united some ten million workers in Poland under the banner of the trade union Solidarity.

---

families and sympathetic fellow laborers staged a strike that not only humbled the giants of the auto industry, but offered impetus to the unionization of steel and electrical workers in the industrial midwest.

After enduring for some fifteen months, the newly established union challenged the government in a most fundamental way, calling for free elections in December 1981. Ten days later, General Jaruzelski, Gierek's successor, dispatched an army across the country and declared a period of martial law that was to last through the close of the following year. With the enforced disbanding of Solidarity, many Poles left the country, some entering the United States. Others, already visiting the United States at the time martial law was imposed, and unable or unwilling to return to Poland, applied for Extended Voluntary Departure status.

There is a wide discrepancy among the most recent estimates of the Polish-American population, the numbers ranging between five and fifteen million.[9] The discrepancies preclude a numerically founded discussion about the relative influences of the old and new Polonias on the community. But discussions concerning the sociological differences between the two Polonias abound. A study published by the National Conference of Catholic Bishops in 1985 argued that the immigrants who arrived after 1939 were more cosmopolitan in outlook and had more years of formal education than did those who entered the United States between 1880 and 1920.[10] The situation is even more complex than stated in this document. The old Polonia of the twenty-first century includes fourth-generation descendants of the earlier wave of emigration, and thus an important further distinction exists between the old and the new: the new consists of Europeans, who for the most part are more entrenched in Poland's politics than are the descendants of the old whose concerns are centered on domestic issues in the United States.

Because of these differences in orientation, members of the old and new Polonias at times have experienced disillusionment, one with the other. The descendants of pre-1920 immigrants have referred to Polish newcomers disparagingly as D.P.s, regardless of whether the people in question were actually "displaced persons" of the war. Derogatory use of these initials describes a group of people who appreciate neither the struggles endured, nor the monuments achieved by the earlier immigrants, and who refuse to acknowledge their postwar indebtedness to the old Polonia. New immigrants have been no less critical of the old Polonia, charging that the old community's members are poorly educated Americans who speak a bastardized form of the Polish language. Recent Polish émigrés have criticized the old Polonia for an alleged lack of concern about current issues in Poland; in 1989, they voiced their disappointment with the old Chicago Polonia for what they saw as its poor response to a call for money to support Solidarity candidates:

> Many recent emigres argue that the response proves it's time finally to dispel the notion of a united, powerful Polish-American community in Chicago that really cares what happens in the land of its forbears.

---

[9] For a discussion of relative sizes of the various periods of immigration and the insurmountable barriers to making such comparisons, see Lopata (1976) and Jaroszynska-Kirchmann (2000).

[10] "The Pastoral Care of Polish Immigrants: Notes From Recent Research" (Washington: Pastoral, n.d.).

> They call it a myth. "The inertia is sad, terrible, frightening," said Bozena Nowicka, who teaches Polish at Loyola University. "Poles here are extremely immature politically. By not putting their money where their mouth is, they're doing nothing to help the struggle for democracy in Poland."[11]

Musically also the two Polonias diverge—not so much in civic displays of ethnicity where choral groups are actually a point of convergence, but in party music at picnics and church festivals. The old Polonia waltzes and polkas, and even takes a few turns around the floor accompanied by foxtrots. The new Polonia, on the other hand, prefers to tango or slow dance to contemporary Polish love songs. The divergence over party music, like that regarding political orientation, is rooted in actual differences distinguishing the European from the American experience. But the disillusionment of post-War émigrés with the old Polonia has produced some widely held stereotypes that are not always grounded in fact. I had the opportunity early on in my study to speak with a church organist, a descendant of the post-World War II emigration. He explained the apathy of his congregation toward classical music, saying that the members were typical of those Polish-American descendants of "uneducated peasants" who had arrived between 1880 and 1924. He further identified them as a polka-loving crowd who enjoyed only bowling, beer, baseball, and bingo. He linked the social-economic background of his congregation to a musical preference, and significantly, with an inability to appreciate classical music. In truth, neither the old Polonia nor the new can lay claim to a greater knowledge or appreciation of classical music. But by invoking a European-derived division of class-based musical taste, the more recent immigrant finds the means to relegate the older community to a sub-standard position—a position far removed from himself. A class-based stereotype that in my experience is more frequently invoked by the new Polonia, its power is not unknown to members of the old who might wish also to distance themselves from a position of low social prestige.

In a dissertation that addressed political and economic leadership in the Chicago Polonia, Charles Emmons (1971, 60) pointed out many examples of division between the old and new Polonias regarding politics and social prestige. When he discussed cultural divisions, however, he concluded with a cautionary statement, ". . . cultural differences [ascribed to a] period of immigration which divide Polonia and which are used in the folklore to account for the division [are stereotypic, and] there is by no means total agreement about or knowledge of the differences."

It would be an over-generalization to suggest that there is a clean social and cultural break between the two Polonias, or to suggest these stereotypes have pervaded the entire community and affected all interaction. Members of the two periods of immigration reside in the same neighborhoods, work together in formal organizations, and intermarry. During

---

[11] *Chicago Tribune,* 14 May 1989, 3.

my fieldwork, I spoke with many descendants of the old immigration who, in fact, have traveled to Poland, donated their time and money in aid-to-Poland projects, and keep abreast of current events in that country. Likewise, new immigrants have joined organizations established by the old Polonia and work alongside the descendants of the old-period immigration in restaurants and churches.

Rather, the divisions within the group are more complex. At the root of the European Pole's contempt for working-class American politics, level of education, and leisure pursuits are the issues of identity and self-representation—issues that affect the old Polonia as well. Music has not remained unaffected by the divisions, boundary delineation, and communication across boundaries that have marked the Polonia's history in Detroit. The questions "Who are the Polish-Americans?" and "How do they differ from surrounding cultures?" have been given answer by a variety of musical expressions. The following chapter introduces those expressions that are heard in the Polish churches of Detroit.

3

The Polish Church: The Sum of All Its Members

Music and Identity in the Church

In 1975 a pastor of one of the Polish churches in Detroit asked, "We have a Polish Mass for Polish-speaking Catholics and why not a polka Mass for Polish-Americans?"[1] It was a rhetorical question. He was responding to another member of the Detroit Polonia who had penned an article criticizing an event known as a polka Mass—a Roman Catholic Mass, the musical parts of which are led by a polka band. The critic, Regina Koscielska, argued against the use of polka music in Polish churches; she reasoned that such an event is not representative of Polish culture because Poles have not traditionally introduced secular practices into the sphere of religious worship. The respondent, Father Francis Skalski, had defended the polka Mass, by invoking his own understanding of Polish culture; he claimed that the Poles have "a tradition of continuing and not containing their religion as in a bottle," and implied that the polka Mass is a significant aspect of Polish-American culture.

Some nine years later, the same critic argued again that the use of polka music at mass in Polish churches is inappropriate:

> Toe-tapping, finger snapping music should not be imposed on a congregation in the name of "culture" unless such music is truly representative of it.... As we have noted, the polka Mass does not reflect the culture or traditions of any one ethnic group [Koscielska 1984, 29].

In Detroit, polka bands are employed at English-language Masses at various Polish churches on one or two Sundays every year. A church's decision to employ a polka band does not often result in published debates, but it can frequently spark some verbal disagreements among members of the congregation. There are parishioners who would side with

---

[1] Francis Skalski, "Polka Mass Is Lauded: An Open Reply to Regina Koscielska," *Polish Daily News*, 15 November 1975, 3.

Koscielska; they typically worship at a neighboring church on the weekend that their own church has scheduled a polka Mass. They, like Koscielska, argue logically that neither the polka itself, nor the use of polka music at Mass, originated with the Poles. Robert Walser (1992, 185) traced the phenomenon of the polka Mass to its 1972 Slovenian origins in the Church of the Holy Rosary in Lowelville, Ohio. Media focus on polka Masses throughout the 1970s centered not on Polish-American churches, but on the Slovenian-Croatian Church of the Resurrection in Eveleth, Minnesota. The pastor of the Church of the Resurrection, Frank Perkovich, initiated the liturgical use of polkas in his parish in order to increase public attendance and involvement at Mass. He noted with pleasure that the parishioners' response at Resurrection was positive: "The people wanted a polka Mass every week, but we had to keep it to every six weeks or so in order not to conflict with the band's nightclub dates."[2] It was Perkovich, not a pastor of a Polish church, who eventually introduced the polka Mass to the Great Lakes area. More than thirty years after its inception, Masses with polka accompaniments thrive among Polish, German, Slovenian, and Czech congregations in the Midwest (Walser 1992, 183). The tunes (both polkas in $\frac{2}{4}$ time and waltzes in $\frac{3}{4}$ time) are in some instances newly composed, and in others adopted from the secular dance band repertory. The adapted tunes themselves reveal a mix of ethnic backgrounds, and typically originate in German-, Slovenian-, and Polish-American dance bands (ibid., 189).

Proponents of the polka Mass who would agree with Fr. Skalski, that the Mass set to polka music is indeed representative of Polish-American culture, are not concerned with the ethnic origin of the dance. Rather, their stance is based on the dance's century-long popularity with urban as well as rural Polish-American communities across the United States. Like the Croatians in Perkovich's parish, the Poles in Detroit have long enjoyed dance music at weddings and in taverns. For them, the dance carries connotations of happy celebrations. Like polka Masses in Minnesota, those in Detroit unfailingly draw capacity crowds. Because, although some parishioners will attend a church other than their own for one Sunday in order to avoid the polka Mass, many people from neighboring parishes will more than make up for the home parishioners' absence, journeying some five or even fifteen miles to attend that same polka Mass.

Arguments both for and against the polka Mass have not focused entirely on the issue of origin. Polka texts, like the tunes themselves, may be adapted from the dance hall to fit the liturgy of the Mass—words may be replaced and poetic forms refashioned so that they conform to a standard appropriate to the parts of the Mass. Walser (ibid., 187) offered the example of a love song sung by the New Brass Polish-American band in which a man promises his fiancée "*With bricks and mortar, a home I'll build you.*" The text, adapted by a musician, Gene Retka, becomes a song of meditation for the Mass: "*With bricks and mortar, a church I'll build you*" (ibid.). Koscielska deemed the secularity of polka texts improper to the Mass setting. She noted that the polka settings of the prayers of the mass employ the same polka

---

[2] "Polka Mass: Worship with a Toe-Tapping Beat," *Polka World,* 15 September 1974, 19.

melodies that are heard at Polish-American festivals and in local bars—the original secular texts of which are familiar to the members of the congregation:

> For example, someone has changed the words to a song used at wedding receptions that all Polish Americans recognize. The song tells of a lady who asks her doctor when to "give"—in the morning, or in the evening?—and the doctor replies. In the refrain, the husband sings that his "old lady" is unable to sleep. The suggestiveness associated with and recalled by this melody causes raised eyebrows and side-glances in the congregations, even though the new words state, "We offer bread and wine..." [Koscielski 1984, 27].

There are members of Detroit's Polish congregations who agree with Koscielska's criticism of newly texted versions of popular secular polkas. Even text settings of newly composed polka tunes are considered by some to be incongruous with the solemnity of the Mass because of the shouted interjections of "Hey!" that are common to the polka tradition.

These textual concerns were indirectly countered by Father Frank Perkovich, the pastor of the Croatian church in Minnesota who emphasized the importance of the polka to the unification of his predominantly Slovenian and Croatian church. In an interview published in 1974, Perkovich explained his reasons for introducing polka music into the Mass:

> What is sacred music?... It's anything that unites a congregation—the people and the priest—in praising God. These songs, these polkas and waltzes, have been cherished by generations of Slovenian and Croatian people. The music is beautiful. It reaches our hearts. So I asked myself, "Why couldn't we change the theme of some of the ballads to convey a religious message?" [ibid.].

The references to good times and memories of secular celebration that were decried by the polka Mass's detractors are the very same references upon which Perkovich relied to unify his congregation in their praise of God. Perkovich's comments do not speak to the textual content or sexual innuendos disparaged by the polka Mass critics.

The use of secular popular tunes in the church is a well-established fact of music history. One can go back to the fifteenth century and find four-part compositions intended for use during the Mass that were based upon popular songs of the day. Composers regularly set a well-known tune to a religious text, placed it in the tenor voice, and surrounded it with complementary parts in the bass, alto, and discant (soprano) voices. It is probable that there were eyebrows raised in church in 1435 when the fifteenth-century composer Dufay set the words of the Sanctus (a movement of the Mass Ordinary) to his own popular love song "Se la face ay pale" (If my face is pale). Protestant churches in later centuries continued this practice. Johann Sebastian Bach borrowed the tune of a German love song when he set the text "O Haupt voll Blut und Wunden," a tune known to many twentieth-century Christians as "O Sacred Head Surrounded." Even John Calvin, whose scruples dictated that he oppose the use of musical instruments in the church because of their worldly connotations, made use of hymns adapted from the pop music repertory. If the use of secular tunes in religious services is nothing new, then neither is the criticism of such practice. Koscielska's denunciation of the use of polkas in the Mass echoes the opinion voiced by church authorities during the Counter Reformation. The Council of Trent (1545-63), though it did not outlaw the use of secular tunes in church composition, did advise the removal of all lasciviousness from church music.

In addition to the problems of incorporating a secular repertory into the liturgy of the Mass, critics of the polka Mass cite the commercialism of the bands as yet another inappropriate factor. Band members may sport the logo of their group on the head of the bass drum, or wear it on their jackets. And, more often than not, they display their recordings on tables in the church lobby and offer them for sale to parishioners after the close of the liturgy.

The published viewpoints of Koscielska and the pastors of the Resurrection and Saint Hyacinth parishes have been echoed by members of the churches of Hamtramck. St. Florian has never featured regular polka Masses, while the Polish parishes of St. Ladislaus and Our Lady Queen of Apostles have offered one or two polka Masses each year. The former pastor of St. Ladislaus Church, the Reverend Stan Ulman, like Frank Perkovich, noted that middle-aged members of his congregation have been greatly moved after attending a polka Mass in their home parish, and have requested that such Masses take place weekly. He attributed their enthusiasm both to their familiarity with polka music and to the high level of energy that is generated by the large crowd in attendance.[3]

The conflict over the polka's appropriateness as sacred music in the Polish churches hinges on the issue of appropriate self-representation by the Polish ethnic group. Detractors of the polka Mass who deplore the use of a secular, highly commercialized, jaunty, drinking music within the Roman Catholic liturgy, find its connections to Polish ethnicity particularly odious. Certainly the placement of the event within fundraising festivals does indeed imply a relationship between the polka Mass and the Polish ethnic group, since the polka Mass is frequently listed alongside advertisements for Polish food tents and Polonia beauty queen contests in festival publicity notices. (Criticism of events that imply a close relationship between the polka and the American Polonia has not been confined to a religious music sphere, but is in fact evident in Polish-Americans' comments regarding the proper representation of the Polonia to the larger United States society. The topic of self-representation and the polka outside of the church will be taken up again in chapter 10.)

Despite the infrequency with which the polka Mass appears on annual church schedules, the conflicts surrounding its use bring out some interesting issues concerning identity and the Polish language church. How is Polish identity dealt with on a week-by-week basis? What

---

[3] Interview, Hamtramck, 14 March 1985.

music is used to express the Polish identity of a parish? The answers to these questions vary from congregation to congregation.

The Archdiocese of Detroit—comprising six counties in southeast Michigan and a Catholic population of approximately one and a half million—ascribes Polish identity to a number of parishes in the region.[4] For the archdiocese, such ascription is based on language use, Polish heritage of the congregation, and devotional styles. These parishes are listed below. Each offers Polish-language Masses, devotional liturgies that have a specifically Polish origin, and/or reconciliation and counseling in the Polish language.[5] The listing offers a good deal of information concerning Polish settlement and dispersal in the metropolitan area. From it, one learns that the earliest churches in the archdiocese were erected in the city proper. The founding of parishes in the city in subsequent years attests to an increasing Polish population, while the establishment of churches that followed, in Hamtramck and the suburbs of Wyandotte, Pontiac, and Dearborn, reveals the further growth and movement of that population. The relatively smaller number of Polish parishes founded in the suburbs after 1920 indicates a general shift in language use, from Polish to English.[6] A Polish mission erected much later in Sterling Heights was established to serve the great influx of new Polish immigrants to that area.[7]

Detroit
St. Albertus (founded 1872)
Sweetest Heart of Mary (1886)[8]

---

[4] The six counties in the archdiocese, Monroe, Wayne, Oakland, St. Clair, Macomb, and Lapeer, cover an area of 3000 square miles.

[5] *Archdiocese of Detroit Directory*, 1990.

[6] 21,031 individuals living in the northeast suburb of Warren identified themselves as Polish-American under the category "Single Ancestry Group" in the 1990 Michigan census of the population. The *Directory* of 1990, however, does not list any Polish parishes in Warren. The lack of Polish churches there suggests that aside from a number of Polish-Americans who presumably travel to the city to attend weekend masses at the old Polish churches, or to the northern suburbs to attend new-immigrant churches, the majority of Catholic Polish-Americans living in Warren are comfortable worshipping in the English language.

[7] Due to the changes brought about in the Catholic church by Vatican II in the 1960s, the archdiocese of a city such as Detroit can establish missions in areas where large immigrant populations have settled. These missions, once established, are expected to serve the settlement for ten years. At the end of that time, depending upon their efficacy, the mission's contract is either renewed or canceled. Chominski, "Polish Mission in Suburbs," *Hamtramck Citizen*, 2 September 1982, 11.

[8] In 1990, both St. Albertus and Sweetest Heart of Mary (along with twenty-one other churches) were deemed "unviable"—both financially and in terms of community service programs—by the evaluating committee of the Archdiocese under then Archbishop Edmund Szoka. Sweetest Heart of Mary, however, was able to rally and challenge this evaluation. In the twenty-first century it stands as a landmark of Detroit's Old Polonia. Its spectacular carved wooden altars and graceful, stunningly colored windows bear witness to the nineteenth-century immigrants' financial sacrifice and determination to thrive in the new world.

St. Josaphat (1889)
St. Hedwig (1903)
St. Hyacinth (1907)
Our Lady Queen of Angels (1915)
Our Lady Help of Christians (1923)
St. Louis the King (1923)
Sts. Peter and Paul (1923)
St. Bartholomew (1925)
St. Stephen (1925)
Our Lady Queen of Heaven (1929)

Wyandotte
Our Lady of Mount Carmel (1899)
St. Stanislaus Kostka (1914)
St. Helena (1925)

Hamtramck
St. Florian (1908)
Our Lady Queen of Apostles (1917)
St. Ladislaus (1920)

Pontiac
St. Joseph (1923)

Dearborn
St. Barbara (1924)
St. John the Baptist (1926)

Taylor
St. Cyril of Jerusalem (1953)

Sterling Heights
Our Lady of Częstochowa Mission (1979)

Detroit's Polish parishes serve increasingly diverse neighborhoods. Albanians, Lithuanians, Romanians, Filipinos, and African-Americans, for example, live in the once largely Polish areas. Despite such demographic changes, many Polish churches have retained their Polish identity to a varying extent—providing liturgies in the Polish language, celebrating important dates in Polish history, and sponsoring Polish-ethnic festivals. And although every parish has a distinct character formed of the sum of its members, musically speaking, the parishes are quite similar. A look at the music of three different Polish parishes

Fig. 3.1. St. Florian Church, Hamtramck

Fig. 3.2. Sweetest Heart of Mary, Detroit

Fig. 3.3. Sweetest Heart of Mary, pulpit

in the metropolitan area reveals a well integrated Polish- and English-language repertory that is in common use.

St. Ladislaus in Hamtramck is a parish of almost eight hundred families, of which more than half are of Polish descent. Four Masses accommodate the people who attend weekend liturgies, and one of the four is in the Polish language.[9] Of the daily Masses that take place the remaining six days of the week, three are devoted to Polish-language liturgies, the other three to English. For special liturgies such as Christmas and Easter, when family members are most likely to reunite and the English-speaking generation travels in from the suburbs to attend religious celebrations with parents and grandparents, the church offers additional bilingual Masses. At these gatherings, two hymns are sung in English and two in Polish; one biblical reading is in English, the other in Polish, and the priest uses both languages in his homily.

St. Florian is larger than St. Ladislaus Church, with over one thousand families. The main Polish element at this church is made up of descendants of Polish immigrants who emigrated before the Second World War, but there are representatives of post-war Poland as well. A majority of Polish-American parishioners warrants employment of the Polish language at two of the four Masses offered every weekend and daily Masses in Polish. As in the case at St. Ladislaus, St. Florian Church offers bilingual Easter Vigil and Christmas Masses.

Our Lady Queen of Apostles is a parish informally referred to by members of the two other Polish churches in Hamtramck as "the one to which the new immigrants go for Mass." Thirteen hundred families constitute the congregation there, seventy-five to eighty percent of them claiming a Polish heritage. The church schedules three weekday Masses and one of every four weekend Masses in the Polish language.

The basis of the Polish hymn repertory in all of these churches is a collection of devotional hymns printed in Poland in the early 1900s, and known as a *spiewnik* (pronounced shpyev' nik) or "little songbook." In the Catholic Church, the practice of congregational hymn singing at the Mass in the vernacular language was broadly implemented only after the close of the Second Vatican Council in 1966. But prior to Vatican II, hymn singing in the vernacular outside of the Mass was practiced regularly by Catholics in Poland. The *spiewniks* contain texts of the Ordinary of the Mass, musical settings of introits, hymns for every church season of the year, music for devotions, psalm tones in Latin and Polish, Latin hymns, and antiphons. Carried from the old country to the new by Polish immigrants, the hymns printed in these small books became part of the established repertory in Polish-American churches following Vatican II. The older *spiewniks*, along with newer Polish sacred compositions that were brought to the United States by more recent immigrants and by tourists returning from Poland, serve as the primary sources from which Polish parishes derive their repertory. Because the old *spiewniks* are not numerous enough to supply every member of a congregation with individual

---

[9] I obtained information on the number of Polish-language masses per week from the rectory offices of each parish during June 2000.

copies, a selection of their repertory appears in a paper booklet (or missalette) that is published at six points during the course of the church year. The booklet, entitled *Pan Z Wami* (The Lord Be with You) contains Mass liturgies and song texts (some with musical notation) appropriate to the weeks included in a particular issue.

In 1991 a new compilation of hymns, the *Spiewnik Stulecia Orchard Lake* (*Orchard Lake Centennial Hymnal*) became accessible to Detroit and Hamtramck Polish parishes. Commissioned by the Saints Cyril and Methodius Seminary in commemoration of its one hundredth anniversary, the hymnal was compiled in 1985 by Władysław Budweil, the music director at Our Lady Queen of Apostles Church, and Joseph Kawecki, the organist at the Masonic Temple in Detroit. The songs in the hymnal are derived from at least twenty-five Polish language sources: six *spiewniks*, eight manuscripts, and eleven various collections of songs and Mass settings, and comprise a repertory of 559 musical settings. Of these, 436 are hymns and the remainder are movements of the Mass Ordinary, devotional liturgies, settings of the Hours, antiphons, and psalm tones. Although the hymnal borrows repertory from older sources, more than a third are post-Vatican II additions to the Polish-American repertory, and include Polish language translations of hymns by American, French, and Spanish composers.

The relatively recent access of Detroit's Polish churches to this printed collection of more than four hundred hymns has not resulted in drastic changes in the sources or styles of the repertory, but rather in the size and scope of that repertory. The Polish churches in Hamtramck that had previously relied on a stock of some one hundred hymns, by 1991 had approximately three hundred selections from which to create the musical portion of their liturgies. This body of hymns includes a greater proportion derived from a post-Vatican II repertory. Differences between pre- and post-Vatican II Polish hymns are more readily noted in the texts which reveal conceptual changes in the Church's understanding of its role in the world, than in the musical settings. The music that was composed for congregational singing in the late 1960s and early 70s does not differ tonally or formally from older hymn writing. Because the newer hymns were often conceived with strummed guitar accompaniment, however, they may contain two or more measures of purely instrumental interlude. Thus the older and newer repertories may be characterized overall as demonstrating either strophic or verse-and-refrain formal structures. The hymns are based on a harmonic system that is rooted in western tonality, the majority written in a major key and ending on the tonic, third, or fifth degrees of the scale.

Melodic motion in the hymns is comprised of adjacent intervals of seconds, thirds, fourths, and sixths. The extension of a melodic idea in some instances is accomplished through the raising or lowering of a part of a phrase by one step (hymn ex. 3.1, meas. 1-2 and 5-6). But lengthy periods of sequencing are rare, and melodic extension more often appears as the result of repetitions and recurrences of two- and four-measure units. Exact repetitions of melody may occur at the beginnings (hymn exx. 3.2-3.3) and ends of hymns (hymn exx. 3.1 and 3.4).

The repetition of melodic and rhythmic units is common to many of the hymns—a technique by which the composers achieved internal integration. It is especially prevalent in the isorhythmic *Serdeczna Matko* (hymn ex. 3.1) that demonstrates repetition of the initial four-measure rhythmic pattern throughout, melodic repetition of the final eight measures, and single pitch recurrences. This melodic and rhythmic repetition that is of course not exclusive to Polish hymn writing appears in much of the Polish hymn repertory.

The majority of hymns printed in the song collections are notated in $\frac{2}{4}$, $\frac{3}{4}$, or $\frac{4}{4}$, and less commonly in $\frac{6}{8}$ time signatures. Displaying, in general, symmetrical phrasing, there are examples of hymns notated with an irregular number of measures. The terms "irregular" or "asymmetrical" in these instances refer to an odd number of measures: five or eleven measures instead of the usual four or eight. Phrases comprised of odd-numbered measures frequently result in music that *sounds* lopsided or loping. Hymn ex. 3.5, for instance, begins with four measures that are repeated, and then closes with five measures. Hymn ex. 3.6 has two eight-measure sections followed by a three-measure close. In both hymns the last asymmetrical sections accompany exclamatory texts, *Alleluja!* and *Nie Opuszczaj Nas!* (Do not leave us!). The manner in which these exclamations have been treated with asymmetrical phrasing is not uncommon in the Polish hymn repertory.

The asymmetry and repetitions of initial and final phrases are the salient features of Polish hymns. Nevertheless, neither feature is exclusive to Polish hymnody; thus one cannot positively identify a hymn as Polish merely by the presence of these features. The accompanying Polish-language text is therefore an important marker by which the congregation may recognize that it is singing a Polish hymn.

The hymns are harmonized according to the voice-leading rules of established western tradition, though there is no specifically set harmonization for any one hymn. The Siedlecki songbook and, on occasion, the issues of the Polish-language missalettes contain hymns notated in two voices, spaced a third, sixth or, more rarely, a fifth apart. Whatever notation is made available to the general congregation, in practice they sing only the melodic line in unison. In a church such as Our Lady Queen of Apostles where one of the Polish-language Masses is celebrated with a choir, the Polish hymns are sung in four-part harmony, with strong congregational participation on the melody.

The directors of music in the Polish parishes in Detroit are largely responsible for the selection of congregational music. In choosing to introduce new songs from Poland into this body of music, the directors are influenced by visiting clergy from Poland, recent immigrants, and fellow musicians and parishioners. In some cases, church members returning from a trip to Poland carry new Polish hymns back with them. Significantly, the directors are also guided by the conviction that, as one of the directors stated, "it is most appropriate that masses in the Polish language be conducted as they are in Poland, accompanied by Polish hymns." This statement is telling: clearly the use of the Polish language in the liturgy is not merely a matter of providing Polish speakers a comfortable format for prayer. If language itself were the sole issue, Kawecki and Budweil could have composed *new* tunes for *newly written*

HYMN EXAMPLES 3.1-3.6

Source: *Zacznijcie usta nasze chwalic Pana Swego*,
printed by the parish of St. Florian, Hamtramck, Michigan, n.d.

Example 3.1. Serdeczna Matko.

Sweet Mother, Guardian of the people, would that the weeping orphans inspire you to mercy! Exiles of Eve, we call to you. Have mercy, let us not stray.

Example 3.2. Witaj Pani.

Welcome Lady, Mother of the Lord Jesus. Patroness in times of need, that we would always make our way to you and accept your assistance. O Holy year.

Example 3.3. Zawitaj, Królowo.

Call on the Queen of the holy rosary, only hope of sinners. Call on the stainless lily. Mother of the rosary, Mary.

Example 3.4. Kiedy ranne wstają zorze.

When the morning star rises. To you the earth, to you the sea, to you sings every element. Great God be praised.

Example 3.5. Wysławiajmy Chrysta Pana.

We glorify Christ who conquered death and Satan. Sun, moon, and creatures with the Creator suffered. Alleluja.

Example 3.6. Matko Pocieszenia.

Mother of consolation, Mistress of sky and earth, to you we sinners bring our hearts and give ourselves over to your protection in the tradition of our fathers; we offer you homage, Holy Mother of consolation, do not abandon us!

Polish texts. But instead, they had compiled *imported* tunes and texts, palpably reinvigorating the congregation's sense of its historical-political ties to Poland. The compilers' decision to introduce new Polish music (i.e., from Poland), into the repertory and the congregation's acceptance of this decision demonstrates a strong determination by the parishes to maintain an identity with *modern* Poland.

The sort of endeavors I have discussed thus far—the self-conscious identification of Polish-Americans with both the United States and the old country—is usually undertaken by members of the second generation and their descendants. The first generation (the new immigrant population) is vulnerable to a different dynamic. Their use of a first language that is not English and their practice of foreign customs place them in a position not shared by succeeding generations. They tend, as a group, to express their faith—singing and praying—solely in Polish. Our Lady of Częstochowa, a mission established in 1979 for the most recent Polish immigrants to the Detroit area, is a case in point. More than twenty years after its establishment, this church still serves a Polish congregation. It offers five Masses every weekend, and eight variously arranged daily masses during the week. Every liturgy is conducted in Polish. There are no English-language Masses. The mission does not offer polka Masses. In fact, the only English-language services offered to the people who attend the mission are the rites of reconciliation and counseling.

The display of Polish heritage by second- and succeeding generations of Polish-Americans in Detroit is greatly enhanced by church choirs. The choirs typically perform in their respective churches at only one weekend Mass. Despite the centrality of congregational music-making at Mass, and the peripheral, almost ornamental, role of the choir in this regard, it is the choir that holds the more prestigious position in the Polish church. Because choir members attend weekly rehearsals, they are trained to sing pieces of greater complexity than those of the congregation, and they participate extensively at holy day liturgies. The choir's function can even extend beyond its particular parish, as it represents the Polish-American church at events that take place outside of the church building. For instance, the choirs are often called upon to sing at a Mass solemnizing the founding of a new organization or building in the archdiocese. Both inside and outside the church proper, the choir's vehicle of self-representation is the Polish hymn.

Yet a third musical marker of ethnic heritage in the Polish churches—the other two being the polka Mass and the Polish-language hymn—is the congregational singing of Polish hymns translated into English. Of all three musical expressions, the English-language version of a Polish hymn is the subtlest indication of Polish heritage. Sung at English-language Masses, the English-texted versions of Polish hymns are considered by musicians working in these churches to be essential to the repertory. The directors share the opinion that translations of Polish hymns, when available in an issue of an English-language hymnal, should be incorporated into the repertory.

Members of a Polish-American congregation do not readily recognize the Polish origins of a hymn tune that has been set with an English text, especially if the hymn tune itself is new or unfamiliar. But the music directors make a conscious effort when introducing the new hymn to announce its Polish origin. If a hymn's Polish origins are publicly acknowledged, it can become part of the representative ethnic repertory signifying the Polish-American identity of the congregation—whether or not it is actually sung in Polish. When translated into English, the Polish hymn becomes immediately accessible to younger generations of English-speaking Polish-Americans; at the same time, it allows the Polish music director to acquaint non-Poles with the melodies and textual meanings of Polish hymns. This second purpose has a converse aspect: Polish-Americans may interpret a publisher's decision to include translated Polish hymns in a mainstream Catholic hymnal as a demonstration of the non-Polish community's acceptance of Polish culture.

The position of the Polonia in relation to the larger non-Polish society is an issue that continually reemerges as a significant aspect in discussions of Polish-American musical styles. Although not as pointedly present in the realm of church music as it is in dance music, the issue has been raised. In a letter to the editor of the *Polish Daily News* (17 May 1975), a member of one of the Polish churches in Detroit described the unjust exclusion of Polish hymns from American hymnals: "It is true that we sing French, German, English, African, Italian, and various other hymns—but no Polish." In 1980, such criticism of Catholic hymn publishers was no longer warranted. Two years after Karol Wojtyla, a Pole, became the head of the Catholic Church, World Library Publications issued *A Heritage of Hymns*, a collection of Slovak, Ukrainian, Spanish, Cuban, Hungarian, Haitian, and Polish hymns, set with English texts by Willard F. Jabusch. Thirty-nine of the one hundred and ten selections are Polish and include both translations of the original texts, and newly composed text settings. Although this hymnal is not held in high regard by Polish church music directors in Detroit—some find Jabusch's translations faulty and the new texts incapable of capturing the spirit of the original Polish—*A Heritage of Hymns* serves as a main source of Polish tunes for English-language missalettes.

From the formation of the earliest Polish parish in Detroit in 1872, the Polish-American church has experienced the gradual integration of non-Polish speaking members on the one hand, and the acculturation of Polish immigrant families on the other. Polka Masses as well as two concurrent traditions of language and hymn repertory have emerged as a result. Other Polish-American institutions—cultural clubs, secular choirs, and dance bands—have been subject to the very same dynamics of change. Their responses to the American/Polish dilemma follow along lines similar to those responses enacted in the religious realm.

4

We Brought What We Could.
We'll Keep What's Good.

Cultural Clubs and Secular Choirs:
Polish or English?

At the beginning of the twentieth century the Polish-American community fostered musical societies that were in some ways no less political in intent than the Polish National Alliance (PNA) or the Polish Roman Catholic Union (PRCU)—two groups which did in fact spawn musical affiliates. Though the constitutions of the various musical societies differ in their wording, they express a number of shared aims: to encourage Polish-Americans to learn more about their Polish heritage, to display the best of Polish culture to Polish-Americans and to Americans of other nationalities, and to preserve and maintain the best of Polish culture for future generations. The constitution from the American Council of Polish Cultural Clubs is an example of the stated intentions of Polish arts societies across the country:

> To perpetuate and to develop the culture created by our forefathers, to encourage higher education and scholarship among people of Polish descent; to foster in Americans of Polish descent a consciousness and pride of their own heritage; to enrich the forming pattern of America's great culture by weaving into it the best from Polish sources of inspiration, and of accomplishment, we associate ourselves together.[1]

An understanding of what is meant by the "best" of Polish culture can be derived from the repertories of these groups. Without exception, they emphasize those forms of music traditionally conceived of as high art in Western European culture: orchestral forms, chamber works, and operas. The arts organizations thus sponsor performances of works by Polish composers Krzysztof Penderecki, Frederic Chopin, Maria Szymanowska, and Stanisław

---

[1] From "Societies, Polish" file in the Hamtramck Public Library, 22 August 1963.

Moniuszko. Additionally, they support choral concerts of Polish Christmas carols, and performances by Polish folk dance ensembles.[2]

There exist a number of organizations in the Polonia that lend financial support to Polish-American performing ensembles and are instrumental in bringing Polish touring artists into the Detroit area. These organizations include the Polish American Congress (PAC), the Art of Poland Associates (an auxiliary of the Founders Society at the Detroit Institute of Arts), the Friends of Polish Art, the Polish American Academic Association, the Polish Heritage Society, and the Polish Singers' Alliance of America. This list contains groups that operate at a variety of levels, from the national to the local. The PAC, for instance, is a federation of some three thousand Polish-American organizations including the Polish National Alliance, the Polish Roman Catholic Union, and the Polish Women's Alliance. The Friends of Polish Art, on the other hand, is a Detroit-based society that is part of a federation known as the American Council of Polish Cultural Clubs. All of the organizations endeavor to support a variety of cultural activities throughout the year, including films, lectures, exhibits of paintings by Polish artists, and musical performances by internationally renowned musicians as well as Detroit-based dance and choral groups.

These cultural clubs and organizations frequently create opportunities to collaborate with non-ethnically-specific organizations in order to showcase their historical presence in America. For example, during 2001 when the city of Detroit was celebrating the three hundredth anniversary of its founding, the Polish American Congress worked jointly with the General Motors Corporation, the Polish American Historical Association (an arm of the academic American History Association), the Hamtramck Historical Commission, and the Jewish Historical Society of Michigan in constructing an exhibit at the Detroit Historical Museum. The show lasted almost eight months, opening the thirteenth of October in 2001 and running into June 2002. "The Polish Presence in Detroit" exhibit featured a collection of artifacts, photographs, and letters documenting Polish-American lives during wartime, in politics and labor, and in music and sports.[3] Opportunities to collaborate in citywide events occur with greater regularity in the annual festivities known as ethnic heritage festivals that are held in larger midwestern cities. In Milwaukee, for instance, from June until the end of August, particular weekends are set aside for specific nationality groups. The public is invited to participate in dancing, reading informational booths, and sampling a variety of foods. Similar celebrations take place in Chicago and in Detroit.

---

[2] Polish dance ensembles in the United States merit an entire book-length history. Essentially not-for-profit dance schools, the majority do not regularly employ live musical accompaniment, and thus the telling of their story lies outside of the scope of the present study. The schools' ties to Poland—their performance of Poland's regional dance styles, display of Polish regional dress, and use of recorded musical accompaniments produced in Poland—as well as their varying blends of Polish with Polish-American dances (polkas, rock, and jazz dance numbers) render them a topic rich for discussion of national identity.

[3] *Tech Center News* (Warren, Mich.) 26, no. 7 (22 October 2001): 1A and 4A.

A network of people who share an interest in promoting Polish-American history and ethnic pride have formed a well integrated Polish cultural arts community in Detroit. It is not unusual for members of any one particular association to participate in the activities of another association as well. Members of the various groups know each other—if only by sight. The integration of membership within the various societies first became apparent to me when I had the opportunity as a non-voting member of the American Polish Cultural Center to observe its meetings. I had already spent several months observing rehearsals and performances of various ensembles throughout the city, and upon entering the spacious meeting hall of the Cultural Center, I recognized familiar faces among the crowd of one hundred and fifty in attendance—people from the board of one of the choral groups, members and officers of another choral group, members of the Friends of Polish Art, musicians from the former Hamtramck Philharmonic Orchestra, and a local Polish radio personality. Several months later, with the intent of documenting the actual overlap of membership among the various organizations, I attempted to acquire a list of members of the American Polish Cultural Center, well over a thousand people. My request for a list of members' names was denied when it came before a meeting of the board of directors, a representative of the board explaining to me that not all members wished to make their membership known. Some refused even to allow their names to be recorded by the organization itself, concealing their identity from the general membership and making anonymous financial donations to the Center. The secrecy is certainly not shared by all of the members, nor is it practiced among members of the various musical ensembles who publicly list general members, financial supporters, and members of their boards. It may be a reflection of new immigration membership at the Center—a reluctance on the part of post-Communist Poland émigrés to have their names placed on a list and given to a stranger for perusal. Despite the unavailability of a roster from one of the largest Polish cultural organizations in Detroit, casual observation reveals that the heads of various musical organizations and members of the Polish folk and art music ensembles are well represented in the sponsoring membership of the clubs of Detroit. Although the Polish-American community is geographically dispersed, the club system is integrated through membership and by a commonality of goals.

Membership in the arts clubs represents both older and more recent waves of immigration. The mixture of old and new Polonias is evident in the bilingual nature of meetings. During the fall months of 1989, the general assembly of the American Polish Cultural Center addressed the volatile issue of whether the meetings ought to be conducted in English or Polish. The democratic fashion in which one hundred and fifty people analyzed and discussed the issue made clear the factors of greatest concern to those present. As with all other issues discussed by the general assembly, such as fundraising, public exhibits, and committee work, the topic of language at meetings—Polish or English—engendered arguments and vociferous speeches in both languages. Many members took a turn at the microphone placed in the center aisle of the room. Others began their arguments standing in front of their chairs and moved to the microphone when urged to do so by a member of the board or by those seated across the room who had difficulty hearing what was being said.

All of the members interested in speaking were eventually heard, even though the meetings had to continue for three or four hours. The chair was careful to recognize all speakers, and each speaker was requested by voices in the crowd to repeat whatever they had said in the other language. At one meeting, a well known member of the old Polonia stood throughout the speeches made by other members, and as each finished, he would shout insistently, "Now in English!" or, "Now in Polish!" During successive monthly meetings, the language issue was discussed a number of times and subsequently set aside. Finally, one evening the board addressed the assembly asking (in English), "Who here cannot understand English?" A half dozen people raised their hands. A motion was made that those people who spoke no English sit together with a translator and that future meetings be conducted in English. Thus, the official decision was made. Still, the Center's newsletters are printed in both languages, and those who are more comfortable speaking in Polish continue to communicate at meetings in that language.

The decision made in this particular case is not as significant as are the two major considerations that propelled the arguments. The first being, does the group see itself, and does it want to be seen by others, as essentially Polish or American? And the second, will the use of Polish discourage the second generation (meaning in this case the English-speaking child of a Polish speaker) from joining and so cause the eventual demise of the organization? The first consideration pertains to identity and self-representation and the importance of language in marking that identity. Bilingualism and the question of whether to use Polish or English are issues that have touched *every* musical style and cultural organization in Detroit's Polish community. The second revolves around attracting and maintaining sponsorship and members—especially young members. For performing ensembles, this consideration ultimately affects decisions involving such issues as the appropriateness of borrowing from American popular styles or including such styles on a program.

Like the national Polish-American organizations, musical organizations and performing ensembles attempt to balance a dual allegiance to Poland and to Polish America. This balance is achieved through choices of musical style and repertory, and through a choice of language in song texts, program notes, and day-to-day work within the organizations. An organization's survival depends upon its ability to reach out to members of the old Polonia and to maintain the support of recent émigrés as well. Its legitimacy as a specifically Polish performing or supporting society relies on a continuation of forms and traditions from Poland's art and folk culture and a continued use of the Polish language.

Since at least the first decade of the twentieth century, musicians in Detroit and Hamtramck who shared a Polish heritage grouped together to form musical ensembles. The choirs and folk dance groups that are active in the twenty-first century are only part of what was once a kaleidoscope of large and small performing ensembles in the city. News clippings from the 1960s and 70s, though they carry only tantalizing bits and pieces of information, bear witness to the active and varied musical life of the Polonia during those years. The community's musical offerings included the Hamtramck Accordiana Band, a number of folk music ensembles

Fig. 4.1. Polish American Congress storefront, Hamtramck

Fig. 4..2 Polish Legion of American Veterans Post 10. The Polonaise Chorale held rehearsals on the 2nd floor in the early 1990s

Fig. 4.3. Members of the Club Filarets representing the Polish Singers Alliance of American, District IV, in Hamtramck parade

Fig. 4.4. Suburban Polonia of Sterling Heights representing the American Polish Century Club in a Hamtramck parade. Note the polka band in the back of the trailer
Courtesy of Clare Savaglio

such as the Laur folk song and dance ensemble, the Lira mixed choirs, a mandolin orchestra, the Hamtramck Municipal Band, and the Hamtramck Philharmonic Orchestra.

This last, the Philharmonic Orchestra, was formed and directed in 1922 by a native of Cieszyn, Poland, Frank Grabowski (1892-1968). The orchestra's repertory did not suggest any particular ethnic affiliation; during the fifty years in which the orchestra was active, it played Sunday concerts at the Martha Washington Theater in Hamtramck, pops concerts, and benefit concerts. The orchestra's link with Poland was, however, evident in its active support of Poland and the Polonia. Through benefit concerts, it provided aid to Poland, the Red Cross, and various hospitals in Detroit. An article printed in Hamtramck's *Citizen* in 1951 (March 22) promised free spring concert tickets to the first one hundred displaced persons who would claim them.

One of the oldest arts organizations still thriving in the Polonia of the United States is the Polish Singers' Alliance of America (PSAA). Leon Blaszczyk, a Polish-American history scholar, has suggested that the PSAA grew out of a tradition of singing circles that was practiced by Poles in Poland during the 1860s. Long before that time, he acknowledged, singing circles and choral singing were enjoyed in Poznania (the Prussian partition), "but they were initiated by the upper strata of the society . . . [and] they aimed at ambitious repertory featuring the vocal-instrumental works of great masters" (Blaszczyk 1981, 52). In 1860 Bolesław Dembinski, an organist and conductor living in Poznania, founded a singing circle that would break from the older high art tradition. His organization was loosely based on the concept of early nineteenth-century choral societies of Germany, the sung entertainments of which were known as *Liedertafel*. Dembinski derived the repertory of this first Polish choral society from the Polish folk song repertory and soon initiated many such societies in the surrounding areas. (Blaszczyk's description of this early repertory makes for an interesting comparison with choirs in the early twenty-first century; I'll return to this topic at the close of this chapter.) By 1892 he had founded the Great Poland Singing Association, and for the next sixteen years acted as its general director.

For the Poles living under the crush of Bismarck's *Kulturkampf*, struggling to maintain their language and to pass it on to their children, the singing circles that sang Polish folk songs were a form of organized resistance. The circles' original male-only format was revised to include female and mixed groups. The groups sang in some instances without accompaniment, and in others instances accompanied by organ, harmonium, piano, or more rarely, by an orchestra (ibid.).

In 1889 an immigrant from Bydgoszcz, Antoni Mallek, brought the tradition of Polish singing circles to the United States. As an émigré from Poznania, Mallek was familiar with Dembinski's Great Poland Singing Association. Newly appointed as the organist and choir director at Holy Cross Church in Chicago, he began to gather around him the youth of the parish who were devoted to the cause of freeing the then-partitioned Poland. He organized them into a choir and established the Chopin Singing Society, the founding choir of the Polish Singers Alliance of America. The constitution of the Alliance of May 1889 stated the following objectives: to familiarize Polish-Americans and non-Poles in the United States with Polish songs and to maintain among Poles in the United States a love of Poland. The aims of the Polish Singers Alliance of America (PSAA) were to be realized through the organization of choral groups in as many communities as possible, through competitions, concerts, and the publication of compositions.[4] Indeed, the Polish history scholar Stan Blejwas (1999, 4) referred to the PSAA as an "ideological organization" that distinguished itself from those Polonian organizations that sold insurance by "the primacy of mission over economics." He quoted from a program of Lutnia Choir Number 4 of Town Lake, Illinois, whose aim at the time of its founding was "to preserve the younger generation from denationalization, to inculcate and to grind into their souls love for the oppressed fatherland, for Polish song, and to respond to the needs that were generally perceived in our neighborhoods" (ibid., 9).

During its history the PSAA has survived two breaks: the first lasting from 1897 until 1908, and the second from 1913 until 1928. The internal dissension worked ultimately to the benefit of the Alliance; during each of the two periods of separation the bifurcated parts worked vigorously to attract more members to their respective sides. When the organization subsequently reunited, it enjoyed a greatly swelled membership. The PSAA grew tremendously—by 1903 it had thirty-five member choirs and almost a thousand members. By 1913 membership had leaped to two thousand, increasing to three thousand in 1920 and peaking at five thousand in 1938 (Blaszczyk 1981, 57). Proud of its numbers, and eager to forge a stronger bond with similar organizations in Poland, the PSAA sought to establish an American-Polish exchange program through the Kosciuszko Foundation. The Kosciuszko Foundation was organized in 1925; its founding coincided with the one hundred fiftieth anniversary of the enlistment of Thaddeus Kosciuszko in the American revolutionary army. Kosciuszko, a Polish military engineer who advanced the American cause, had become a symbol of alliance between Poland and the United States. And the foundation that takes his name specializes in cultural and educational exchanges between the two countries. With the support of this group, the PSAA devised a plan in which student directors from the United States would study conducting in Poland while experienced conductors from Poland would travel to the U.S. to guide the PSAA (ibid., 61). Unfortunately, World War II put an end to these plans, and after the war the ties binding Polish and American singing circles weakened considerably. Nevertheless, official links between Poland and the PSAA can be found in the Alliance's International Conventions that are held every three years. The PSAA Conventions provide a stage upon which the member choirs gain an opportunity to listen to and compete against one another. A convention typically lasts five days and usually includes meetings, rehearsals, choral competitions, a grand ball, an awards ceremony, a joint concert of all competing choirs, and a Roman Catholic Mass. The majority of the judges at these conventions are professional musicians who emigrated from Poland

---

[4] In Blaszczyk 1981, "The Polish Singers' Movement," taken from the Constitution of the Polish Singers' Alliance of America, New York, 1952.

Cultural Clubs and Secular Choirs

after the war. Unofficially, the PSAA maintains ties with Poland through its post-war emigrant members, and through its repertory.

It would seem that the PSAA had seen its glory days prior to the Second World War. Once an umbrella organization with two hundred choirs, the PSAA by 1991 had less than fifty. In 2000, that number stood at forty-six—forty-three in the United States and three in Ontario. A look at their distribution in the United States is instructive: not surprisingly, member choirs of the PSAA have endured where the Polish-American population is most concentrated and quite active.

District I	**Eleven Choruses**[5]
Chicago, Illinois	Filareci-Dudziarz, mixed
	Filharmonia, mixed
	Kalina, female
	Filomenii, male
	Echo, female
	Paderewski, mixed
	Lira, female
Gary, Indiana	Chopin, mixed and female
Phoenix, Arizona	Paderewski, mixed
Milwaukee, Wisconsin	Nowe Zycie, mixed
District III	**Four Choruses**
Cleveland, Ohio	Harmonia-Chopin, male
	Halina, female
Johnstown, Pennsylvania	Kolko Młodziezy Polskiej, mixed
	Polish Heritage Choir, mixed
District IV	**Seven Choruses**
Detroit, Michigan	Filarets, mixed and male
Hamtramck, Michigan	Polonaise Chorale, mixed and female
Troy, Michigan	Lutnia Singing Society, mixed and female
Grand Rapids, Michigan	Polish Heritage Society, mixed
District VI	**Four Choruses**
Syracuse, New York	I. J. Paderewski, mixed
	Symfonia, female
	Polonez, mixed
Utica, New York	Filarets, male

---

[5] From the PSAA internet site of 1999.

District VII	**Nine Choruses**
Passaic, New Jersey	Chopin, male
Brooklyn, New York	Jutrzenka, female
	Hejnal, mixed
Philadelphia, Pennsylvania	Paderewski, mixed and female
Hempstead, New York	Oginski, male
New Britain, Connecticut	Polonia Paderewski, mixed and female
Wallington, New Jersey	Aria, mixed
District IX	**Eight Choruses**
Buffalo, New York	Chopin, mixed
	Polish Heritage Circle, male
	Kalina, female
	I. J. Paderewski, mixed
Niagara Falls, New York	Echo, mixed
Hamilton, Ontario	Symfonia, mixed
Lackawanna, New York	St. Hyacinth's Choir, male
Cheektowaga, New York	Quo Vadis, mixed
Junior Choruses	**Three Choruses**
Hamilton, Ontario	Uśmiech (Smile)
Mississauga, Ontario	Radość (Joy)
Philadelphia, Pennsylvania	Adam Mickiewicz

There are a good number out east, with four in Buffalo alone, three in Syracuse and two in Brooklyn. One junior ensemble and four adult groups work out of Pennsylvania. Michigan accounts for seven choirs in the midwest, and other strongly Polish cities such as Milwaukee, Chicago, and Gary, Indiana make up the bulk of the remaining groups. The names of these various choruses speak to the goals of the American Council of Polish Cultural Clubs with which I opened this chapter. Thirteen take their names from the Polish musicians and composers Frederic Chopin and Ignaz Paderewski, while one uses the name of the great Polish poet and statesman Adam Mickiewicz. Others, such as the Polonaise (a dance form practiced by sixteenth-century Polish nobility), Philharmonic, and Symphonia, clearly relate to a classical music background.

The three choirs listed for the Detroit metropolitan area—the Lutnia Singing Society, the Club Filarets, and the Polonaise Chorale—present us with histories that are not uncommon to other chorus members of the PSAA. Beginning as male-only ensembles, early on they spawned affiliates in dance, drama, and women's organizations. In the case of each choir, a body of non-singing members acts as a decision-making board that provides financial support and direction to the performers. The Lutnia Singing Society is the oldest of the three. Organized

Cultural Clubs and Secular Choirs 47

by twelve Detroit residents in 1908, it was originally a male chorus, but formed female adjunct groups during each of the World Wars when male membership was depleted. In the mid-1930s the Lutnia Singing Society considerably expanded its membership to include a boys choir, an auxiliary club for young men, and a young girls' dance class. By 1958 the society had seventy singers and two hundred and fifty supporting members. Their performance venues expanded to radio in 1933 and local television in the late 1940s. But the bulk of their schedule has, for most of its existence, centered around in-community events, such as dates honoring Polish composers, celebrations of significant dates in Polish history, civic parades, religious solemnities, and community outreach performances. In 1981, disagreeing over questions of administration within the group, the Society divided into two parts—one section of the original membership continuing under the name Lutnia, and the other constituting the new Polonaise Chorale, under the directorship of the former Lutnia director, Bronislaw Siarkowski.

Like Lutnia, the Polonaise Chorale places a great deal of its energy into performing for the Polish-American community and, like Lutnia, it acts as a voice for that community representing it to the larger Detroit area. The Chorale's first public appearances of 1981, a series of six Christmas concerts, became an annual tradition among Canadian and Detroit audiences. It followed this initial series with performances celebrating the anniversaries of the founding of the Saints Cyril and Methodius Seminary in Detroit (1885), the establishment of the Polish Boy Scouts (Hacerstwo) in this country, and the fortieth-year commemoration of the Battle of Monte Casino.

The Club Filarets, the third Polish choir in Detroit, was founded in 1935 by three students and was affiliated with the Society of the First Brigade of the Polish National Alliance. The founding students' original intention of identifying themselves with Poland is evident in the motto they chose for their newly established choir: "For Fatherland, Learning and Virtue"—words taken from their Polish patron poet Adam Mickiewicz. In its early years the Filarets, like the Lutnia Singing Society, was a sprawling, multi-faceted organization. It presented choral and orchestral concerts together with its affiliate the Filaret Orchestra, and its members took part in the Club's soccer and volleyball teams, dramatic presentations, and cultural and educational programs. Money raised at these events was donated to Polish as well as American causes—Polish orphans, disabled veterans, and Polish-American students' educational funds. Women sustained the club during the war years, and the post-war periods entailed renewed drives for membership. In 1953, the Filarets became a member of the PSAA.

The majority of the members in each of the three choirs are second- and third-generation Polish-Americans; however, post-war émigrés comprise a small portion of the singers. Of mixed memberships, all three choirs have come under the influence of both the old and new Polonias. Bronisław Siarkowski, who led Lutnia and then the Polonaise Chorale for thirty years, was a member of the post-War wave of immigration. A concert organist, conductor, and composer, he emigrated from Katowice, Poland in 1962. Under his direction, Lutnia recorded its first album in 1976, *The Pride and Spirit of Poland*. After his death, the choir, by then known as the Polonaise Chorale, came under the musical direction of his daughter Ewa

Siarkowska-Depa. Lutnia had to reorganize and seek a new director after the group's bifurcation in 1981. Since that time, it has drawn its leadership from among both recent émigrés and descendants of the older wave of immigration.

The Filaret's director, Władysław Budweil (born in 1921), immigrated to the United States from Europe in 1950 during the great post-war migrations. Budweil, who survived internment at Auschwitz and then Buchenwald, remained in Germany for five years following the end of the war, teaching music to Polish children. He then settled in Detroit where he acquired the post of organist and music director at the Polish church Our Lady Queen of Apostles. Budweil spent some twenty years developing the choirs in that parish before he took on the added responsibility of directing the Club Filarets in 1976.[6] Both the parish choirs and the Filarets have benefited from their director's joint duties: Budweil has frequently brought the groups together in concert, integrating Polish-American musicians from the city and suburbs.

Under Budweil's leadership the Filarets have made two recordings: *Poland's Songs of God and Country* (1966) and *Poland Lives Forever* (1985). The second carries a dedicatory note on the album jacket professing the choir's loyalty to the United States: "[it] is a gift from the Filarets to Detroit's Polonia. It is also their contribution to America's bicentennial celebration." Such patriotic gestures on the part of an immigrant group may seem at first too commonplace to merit attention. They gain significance, however, when viewed against a one-hundred-year backdrop of Polish-American almost over-compensatory affirmation of loyalty to the United States. Not unlike other South and Central European immigrant groups, Polish-Americans have been accused of un-American activities in the workplace and in politics. Their affirmation of an asymmetrical dual loyalty that gives first allegiance to the United States has been expressed in statements made by formal organizations. Typically, these statements offer statistics showing that Polish-American numerical representation in the U.S. armed forces is out of proportion to its numbers in the United States population. (This sort of affirmation of allegiance is common among national heritage groups in the United States and can be found in any number of ethnic group histories published since the 1940s.)

Mieczysław Haiman, a Polish-American history scholar cited just such statistics in his response to a congressional inquiry, dated November 1945. He compiled numbers from a series of questionnaires he had sent to some eight hundred Polish American Catholic churches in the spring of 1944, and compared these with statistics he had gathered from the Polish Institute of Arts and Sciences in America,[7] a Polish daily in Milwaukee, and the Polish Chicago newspaper *Zgoda*. From these, Haiman concluded that Polish-Americans who constituted only four percent

---

[6] *Polish Daily News* 23, no. 5 (1990): 6.

[7] Also known as the Polski Instytut Naukowy w Ameryce, the society was founded in 1941 by a group of scholar-members of the Kosciuszko Foundation. Its purpose is to promote Polish scholarship and appreciation for Polish culture in the United States.

Cultural Clubs and Secular Choirs 49

of the country's total population made up over eight percent of the U.S. armed forces.[8] When Charles Rozmarek, president of the Executive Committee of the Polish American Congress, dedicated the members of the PAC to efforts on behalf of the allies in the Second World War, he affirmed the Polish Americans' loyalty to the United States:

> Our consistent record as loyal Americans stands for all to behold. It is clean and unblemished. We are proud to note that no Polish American has ever been engaged in any sabotage or in any subversive activities. In proportion to our numerical strength, we constitute the highest percentage of volunteers in the air-force, in the navy and in the army. . . . On the home front we are also purchasing more than our quota of War Bonds. So far we have purchased over eight billion dollars worth of War Bonds. In the city of Chicago, for example, government statistics reveal that Americans of Polish descent led the parade of all groups in the purchase of War Bonds.[9]

As patriotic Americans, the Filarets were careful to express their first loyalty to the United States through the dedication of their second album. They did not want the title of that album—which took its name from the words of the Polish National Anthem, "Jeszcze Polska nie zginęła póki my żyemy . . ." (Poland still lives while we are alive)—misconstrued as a gesture of sole allegiance to Poland. And yet, all three of Detroit's Polish choirs have felt a responsibility to make Americans aware of the political situations in Poland. Following the Polish government's check of the Solidarity movement in 1981, the Polonaise Chorale elected to donate the proceeds from a concert to a relief project for Poland. As the president of that ensemble, Ewa Siarkowska-Depa explained in a statement printed in the choir's 1987 program notes: "Since several of the singers have recently come from Poland, where they were active during the Solidarity movement, the chorus has given several performances in support of Solidarity."

At the time I began attending and observing rehearsals of the three choirs, all were rehearsing on a regular, weekly schedule in Hamtramck places of business.[10] One choir rehearsed in a restaurant that was owned by one of its members, another rented the upper

---

[8] Haiman, "The Polish American Contribution to World War II," *Polish American Studies* 3, nos. 1-2 (1946): 35.

[9] This statement can be found in the keynote address of the Polish American Congress of 1944, *Selected Documents* 1948, 5. The reader may wonder at Rozmarek's assertion that no Polish-American has been involved in subversive activities. Certainly he knew that the assassin of President McKinley was the Michigan-born Polish-American Leon F. Czolgosz. But I would imagine Rozmarek was speaking with reference to the Second World War only. In any case, his eagerness to place Polish-Americans in a positive and patriotic light is quite clear.

[10] In the late 1980s Lutnia changed its rehearsal space, but remained in the Detroit area. In 1991 they moved to a northwest suburb of the city, following the general pattern of Polish-American relocation from the city to outlying areas. The Polonaise Chorale moved there soon after.

floor of a Polish Legion of American Veterans bar, and the third rented the back room of another bar. Rehearsals in these makeshift surroundings usually began informally as members arranged chairs in semi-circular rows around a piano. The first rehearsal I attended was the first of the fall season, and people were coming back from a two-month summer break, telling each other about various travel experiences and passing photographs around the room. Members greeted each other with hugs and handshakes, and the atmosphere was one of a family reunion. Because the temperature outside was very warm that evening, the choir decided to rehearse in the large, air-conditioned supply room behind the bar instead of in their usual space upstairs. The move resulted in some interference for the rehearsal, as the sound of patrons singing in the adjacent barroom filtered into the supply room.

This rehearsal was very similar to many that I would attend during that year. Choir rehearsals typically opened with several announcements, questions and discussion about upcoming concerts. The next ninety minutes were spent rehearsing music. The rehearsals, although intensive, took on the aura of a social club during breaks. One choir, on the occasion of its reunion after a summer vacation extended its first rehearsal into an evening of celebration. The rehearsal of another lasted well beyond its regular finishing time of ten o'clock. The choir members, who had been seated throughout the rehearsal, stood up at its close and began singing Polish Christmas carols in four-part harmony from memory, calling out the title of another song as soon as the previous one had been finished. Though some people had come only one or two miles to rehearse, others had traveled five or ten miles. Their willingness to remain in each other's company and sing Polish carols that September evening, long after the required rehearsal had ended, strongly indicated that the ethnically-based music ensembles had remained a vital institution in the social lives of even third- and fourth-generation descendants of the immigrants.

Choir rehearsals were conducted, for the most part, in English. Descendants of the earlier waves of immigration vary in the extent they speak and read in Polish. Many speak what they refer to as "kitchen Polish"—a limited use of the language sufficient to describe day-to-day events, but lacking the level of sophistication necessary to discuss more abstract topics. Thus the use of two languages during rehearsals was an informal and seemingly unselfconscious logistical response to the problem of communication among people who speak one or the other language. The differences in the members' various abilities to speak either language did not result in any antagonism or show of impatience. Any comments or questions spoken in Polish by choir members were answered by the director in Polish and then translated into English for anyone who could not understand Polish. If the directors themselves slipped into Polish, they immediately translated what they had just said into English. In the case of one director who spoke very little English, the rehearsal was conducted in Polish, and one of the Polish-speaking members of the ensemble translated all of the director's remarks into English. This same bilingualism occurred at board meetings of the choir, where members made an effort to relay information first in one language, and then in the other.

The use of two languages sounds more cumbersome in its description than it actually is. The choirs, after all, are not wrangling over a decision about which language to use—as was the case at the American Polish Cultural Center. Their use and translation are expedient, and not at all self-conscious. Musical concerts are a different matter, because in the public eye language use becomes an emblem by which the choir marks its Polish and Polish-American identities. Because the intent behind the concerts is as much education of the audience as it is entertainment, customarily a choir member or the director introduces each song or set of songs to the audience with a statement about its origin, history, or significance. Depending on the audience, this information may be imparted only in English, or in other cases, in Polish and then translated into English. Never are the introductory comments made only in Polish. While the audiences at Polish community benefits are Polish-American, the choirs perform also for general audiences—especially during the winter holiday season. Bilingualism in the case of performance is as important in self-identification as are choices of costume and repertory.

Concert dress of the choirs is uniform—either formal in the style of the western European art music tradition, or designed to represent the traditional clothing of Poland. Traditional garb in Poland varies from region to region, and the choirs expend a good amount of effort in researching and replicating regional folk dress. Again, with an intent to educate their listeners, the choir provides the audience with information about their concert dress, either in printed form in the concert programs, or verbally while on stage.

The choirs have a number of regular avenues of performance open to them: they perform at civic events at which ethnicity plays a significant role. For instance, they have sung at Detroit's ethnic festivals on the waterfront and at Polish festivals in the suburbs north of Detroit. Typically performances at such events entail a twenty- or thirty-minute program outdoors. The choirs perform standing on risers in front of a sound shell, and present their songs as fair-goers pass by or take seats on available benches or chairs to listen for a while. Memorial Day and Labor Day parades provide another forum for a public appearance, where members may march silently behind a banner bearing the choir's name.

Historical anniversary celebrations offer yet another performance opportunity, and, as a tradition, reach back into the earliest days of the PSAA. The First Chopin Singing Society of Chicago, within its first twenty-five years of existence, sang at 215 patriotic commemorations. The pattern thus established, in 1910 the PSAA choirs performed at the unveiling of statues erected in Washington, D.C. to the memories of Polish and American patriots Thaddeus Kosciuszko and Kazimierz Pulaski. Nationwide, they presented concerts marking the five hundredth anniversary of the Battle of Grunwald (Blejwas 1999, 11). These types of commemorations, like the civic events, require that the ensemble constitute only a part of one or two days of scheduled events. Choral concerts, in contrast, are comprised only of choral music. They provide the choir director with more freedom in choosing repertory. He or she may count on a lengthier program and on a stationary audience that is presumably prepared to stay and listen for sixty or ninety minutes. The place of performance—a recital hall, church narthex, or even a low-ceilinged reception hall—allows for dress rehearsals and sound checks prior to the actual concert, and thus offers the director greater control over sound production as well. Thus a six- or seven-minute work by Moniuszko, or a sparsely textured religious piece from the seventeenth or eighteenth century may be sung to its greatest artistic advantage. Nevertheless, in spite of all of the advantages presented by the choral concert, the choirs cannot afford to limit themselves solely to these more controlled situations. The ethnic festivals, parades, and historic commemorations provide choruses with potential audiences of thousands to whom they might showcase "the best" of Polish culture.

The repertory of twentieth- and twenty-first-century PSAA choirs reminds one of Blaszcyzyk's description of pre-1860s Polish choral groups in Poznania that featured "the vocal and instrumental works of great masters." But it shows the influence of the Great Poland Singing Association as well. Dembinski's post-1860 reliance on folk songs is mirrored in a twentieth- and twenty-first-century repertory that comprises examples of traditional Polish folk (village), political, sacred, and classical music. Over the past one hundred years, the Detroit choirs have amassed a substantial library, including pieces published in the United States, some printed in Poland, and a great many handwritten, xeroxed arrangements—the creative work of musically educated directors. From this vast repertory the directors choose pieces by which they hope to communicate pride in the Polish heritage and to share the most laudable elements of Polish culture with the American public. One of the directors explained to me that the aim of his choir was to show to others the "true music" of Poland—beautiful compositions and regional folk music that he had arranged in two-, three-, and four-part harmonies. Whether recent arrangements for choral groups, or in original format, the repertory reflects a wide variety of sources, both chronologically and with regard to subject matter. Although I am offering here a look at the repertory of only one of the choirs' libraries, its holdings are typical of all three groups. The ensemble's librarian had categorized the entire repertory as follows: Theme Song; Patriotic; Early Sacred; Recent Sacred; Stylized Arrangements of Folk Music; Polish Christmas Carols; Contemporary Poetry about Solidarity.

This repertory reveals a strict commitment to the learning and presentation of Polish music and a disregard for Western European and American compositions; of the Early Sacred category, only one selection is not by a Polish composer, "Ave verum" by Wolfgang Amadeus Mozart—but its text has been translated into Polish. Other early sacred music includes a sixteenth-century song by Wacław Z. Szamotul and a seventeenth-century "Ave Maria" by Bartłomiej Pękiel. The category "Recent Sacred Music" includes songs composed within the last thirty years, such as a Mass Ordinary by Jan Maklakiewicz for choir and organ, and a work by Bronisław Siarkowski, composed in honor of the visit of the Polish Pope John Paul II to Detroit in 1987.

The songs are arranged in two-, three-, four-, and six-voice harmony according to the rules of traditional western part writing. Two songs from the repertory are included at the close of this chapter. The one entitled "Kukułeczka" (ex. 4.1) is as well known in Poland as it is in the United States Polonia, and has been recorded by Mazowsze, one of Poland's

Cultural Clubs and Secular Choirs 53

foremost regional song and dance ensembles.[11] Arranged for three women's voices, it is a light, playful piece. Its emphasis on beat two of the three-beat measure is reminiscent of a mazurka. The Hofman arrangement (ex. 4.2) of an opera chorus follows the rhythmic pattern of a *krakowiak*—a strong $\frac{2}{4}$ march with, again, an emphasis placed on the second eighth-note beat of the measure. Composed for four voices—soprano, alto, tenor, and bass—its text is patriotic. The texts of arranged folk music frequently feature elements from various dialects.[12] Whether the songs were originally transcribed with the regional dialect intact or the elements of dialect were incorporated later with an attempt at local color is not known. In any case, the inclusion of dialect enhances the provincial or "folksy" nature of the songs. The category "Patriotic Songs" contains material much older than the Solidarity song ("Żeby Polska," by Włodzimierz Korcz). The patriotic texts are derived from the situations of eighteenth- and nineteenth-century partitioned Poland. The majority of the song texts are in Polish, excepting certain of the religious songs, which are in Latin, and the English-language Christmas carols used at seasonal concerts.

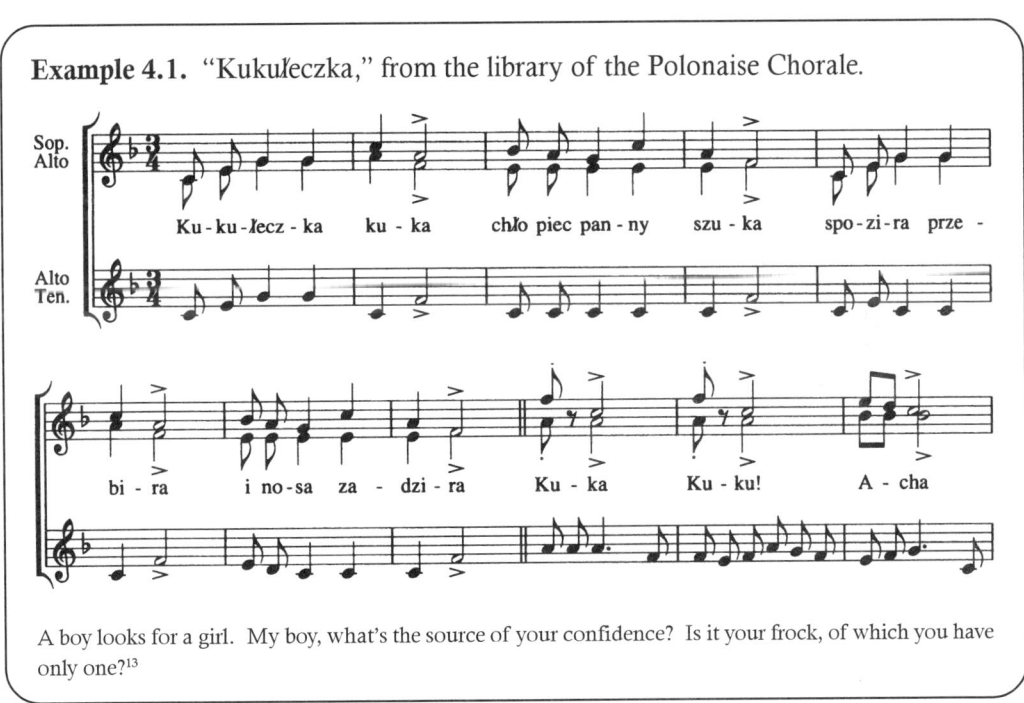

Example 4.1. "Kukułeczka," from the library of the Polonaise Chorale.

A boy looks for a girl. My boy, what's the source of your confidence? Is it your frock, of which you have only one?[13]

---

[11] Mazowsze, founded in 1948, was one of Communist Poland's foremost "folk" ensembles, and was patterned upon the Soviet dance group Moiseyev.

[12] I am grateful to Dr. Frank Gladney for bringing to my attention the use of Polish dialects in the stylized text arrangements of traditional folk songs.

[13] I have included in my translations the continuation of the texts beyond those measures which appear in the abbreviated exx. 4.1 and 4.2 in order to provide a fuller rendering of both songs' meanings.

Example 4.2. Excerpt from "Marsz kosynierow" by J. Stefani, arranged by Karol Hofman, from the library of the Polonaise Chorale.

Farther brother, eagerly farther. The harvest opens for us. Let's throw the plow and coulter.
We must fight, since such is the lot that has fallen to us. Let he who wants to, farm.
Let the old man look after the field. We the plowboys, the cottagers, throw [aside] the plows
Take up the pikes.

Onward brothers without fear. No more will it be as it was.
The enemy shudders before peasant strength. The dear sun will rise over the fields.
The fortunate day will come soon. The Day of Brotherhood and Freedom
Of a Reborn, Young Poland.

For what kind of a guy, only a Krakowian peasant.
The proud soul in us does not fear the nobleman. They oppressed us enough. Let's not endure
Any further injustice. Let us grab axes. Everyone come the way of Kosciuszko.

The choral groups are firmly linked to Poland through performances of a largely European-composed repertory and by their membership in the Polish Singers' Alliance of America, an organization that has its roots in the traditions of the singing circles in Poland. It is this traditional association with Europe, I believe, that allows the choirs to represent the Detroit Polonia at official presentations and celebrations of the community's national origins. In addition to singing at ethnic festivals, they perform at receptions honoring visiting religious and political dignitaries. The choirs' primary mission—or, the reason for their existence—remains what it was at the beginning of the twentieth century: namely, to preserve and maintain for their children, and to show American society what they consider the best of Polish culture. In this purpose, the choirs—as an institution—are at odds with another representative institution of Polish-American culture: the Polish-American dance band and its mainstay—the polka.

Fig. 5.1. Lutnia Chorus during its heyday, under the directorship of Bronistaw Siarkowski. Production of "Memories of Poland" ca. 1968. Joann Nawrocki is seated to the right of the director. Joan Hickey is standing in the 3rd row, 1st woman on the left
Courtesy of Lutnia Archives

5

Lutnia

*The Story of One Choir**

Lutnia is the oldest of the three choirs in Detroit. Founded in 1908, it is in fact the oldest Polish choir in the state of Michigan. But it is also an institution the heyday of which is long past. Although unique in the particulars of its founding and its performing career, Lutnia is not unlike its fellow choirs in Detroit or Chicago, at least not with regard to its goals and cultural affiliations. This chapter seeks to narrate the history of one choir, Lutnia, and to provide some reflections of four of its remaining members, Jean Nash, Joann Nawrocki, Joan Hickey, and Toni Colasanti.[1]

Lutnia's founders, deeply appreciative of the choral singing tradition, sought to create a formal singing organization that would exist outside of the church. In August 1908 six men met in one of Detroit's halls with the intent of organizing a choir. Their full names do not appear in Lutnia archival materials, but are listed merely with first initials and last

---

* My position regarding this particular choir went well beyond that of observer. Some years after I had initially contacted the group, interviewed members, and attended rehearsals and board meetings, I received a call from Barbara VanHulle, a member of Lutnia, who offered me part-time work as the choir's new director, a position I held for two years. I did not take a strong leadership role in the ensemble—the members themselves presented me with the repertory they wished to cover during rehearsals, and it was they who suggested a number of performance venues. My job entailed rehearsing the choir—at that point more accurately described as an octet of women's voices—and directing and accompanying its performances at various senior centers and churches. During these two years, I was able to observe at close hand the women's great dedication to their task and discuss with them their motivation for performing.

[1] A word concerning my transcription of group interviews: Nash, Nawrocki, Hickey, and Colasanti form a close-knit group whose personal ties in some cases reach back to the 1960s. The camaraderie between the women and their interest in each other's statements cannot be adequately brought out when transcribing the interviews. I've tried to provide some of the emotional content of the situation by transcribing interruptions or places where one woman would finish another's sentence. But the general flavor should be understood—often while one woman spoke, the others were making sounds of general agreement.

names, as B. Kawecki, Wojciechowski, R. Beger, M. Zaporski, and F. Freda. They intended that Lutnia endure solely as a musical institution; it was not meant to double as an insurance group, or a religious or political society. From the beginning the six men acted in earnest about establishing a rather formal organization: at their first meeting they set a date for the following week when each would bring with him other interested persons and together they would elect officials. That following week, not only did they select officers and choose their first director, but they also took on the motto *Gora Piesn!* (Hail to song!), and agreed to address each other with the term *kolega* (colleague).

Lutnia survived its first year without funding. Its continued existence rested entirely on the cooperative efforts of W. Osmialowski, who agreed to direct the all-male group for free, the owner of the Polonia Hall who allowed the group to use his building without rental charges for weekly rehearsals, and the regular attendance of the men themselves. The choir's first season of rehearsals resulted in two concerts, one in December, and the second in August. In the fall of their second season, they became a chorus member of the national Polish Singers' Alliance of America, and in 1911 they were ready to take part in their first PSAA convention.

Lutnia was begun by and for men. It is unknown when women may have first expressed an interest in joining, but approximately six years after establishing the organization, men accepted female members. The women were members only in a restricted sense, however. They could not cast a vote concerning organizational issues, nor were they allowed to sing under the Lutnia name. Instead, Lutnia took them on as an affiliate—a women's chorus known as Halka. Those lists of names on programs that are still in existence reveal that in 1915 Lutnia had twenty-one members and Halka, thirteen. Halka and Lutnia rehearsed separately from each other. And although the men's and women's choruses participated in the same concerts and competitions, they usually performed at these events as two separate bodies. Exceptions to this their regular form did occur, however, at least as early as 1916; the acceptance of women into the organization had made the mounting of large-scale productions of Polish operas and operettas feasible for the first time. The first opera men and women tackled together was Stanisław Moniuszko's *Halka*. Composed in 1848 and referred to by musicologists as Poland's first national opera, its title provided Lutnia's female affiliate with a name. Other dramatic performances for which women's voices were required followed upon this initial success and included the operas *Flis* (The Raftsman), *Hrabina* (The Countess), and *Verbum Nobile*, all by Stanisław Moniuszko.[2]

Despite the great deprivations under which Americans struggled in the Depression years, or maybe because of these deprivations, Polish-Americans sought the camaraderie of choral groups in ever-greater numbers. By 1933 the men's chorus had grown to include forty-nine

---

[2] Moniuszko (b. Minsk 1819, d. Warsaw 1872) is the foremost composer of Polish operas and symphonic works in the nineteenth century. Along with *Halka* of 1848, his operas include *The Raftsman* (1858), *The Countess* (1860), and *The Haunted Castle* (1865).

members. There is no evidence of Halka's existence during the 1930s, and we find women associating with the group in a new role. In April of 1933 women formed a Ladies Auxiliary (*Grono Pan*). This was a non-singing affiliate whose efforts supported the financial upkeep of the Lutnia Singing Society. By organizing and selling tickets for picnics and social dances, the Auxiliary raised funds for the director's salary, the purchase of uniforms, and travel to conventions. In a number of instances, they were able to donate some of the monies raised to Polish Veterans organizations.[3] *Grono Pan* was quite active during the thirties and managed also to establish folk dancing classes for girls. These were peaks years for the choir. Although there are no numbers available from the late thirties, the addition of youth affiliates suggests that the organization continued to increase in overall size. In 1937 the men established a Youth Circle (*Kolko Mlodzieży*) which was meant to provide older boys with an opportunity for musical socializing—boys Lutnia intended would one day join the men's chorus. Nevertheless, despite Lutnia's many programs in the 1930s, the 1940s ushered in a new era; in the way of all "best laid plans," the men's intentions for further expansion were upset by world events.

With the entry of the United States into World War II, at least thirty-five Lutnia men were called up to serve, depleting the group's membership. In response to this, the choir's personal crisis, the women reinstituted their choir (that had fallen by the wayside during the twenties) and engaged Ed Adamski in 1943. He served as the women's temporary director until, in the fall of that same year, he handed over full directorship to Kazimierz Obecny. After the war, certainly the men must have experienced some dismay as they looked upon Lutnia's greatly reduced ranks. Still, men's and women's choruses did not join forces; they would remain separated into the 1960s.

Beginning in the late 1950s and continuing through the early 1980s, Lutnia's membership was enhanced through the initiation of new female singers, one or two at a time. (Those women who joined prior to 1968 formed what was then known as the Lutnia Girls Glee Club.) In some cases then current members invited acquaintances to accompany them to rehearsals; in others, a singer sought out the group herself. Jean Nash recalled an invitation extended to her by one of Lutnia's long-time members:

Jean: [I began, thanks to] my little friend Ewa [Pencach]. She sang in our choir at church, and one Christmas, she said they needed people for their [Lutnia's] Christmas program. And that brought back so many memories of having been raised in Canada . . . and the Polish *kolendy* [carols]. Back when we were kids, the priest used to go from house to house during the Christmas season with ushers. And they would [laughs], they would sing Christmas carols in parishioners' homes. . . . This

---

[3] Picnics and dances are a well-established form of fundraising among the Polish choirs. And incidentally, both types of events provide work for the local dance bands which perform live music. Dues required of members as late as the 1980s amounted to only $12 per year, and certainly could not cover the cost of uniforms or the director's stipend.

was in Toronto. And then every parishioner would have a toast, and by the time the priests and ushers were done [laughter] . . . I mean the snow was melted and they were lucky if they got back to the rectory after all that. But it was always fun.

Joan: Now were these Polish songs they were singing?

Jean: Yes. This was a Polish church. We went to St. Stanislaus Church in Toronto. So that was part of our Christmas tradition. So when Eva told me they needed somebody to join the choir at Christmas time, I joined. And it was just so, so great hearing Polish Christmas carols again.

Like Jean, Toni Colasanti also received an invitation from a member of her regular church choir.

Toni: I was sitting at our church choir at St. Hyacinth's (which is a Polish church choir) and Mary [Kozlowski] asked me if I would join with her group. She had already sung there, she belonged, and that's how I got to know Joann, through Mary. And I just started going there. Then Joan joined . . .

Joan: I was there before you. Mary and I joined together [general agreement].

Toni: So it was Mary that talked me into coming. And I love music, I love playing music. Both my parents are Polish. My mother came from Poland when she was little, and [music] was just something we did. But I remember, in our neighborhood on Christmas Eve, there would be two or three groups of four or five young people going from door to door, ring the doorbell, and start singing these Polish carols. And naturally, my father and my mother would give them whatever change or money they had. No sooner would they leave, maybe within another half hour, another group came. And I guess that was just something I *wanted* to do when I got to be sixteen years old. (My mother said [only] when you're sixteen [laughter].) I miss it now. I *really* miss it.

Joann: Well you built up a camaraderie . . .

Toni: Of people, when you sing.

Joann Nawrocki's ancestral ties to Lutnia reached back to the choir's origins. Her grandfather's brother Bolesław Kawecki was one of the founding members. But she was unaware of her family connection at the time she joined. She could not recall exactly what brought Lutnia to her attention—at the time she joined there was at least one other PSAA choir in existence (Club Filarets), but she remembers her motivation in seeking it out:

> I never knew that my great uncle had any involvement with Lutnia. In fact, I didn't even know about Lutnia until I was . . . probably twenty, and I was singing at St. Thomas the Apostle in a church choir. . . . I don't even remember how I heard about Lutnia, [but I remember telling the organist there that] I wanted to join a Polish choir, and I was going to join Lutnia.

> But it wasn't until I got involved in fact in [writing] one of the anniversaries of Lutnia's history that I found my great uncle's name. Then I asked my mother, could that be a relative, and she said "Yeah" [*laughs*].

Joan Hickey's description of her earliest encounter with Lutnia resembles that of Toni, Jean, and Joann. She joined alongside of a friend from her church choir. Like Joann, Joan did not recall when or where she had first heard of the organization, whether she had read about it in a local Polish newspaper, or the *Michigan Catholic*. Although the women joined at different points in their lives, their stories are similar. For each had had choral experience as a youngster, and each had expressed a desire to emulate something they had seen as children.

It was not until 1968 that the Lutnia Singing Society accepted its first female voting members, and not incidentally, elected its first woman president, Joann Nawrocki.

> *Joann*: I was the first woman president.
> *Paula*: Of the whole group? Not just the Girls Glee Club?
> *Joann*: Right.
> *Toni*: The chauvinists had finally settled down [*laughs*].
> *Joann*: It was a great revolution when it happened, because the old guard just couldn't accept a woman.
> *Paula*: Did you make it by election?
> *Joann*: Yes, it was by election. But it was the first time the women voted [*laughs*].
> *Joan*: So you see who had the clout.
> *Joann*: A lot of the men voted for me too. Because, actually it was Richard and Ted who decided they were going to make me president.

It was perhaps the changes in societal views in general that influenced a change in Lutnia's view of its own gender-divided membership. Certainly, Toni's use of the word "chauvinist" places the election within the context of women's rights struggles of the late 1960s and early 1970s. And Joann's statement, that two male members of the group instigated her nomination, supports the argument that the men themselves no longer viewed Lutnia as a male-led organization. Membership lists are unavailable for 1968—the year of Nawrocki's election—but those of the next few years reveal a membership rather evenly distributed between men and women.[4]

Lutnia's finances, like its trends in membership, fluctuated in step with larger societal trends. These changes in the financial status of the choir generated a few changes of address. The choir's first rehearsal space proved temporary and set a pattern for future movement, as the group would shift its headquarters many times during its ninety-year career. In the

---

[4] Program photographs in 1970 reveal a membership of twenty-one women and seventeen men. By 1983 these numbers had dwindled to eighteen women and thirteen men.

1930s members acquired a clubhouse on Palmer and Chene in Detroit. It was a significant move, because these quarters served as more than merely rehearsal space; there, in addition to conducting their regular rehearsals, the group scheduled literary as well as musical evenings for its members' benefit. But financial concerns forced them to give up the clubhouse in 1942 and move into a smaller establishment on Medbury and Chene. The group's fortunes changed again in the post-war American economy, and in 1950 it purchased a grand, three-story house at 1819 East Grand Boulevard at the corner of Moran. Lutnia members made full use of the house's ample dimensions, converting its space into eight meeting rooms, a bar, and a rehearsal hall. The Grand Boulevard mansion served as home until 1976, when financial considerations once again required the group to move out. By the mid-1980s when I first began attending rehearsals, Lutnia had moved to another temporary rehearsal space: a Polish restaurant in Hamtramck, owned by a couple who sang with the choir. Anthony Kulick, owner of the Golden Duckling, closed the restaurant early on Wednesday evenings. Choir members, admitted after hours, would quickly convert the interior, pushing aside tables, and forming a semi-circle of chairs around an upright piano that stood against a side wall. By 1992, when I'd looked the group up again, they had already established another rehearsal space in a large barroom at the back of the American Polish Cultural Center (APCC) in Troy, a northern suburb. This building, replete with carved wooden columns, slate floors, and lighted showcases, had originally served as a privately owned architectural museum. The APCC refashioned the building so that it served the suburban community as a Polish restaurant and rental hall. For Lutnia, it served as a headquarters.

Every week choir members, myself included, entered the bar by a back door so that we would not disturb any of the entertainment going on in the front rooms. As quickly as possible, we converted the available space, rearranging chairs and tables, and unlocking the piano. (The instrument belonged to Lutnia; locked and stowed up against the barroom wall, it was not available for use by APCC patrons during the week.) We retrieved our music from a set of cupboards in the bar. The seven or eight women present conducted a business meeting, either at the beginning of rehearsal after the set-up process was completed, or during the middle of our two-hour session when I called a break. During the business meeting, I remained silent. They communicated with each other in both Polish and English, as at least half of our company felt either equally comfortable in both languages or a little more so in Polish. Topics covered included plans for future conventions or performances, as well as fundraising. When this part of the evening came to a close, we resumed singing. As director, I selected most of our music from the Lutnia library (a standard Polish choir repertory, described in the previous chapter). To this body of songs we added selections chosen for our entire circuit by the PSAA, and from my own collection I added a translated (Polish) arrangement of an old standard, "Cocktails for Two."

Despite the long-standing friendships of the women present, the members worked hard at their musical task all evening with very little side conversation. Our rehearsals focused on rather standard musical elements: intonation, rhythm, enunciation of text, phrasing, and style. The only interruptions to our sessions were the sounds of a bingo game seeping into the bar through a somewhat problematic public address system. At the close of rehearsal, we returned the furniture to its usual position, and then saw each other safely out to our cars in the parking lot behind the building.

In eighty-four years the choir had moved its headquarters at least seven times, but consistently it remained in Polish "territory"; its final headquarters in the suburb of Troy was situated in an area populated by Polish-Americans who, like the choir members, had moved out of the city of Detroit. In addition to its many changes of address, Lutnia also experienced a high rate of turnover in its musical directors, especially since the 1980s. My immediate predecessor, a recent émigré from Poland, directed the choir only a few years. The perils she experienced in her own neighborhood forced her to reconsider leaving the house and traveling more than twenty miles round trip on rehearsal nights. I directed the group for only two years before I left for a teaching position. The last choir director, a graduate student in music, led the group during its last two or three years, until dwindling membership made the singing of choral repertory impossible. (In contrast to Lutnia, the Club Filarets remains a uniquely viable organization in the year 2000. This is due, I believe, in great part, to the consistent leadership provided by Władysław Budweil, who has served as the Club's director since the 1970s. His personal dedication to the group has inspired a similar loyalty and fortitude among group members. Nevertheless, the average age of membership is relatively high, and without the influx of youth, the future of Club Filarets does not appear favorable.)

The financial struggles as well as the logistics involved in keeping Lutnia afloat—namely, the searching out of adequate rehearsal space, engaging a director, and maintaining a strong membership—were everyday concerns and the subject of group business discussions at rehearsals. Vital to the group's very survival, these concerns were nevertheless only the means by which the choir might pursue its main objectives: musical excellence and the demonstration of pride in its Polish heritage.

Lutnia's members measured their progress with regard to musical excellence through competition with other Polish-American choral groups. The choral conventions that are sponsored by the Polish Singers' Alliance of America (PSAA) and take place every three years comprised the centerpiece of Lutnia's competitive efforts. Probably more than any other performance activity, the convention's competitions kept the choruses focused on the honing of their musical skills, vocal unity, and group precision. Competition pieces demanded concentrated study of a choir and its director. Traditionally, a competing choir chooses one piece from its own repertory, and then studies two or three others assigned by the PSAA circuit. A choir does not learn until a week or so before the convention takes place which of the circuit's assigned pieces will be used in actual competition. Those pieces not used in competition are sung by a mass chorus made up of all competing groups at the close of the convention. Circuit sponsors maintain secrecy about the assigned pieces because they hope to encourage the choirs to give equal attention and study to competition and performance numbers alike. This is the circuit's method of ensuring a fine closing performance.

The level of difficulty of the chosen repertory requires that the singers, who for the most part have not received formal musical training, nevertheless learn to sing complex rhythms, unusual and dissonant harmonies, and the correct enunciation of Polish texts. Because scheduled rehearsals occur only once a week, some practice reading their music at home. Those who cannot read music must learn through repeated listening and correction by the group's musical director. After a group has memorized the competition pieces, it then begins readying its stage presentation. Convention judges award points for uniformity and discipline in appearance as well as in sound. As important as the singing itself is the way a group walks onto the stage and situates itself on the risers. Dress at these events is not Polish regional clothing, but rather a formal costume of the group's choosing. Men wear dark suits, and women formal gowns, of a single color.

The first time Lutnia attended the convention as a mixed chorus, the women recalled they lacked money for stage clothes. All the group's funds had been spent toward bus fare for the group's travel to and from the event:

Joann: That was the first convention we went to, and we were so poor. . . . We had to have uniforms.
Joan: Uniforms everyone'd look good in.
Joann: So we ended up ordering these blouses for three bucks, and then the girls all made [skirts].
Joan: We were the poorest group there.
Toni: But we looked good!
Joann: And we won. We won two first places!

Trophies awarded at the event and the recognition of PSAA judges and one's peers only accounted for a portion of the joy Lutnia members derived from the conventions.

Joann: I would enjoy being in a choir when you got it right. You know, that *sound*.
Jean: Yeah, the result.
Joan: The result was mind-boggling to tell you the truth.
Joann: I know that when we did that piece that we call the Chinese song, it was so hard, it was six- or eight-part harmony for girls.[5] Each section was split, and I thought to myself, we are never going to get this right. But when we sang it [at competition], and you knew you had it right. You *knew* you *had it*.
Joan: The feeling of satisfaction is unbelievable. . . .
Joann: Right. And it's a real sense of accomplishment, because it takes each individual contributing, and that's the wonderful part. . . . It's not one person or two people. It's everybody.

---

[5] Lutnia choir members do not recall the actual title of the "Chinese Song." The composition may have incorporated a pentatonic scale pattern—thus their description of it as "sounding" Chinese.

The Story of One Choir

The triennial PSAA conventions are certainly central to the choral group's efforts, but they are substantially an in-house event—choruses sing for each other. Another whole aspect of Lutnia's career has taken place in more public-centered performances, where the display of Polish culture and music is paramount. In 1910, one of Lutnia's earliest concerts marked the five hundredth anniversary of the Battle of Grunwald. For Polish patriots, the commemoration of Grunwald recalls the triumph of Poles and Lithuanians over the occupying forces of Teutonic Knights and their West European allies in the fifteenth century. The proceeds from this concert were divided between an orphanage and a Polish-American college, Alliance College in Cambridge Springs, Pennsylvania. The choir's emphasis on Polish heritage, begun with this nod to the victory of Lithuanians and Poles at Grunwald, continued into the 1990s. As one Lutnia member pointed out,

> You want to do a variety of the music that is your heritage. And most of us who belong to Polish choirs were Polish heritage. So we did everything from fifteenth century to things that our directors would write for us—contemporary—and you did it because it was a representation of the culture. You have to know the history to know where you're going.[6]

In 1933 Lutnia began a series of Christmas broadcasts on radio, singing Polish carols interspersed with spoken narratives in both Polish and English. Like the annual broadcasts and live Christmas concerts, summer ethnic festivals became a regular staple of community leisure pursuits. The choir also scheduled special performances to mark the anniversaries of such famous Poles as the musician Stanisław Moniuszko and the scientist Mikolaj Kopernik (Copernicus). In addition to celebrating dates in Polish history, they participated also in commemorations of Polish-American and Catholic history in Detroit. In June 1972, for example, during the celebration of a traditional Catholic holy day, Corpus Christi, the choir processed to three different churches in Detroit, forming a long parade down the city streets. The next year they were on hand at the anniversary of the founding of one of the city's oldest Polish parishes, St. Albertus Church. There they performed a repertory of medieval and renaissance religious music.

Of all of Lutnia's public performances, two stand out in the collective memory of the organization. The first was a series of concerts they performed with the Detroit Symphony Orchestra. An expensive undertaking, the series began in 1951 and finished in 1966 with the millennial commemoration of Poland's founding as a country. For these concerts, Lutnia wished to enhance its sound as well as its visual presence and to that end it accepted temporary singers from other choirs, including members of the Club Filarets and Our Lady Queen of Apostles Church. Underwritten by Lutnia and its supporters in the community, the series never made money, but the performances were a matter of great pride to the organization.

---

[6] Joann Nawrocki, interview, 21 March 2002.

> We were the only group that they [the DSO] dealt with. Actually Lutnia would sponsor the concert, and then we would get whatever receipts from the tickets were left. We always lost money in those concerts. But it was the prestige. [The concerts] were unprecedented in Michigan.[7]

Lutnia's officers do not recall how the concerts were initiated, but they acknowledge that, as the oldest Polish cultural organization in the state of Michigan, their contacts with the Detroit Symphony Orchestra board held some credibility. Former Lutnia members are quite certain it was their own board of directors that approached the symphony, and not the other way around. They maintain that other organizations similar to their own had approached the symphony at various points in time, but were turned down. Presumably Lutnia's supporting members both carried enough social prestige to request such a joint venture and had the financial resources necessary at that time to underwrite it.[8] The conductor of the Detroit Symphony Orchestra at the time of the series, Valter Poole, usually led the performances that took place in Detroit's Ford Auditorium. In February 1955, however, Leopold Stokowski replaced Poole at the podium, when he came to Detroit in order to direct the U.S. premiere performance of the *Symphony of Peace* by Andrzej Panufnik.[9] Lutnia members point with tremendous pride to their participation in that particular concert.

These collaborations between the Detroit Symphony Orchestra and Lutnia are an example of the intersection of the ethnic group and a more general (non-ethnic) arts organization. The choir's eagerness to perform with the orchestra, clearly demonstrated in their willingness to underwrite repeatedly a venture that they knew from experience could not mean financial gain, points up the importance of this type of intersection for the ethnic community. For Lutnia, the concerts spelled an opportunity to share their pride in their Polish heritage with a general, classical music audience. Their concerts also signified for them a coming of age: the Detroit Symphony Orchestra had recognized the musical level achieved by the ethnic organization and had accepted it as a credible musical partner.

Soon after the series with the Detroit Symphony had ended, Lutnia embarked on yet another large-scale endeavor, a musical-dramatic production entitled *Memories of Poland*. This presentation of a Polish courtship and wedding initially drew large crowds and began with a series of eight performances in 1968. Programs provided the audience with a description of the pieces that were to be performed. I have reproduced below a synopsis of the information presented to the audience in a 1969 program. The production was directed by Bronisław Siarkowski, and included dance demonstrations performed by Wawel, a local Polish folk

---

[7] Ibid.

[8] Singing members of Lutnia describe supporting members as "business people, politicians, and doctors."

[9] Sir Andrzej Panufnik (b. Warsaw 1914, d. Twickenham 1991) composed the *Symphony of Peace* in 1951. It debuted that same year in Poland. Of the three movements, only the first and third feature a chorus.

dance ensemble led by Richard Kubinski. Lutnia, at the time of this performance in 1969, comprised forty-nine singing members.

The first half of the program consisted of fourteen selections, listed and described as follows:

Hasło by St. Raczka and L. Rydla.
We cry out to Polish Song to rise from the hearts of its people and drown out the sounds of war.
Gwiazdzista Noc (*Starlit Night*) by P. Maszynski (1855-1934), a former director of Lutnia.
Zielona Lacka, Piekny Kwiat (*The Green Meadow*) by T. Czerniawski. A love song.
Juhasi (*The Polish Shepherd*) by J. K. Lasocki. A folksong depicting teasing between boys and girls.
Chciał Gęby (*He Desires a Kiss*) by S. Kazuro. A comical love song.
Guest artists, violinist Noreen Smialek Sinclair, accompanied by pianist Marta Szynal Dyczewski, performs works: *Mazurka in G Major* by Emil Mlynarski, Director of the Warsaw Opera and teacher at the Curtis Institute in Philadelphia; "Romance" from the *Second Violin Concerto* by Polish composer Henryk Wieniawski; and *Oberek* by twentieth-century Polish composer Grazyna Bacewicz.
Shenandoah. A traditional American song.
Selections from the *Sound of Music* by Rodgers and Hammerstein.
Już sie Zmierzcha (*Twilight Descends*) by W. Z. Szamotul, a sixteenth-century motet.
Noc (*Night*) by J. Gall.
Warsaw Polonaise by T. Sygietynski.
Nie Chcę Cie Kasiuniu (*I Don't want you, Katie*). A comical folk song by S. Wiechowicz.

With the exception of two selections, all of the pieces that made up the first half of the evening's program were by Polish composers. They provided a wide range of styles, including eight songs from the folk music repertory and eight classical pieces. Each of the fourteen is described with at least as much detail as I have reproduced here; clearly the program notes were intended to educate the audience, or at least enhance its enjoyment by sharing with it the general meaning of the Polish texts. The second half of the program breaks with the pre-intermission pattern. No written explanations are offered; Part 2 merely lists the singers' names under the title "Courtship and Marriage in a Polish Village." Presumably the dramatic and contextual aspects of the presentation would render the scenes meaningful.

For choir members with whom I spoke, the most memorable performance of *Memories of Poland* occurred in the early seventies. The president of Lutnia at the time, Joann Nawrocki, along with a Lutnia member, Albert Owsiany, applied for and received a Detroit Model Neighborhood Agency Grant from the city in 1971. Award money in hand, Lutnia was able to extend its resources well beyond its usual limitations. Nawrocki traveled to Poland where she purchased examples of regional folk dress—boots and vests—so that choir members might have models for their costumes. Lutnia, well adapted to producing shows on a shoestring budget, constructed and painted its own scenery.[10] The women sewed their costumes, patterning their design after the examples purchased in Poland. They made their own boots as well—spat-like apparatuses that fitted closely over their shoes, and were laced up around the lower leg. Free of its usual financial constraints, Lutnia was able to offer its performance to the public free of charge. The concert took place at St. Stanislaus Church on Chene in Detroit, and Lutnia members recalled that one thousand people attended while another thousand were turned away for lack of space.

Lutnia thrived for more than ninety years on just such resourcefulness of its members. Makeshift rehearsal spaces, home-sewn costumes, and hand-crafted stage sets have marked the history of all three Polish choirs in Detroit. The requirements for keeping these large musical groups afloat have left them especially vulnerable to changes within the community itself. The stream of Polish population from city to suburb has been echoed in the changing addresses of the Lutnia Singing Society, as it moved from the city of Detroit, to Hamtramck, and then to the northern suburb of Troy. In the 1980s and 90s the majority of members willingly drove ten or fifteen miles one way to attend weekly rehearsals; during the winter heavy snows made the journey especially perilous. And yet the members themselves argued that distance was not affecting the organization's numbers. They insisted choir practice had always required an effort on the part of its members. (Nawrocki recalled taking three buses in the 1960s in order to attend rehearsal.) Rather, they explained the reason for the group's imminent demise as a change in youth's attitudes with regard to singing itself. They spoke of the present as a "different era" and recalled a time when men in particular enjoyed singing.

> *Jean*: I still remember picnics when the guys would all of a sudden break into song.
> *Joan*: Oh yeah. At our clubhouse, my God you never knew. All of a sudden someone would be bursting out into song.
> *Joann*: I think a lot of it was because we were brought up to sing in church. You're used to singing, and you want to sing, and so you look for places to sing. . . . I don't think the generations coming after us have got that same background. They don't sing in church. They don't sing in choirs.
> *Joan*: You can't compare people today to what they were twenty-five or thirty years ago. Our lifestyles are different.

In the springtime of 2002 Lutnia was inactive, but had not yet made the final step toward disengaging itself officially from its parent organization, the Polish Singers' Alliance of America. An institution originally founded by six men was drawing to its conclusion with a remaining

---

[10] Scenery for the 1969 production was constructed and painted under the direction of Ted Kowalski, Al Owsiany, and Jim Reesman (program notes, 27 April 1969).

The Story of One Choir 69

membership of only five or six women. At the end of our interview in March 2002, the women invited me to accept responsibility for the Lutnia archives—library of repertory, programs, and photographs. I questioned them then about the possibility of the group continuing. They answered that anything was possible, but not probable.

Joann: It could happen.
Toni: Anything could happen.
Joan: If you can dig up people.
Jean: But digging's the right word [*laughing*]. That's it exactly. Those of us who can still walk.

6

You Wanna Dance, or Something?

The Polka in the Mainstream and the Ethnic Market

It is not unusual in the history of dance to find a popular step that has graced the dance hall and the stage, as well as the family parlor. Thus it has been with the polka, a dance whose history has occupied two realms—one highly commercialized, driving and driven by mass-marketed tastes, and the other, ethnic-group specific and locally generated. During the last one hundred and seventy years, the polka has twice risen to a position of international focus and acclaim and then subsequently settled into the domain of national, more localized entertainment. Its nationwide appearances during the past two centuries have assumed a variety of contexts—from staged representations of a controversial European import to the sweet wholesomeness of Lawrence Welk's Champagne Orchestra on network television.

Almost from its birth in the mid-1800s, the polka sparked international interest. The impresario Johann Raab introduced the polka—generally conceded to be an invention of Bohemian peasants—to audiences in Prague in 1837. Three years later, he took it to Paris to the Odeon Theater and to the Théâtre de l'Ambigu Comique. Tremendously popular on those stages, the polka appeared in March 1844 at the Parisian Opera; its status as upper-crust entertainment had been firmly, if fleetingly, established. The dance was exhibited at Her Majesty's Theater in London one month later.

Londoners seem to have greeted the new dance with mixed emotions—a sort of disdainful interest. A music critic for the *Illustrated London News*, M. Jullien, author of a column entitled "New Music," commented:

> It is [a] waste of time to consider this nonsense. The weather-cock heads of the Parisians have been delighted always by any innovation, but they never imported anything more ridiculous or ungraceful than this Polka.

> It is a hybrid confusion of Scotch Lilt, Irish Jig, and Bohemian Waltz, and needs only to be seen once to be avoided for ever![1]

Evidently Jullien intended his criticism to be read by his fellow critics and not by the eager, if undiscerning, regular reader, because one week earlier the classifieds section of that same *News* carried an advertisement for Jullien's own recent composition "The Polka" for a price of two shillings.[2] Those who did purchase Jullien's latest work may have been seduced by such newsy items as the following which reveals the fashionable, even faddish, status of the polka in Paris:

> We have received from Paris, by the last post, the accompanying sketch of the new dance recently imported from Bohemia into the French metropolis, entitled the Polka, and which, to the exclusion of all other considerations—Legitimacy, Tahiti and the Right of Search not excepted—has seized this volatile and light-hearted people universally by the heels. . . . Our daily contemporary the *Times*, thus alludes to the rage which prevails in Paris with regard to this most recent innovation. "The Paris papers are destitute of news. Our private letters state, that 'politics are for the moment suspended in public regard by the new and all-absorbing pursuit—the Polka.' . . . This is an unfortunate diversion for the war party, whose subscription for the sword of honour for Admiral Dupetit Thouars will be put *hors de combat* by this fascinating novelty."[3]

The sketch mentioned in the press (see fig. 6.1, "Polka Dance") was accompanied by a brief description of the dance's numerous figures and an actual musical example composed by Jacques Offenbach.

The polka was only one in a series of dances imported to the United States from Central Europe, but achieved a degree of popularity not shared by the others. Its appearances on the New York stage are documented in a number of diverse sources, including published personal accounts and popular magazines. It found its way into the engravings of an 1844 issue of *Knickerbocker*, and was fodder for an essay in *Putnam's Magazine* in December 1853, nine years after its introduction to the United States. Joseph Ireland, an American collector of theater

---

[1] *Illustrated London News*, 13 April 1844, 234.

[2] 6 April 1844, 224. Monsieur Louis Jullien was an extremely popular figure in Paris and London at the time he composed this polka. He was a master showman and conductor who greatly popularized the promenade concert in Europe and later, in America. His orchestral hodgepodges of Mozart, Beethoven, fireworks, opera arias, barking dogs, and stage antics, aimed at entrancing and exciting the middle-class concert-going public, were replete with polkas in 1844, 1845, 1846, and beyond. For an interesting read about this fascinating musical counterpart to P. T. Barnum, see Adam Carse's *The Life of Jullien* (Cambridge: W. Heffer and Sons, 1951).

[3] *Illustrated London News*, 23 March 1844.

Fig. 6.1. "Polka Dance"
Courtesy of *Illustrated London News*, 23 March 1844, 84

announcements and playbills, noted the appearance of "Polka-mania" at Niblo's Garden in New York in June 1844. He wrote, "A sketch entitled 'Polka-mania,' founded on a prevailing saltatory epidemic, was produced on the 17th, and received with great applause, more from the novelty and execution of the Polka-dance, than from any intrinsic merit of the piece" (Ireland 1866-67, 422-23). Ireland mentioned another performance of the polka by a traveling girls' troupe from Vienna in December 1846. His last notation concerning the stylish dance is a report of an exhibition performance given at the Bowery in August 1847 by a Miss Turnbull and a Mr. G. W. Smith. According to Ireland, a riot broke out in the theater that night. Riots were not uncommon at the Bowery, and this particular one seems to have had little to do with the polka dance. Rather, it had to do with a misunderstanding between Turnbull and Smith. The rioters destroyed some of the theater property, and were only stopped when a large contingent of police stepped into the fray. The unfortunate Mr. Smith, though pelted (Mr. Ireland does not say with what) was able subsequently to finish the engagement.[4]

From the time of its formal introduction until the end of the century, the polka inspired over a dozen compositions by Richard Strauss, Sergei Rachmaninoff, Antonin Dvořák, and Bedrich Smetana, and became a staple of American military bands. But by 1900, the popularity of the dance had at last faded from the American stage; it no longer garnered either the accolades or criticism that it once had. Once the flames had been fanned, Western interest in the polka had spread like wildfire over Europe, crossed the Atlantic, and burned brightly in America for some fifty years. And although one could not expect that it would ever again achieve similar international status, the polka rose to great national popularity for a second brief period in the United States in the late 1930s. The media through which the polka was exhibited during this second period were radio, jukebox recordings, and sheet music.

Coincidentally, the second wave of the polka's popularity, like that of the first, was initiated with Czech music. It was not uncommon during the 1930s for publishing companies to send an agent to Europe with the task of searching out novelty tunes and dance genres that could be published and recorded for sale in the United States. Elliot Shapiro, a partner in the Shapiro and Bernstein publishing firm, for example, made annual trips abroad in search of new music for publication. In 1939 he acquired the copyright to a tune that came to be known as the "Beer Barrel Polka."[5] Composed by Jaromir Vejvoda with Lew Brown and Wladimir A. Timm, the "Beer Barrel" is a Czech-style polka. It led the renewed craze of the dance form, appearing for the first time on *Billboard*'s list "Songs with the Most Radio Plugs" on

---

[4] Ireland, ibid., 468 and 504. The Bowery survived this riot in August. It shut down at the close of the season and reopened in September, repainted, with new appointments and chandeliers, and a new (painted) drop curtain. Prices at this time were twenty-five cents for a box seat and twelve and a half cents to sit in the pit. (The same year, 1847, the new Broadway Theatre asked a dollar for its best seating, fifty cents for family seating in the third tier, and a quarter for seats in the gallery and "colored gallery." Ibid., 492 and 500.)

[5] In addition to the "Beer Barrel Polka," the firm of Shapiro and Bernstein enjoyed success with Eddie Fisher's recording of "Oh, Mein Papa" for RCA Victor.

20 May 1939.[6] In the 6 January 1940 issue, *Billboard* advertised that the "Beer Barrel Polka" had appeared on its Best Selling Sheet Music lists for thirty-one consecutive weeks from the fifteenth of April until the fifteenth of September, and for twenty weeks in 1939 on the record buying guide's "Going Strong Classification."

A large number of polkas were quickly recorded and issued on the basis of the "Beer Barrel's" success. Thus, a 1941 *Billboard* chart, "Defense-inspired Tunes," included the following offerings from the Columbia and Okeh labels: "Army Rookie Polka," "Army Polka," "Army Hostess Polka," "Yankee Doodle Polka," and "Soldier's Sweetheart Polka." The Victor Recording Company certainly did not dawdle behind Columbia and Okeh; its advertisements in *Billboard* list over two dozen polkas in 1941. These appear, however, under such headings as "International Novelties," "Continental Gems," or "Polish." Marketed as international musical novelties, these polkas rarely appeared on a best-seller list, and did not attain a status equal to that of the "Beer Barrel," "Friendly Tavern," or "Yankee Doodle" polkas.

The next polka to attain a degree of mainstream popularity was another Czech-style piece, the "Pennsylvania Polka," which was recorded by a number of different performers, including Horace Heidt and the Andrews Sisters. A third polka to achieve similar, albeit short-lived, success was the "Victory Polka," which appeared on a January best seller sheet music list. "Beer Barrel" appeared again on the 1944 *Lucky Strike Hit Parade*, but by that time the genre's potential for chart success, so strong at the end of the 1930s, seems in retrospect to have been a singular occurrence. Only two more polkas, both released in 1948, "Too Fat Polka" and "Last Polka," were to be the subjects of mainstream marketing. By 1950 the polka had fallen from the realm of the general, national market for the second time.

The polka, though it could no longer claim a competitive position among mass-marketed popular music, did not disappear. It drifted, rather, along with other favorite genres of the big-band era, into a milieu of nostalgic musical entertainment. Between 1955 and 1971 the music director Lawrence Welk appeared on a network television program, *The Lawrence Welk Show*, that was devoted to just such entertainment. Welk's Champagne Orchestra offered television viewers and live audiences alike a Saturday-night dance date, where polkas peppered a repertory of sweet renditions of popular standards, stylized versions of country songs, hymns, and ballroom and tap dance pieces. On this format, the polka had a less mainstream appeal than it had during the early 1940s. Like the record companies' international and novelty releases, Welk's shows had an ethnic flavor, due to his focus on accordion solos, vocal solos

---

[6] *Billboard* determined its lists by means of a system of surveys. For instance, "Records Most Played on the Air" provided titles of the recordings played over the greatest number of radio broadcasts as determined by a weekly survey of twelve hundred disk jockeys across the United States (*Billboard*, 3 January 1948). Such lists have since been called into question. Simon Frith, for example, has noted that the *Billboard* charts are a crude measure of a piece's popularity, as they created rather than reflected consumer taste (1987:137-38). A similar point was made by Michael Goldberg in an article in *Rolling Stone* (1991). The weakness of the charts in reflecting consumer tastes does not, however, detract from the significance of the polka's being marketed at all, and with some degree of success, to the non-specifically ethnic public beginning in the late 1930s.

sung in Spanish, and Welk's own lilting German accent.[7] The polka enjoyed then only two periods of popularity in the history of highly visible (saleable), mass-marketed music in the United States. These episodes (and to a smaller extent, that of the Welk years) are reference points against which present-day polka musicians measure the recent status of the genre.

While the national taste for polkas was confined to two periods, the preference for the genre among particular nationality groups has continued since the 1910s. Documentation of the genre in ethnic communities is comprised of recordings and published music, and has been greatly enhanced with the publication of Richard Spottswood's *Ethnic Music on Records . . . 1893 to 1942* (1990). Spottswood's work makes available the information printed on the labels of foreign-language records produced and released in the United States, including those intended for sale to a "Polish" (Polish-American) market. The information that Spottswood culled from record labels, record company files, and the archives of private collectors includes matrix and catalog numbers, names of the recording musicians, instrumentation, titles of pieces (with the English translations), take numbers of released recordings, and the dates and locations of the recording sessions. Spottswood's compilation enables us to ascertain the extent of the polka's popularity among the various ethnic groups.

A tally of those recordings labeled "polka" in Spottswood's compilation between 1915 and 1942 (see table 6.1, p. 78)—presumably there are polka recordings not labeled as such—results in the following numbers of polkas recorded for each group: Polish with an overwhelming lead of some 1180 recordings, Italian with 459, followed by Spanish with 430, German with 408, and a Bohemian category of 397, Ukrainian with 339, Scandinavian with 134, Russian with 124, and Slovene with 87. The rest (Slovak, Swedish, Finnish, and Serbo Croatian) are each represented by under fifty polka recordings. With so broad a market for the polka, it is understandable that the record companies created a multi-ethnic category, a so-called International series under which they sold dance recordings to a non-specific ethnic population. This category alone contains 237 polka titles prior to 1943.

These fourteen foreign-language categories reflect a wide base of listeners whose impact on the various *Billboard* charts cannot be overlooked. One *Billboard* writer analyzed the national success of the "Beer Barrel Polka" in 1941 (September 27, 30):

> One of the outstanding "freaks" to capture the phonograph-playing patrons was "Beer Barrel Polka," especially as done by Will Glahe's Musette. The polka tempo, together with the orchestra's rolling, almost martial instrumentalizing, hit tavern habituees right between the eyes. [The] tune had an international appeal, too, and was as popular with our Spanish-speaking neighbors as ourselves. It was the first time that anything resembling a polka gained such widespread popularity.

---

[7] For more on Welk's rural upbringing in German-speaking Strasburg, North Dakota, see his 1971 autobiography, *Wunnerful, Wunnerful*.

The writer's reference to "tavern habituees," zeroed in precisely on an area where the mainstream American market and the ethnic American market intersected: certainly patrons of taverns in German-, Polish-, Slovenian-, Hispanic-, Italian-, or Czech-American neighborhoods would have enjoyed listening to the new "Beer Barrel Polka" on the jukebox. In other words, what some analysts in the industry may have considered to be an overnight sensation can be better explained as a brief melding of popular ethnic traditions with general mass-marketed tastes.

Taking all of the foreign-language series into consideration, national trends reveal a steady increase in the number of polka recordings from the mid 1910s until the late 20s, followed by a sharp drop in the Depression era when the industry faltered, and an upswing around 1940. Against this backdrop, the Polish-language recording may be compared. The first polka recording released in a Polish-language series was made in 1911, followed by eight more in 1915. The numbers increase somewhat steadily to thirty-eight in 1924, jumping to sixty-six the next year and reaching a peak of 117 in 1929. They decrease dramatically to eight in 1935, returning to eighty-five in 1940. The comparative table on the following page, a year-by-year compilation of polka recordings for four nationality groups, not only demonstrates the highs and lows of the recording industry between 1915 and 1942, but indicates also the differing emphases with which the industry marketed the genre to these groups. The relatively large number of Polish polkas recorded prior to 1943 explains, in part, the potency of this particular dance as a symbol of Polish ethnicity in the twentieth century.

A large number of companies had invested in the recording of ethnic series by 1942. Those that recorded for the Polish-language market included Bell, Brunswick, Columbia, Decca, Edison, Emerson, Odeon, Okeh, Pathé, Polonia, Victor, and Vocalion. The Columbia, Victor, Okeh, and Vocalion labels offered the bulk of Polish recordings that were made for the most part in New York, Chicago, and Camden, New Jersey. After 1942 more recently established companies like Continental, Dana, Spiro, and Harmonia helped broaden the array of ethnic polka recordings.

By assessing Spottswood's discography, it is possible to trace trends in Polish-American dance music instrumentation. Despite a small number of early polka recordings that were made by solo tenors with orchestral accompaniment, the genre is primarily presented as purely instrumental music, and it is most often recorded on the flip side or as part of a set of other popular dance types, including the waltz, schottische, and mazurka.

There is no typical recording ensemble of the Polish polka prior to the late 1920s or early 30s, after which time certain combinations of strings, winds, percussion, and brass become standard. The instrumentation ranges from solos to ensembles of nineteen or twenty. Even among the great variety of possible combinations, however, certain instruments, such as the accordion, violin, and clarinet, are more regularly included than others in the ensembles; recordings as well as published music sources show that these instruments maintained characteristic functions from ensemble to ensemble. A melodic core of violins, clarinets, or both—often with an added trumpet—sang out a dance tune over supporting harmonies that were provided by brass (trombones or tuba), strings (second violin or viola—the viola

Table 6.1
Polkas Recorded and Designated for a Particular Ethnic Group*

Year	Polish	Italian	Bohemian	German
1915	8	–	6	3
1916	4	6	–	2
1917	18	8	–	5
1918	12	12	5	3
1919	18	27	1	–
1920	22	24	9	2
1921	25	16	8	–
1922	26	23	7	6
1923	35	25	15	44
1924	38	27	30	40
1925	66	25	33	27
1926	89	26	62	57
1927	85	54	40	43
1928	99	56	20	28
1929	117	32	12	20
1930	86	21	5	14
1931	69	36	9	1
1932	40	7	2	7
1933	52	5	8	6
1934	27	1	12	13
1935	8	–	7	5
1936	14	–	11	10
1937	27	–	8	–
1938	20	1	7	12
1939	42	7	6	12
1940	85	7	16	9
1941	77	–	42	38
1942	44	13	16	1

* Compiled from information provided in Spottswood 1990.

disappears from recordings after 1932), or accordion or piano. The bass and rhythm sections consisted of string bass, banjo, guitar (early 1930s), or tuba, and drums.

As early as 1920 the accordion was an important element of dance music recordings, both in ensembles and as a solo instrument.[8] The names of accordionists Jan Kreselski (who also recorded under the name of J. Kressel for the Slovak series), Jan Wanat, Casimir Littmann, Jozef Pawlak, the Balbanowy Brothers, and the concertina player Matt Pajakowski regularly graced labels produced in the early and mid 1920s. With the exception of the Wanat-Littmann

---

[8] In this study I use the term "accordion" to refer specifically to a piano accordion, where the right hand plays on a vertical keyboard and the left hand depresses buttons. "Concertina" in this and following chapters refers to a squeeze box, the notes and chords of which are produced by pressing buttons on *both sides* of the bellows.

accordion duo and the Balbanowy quartet (four accordions with woodblock accompaniment), every one of the ensembles featuring these musicians included a clarinet, a violin, or both. The violin and clarinet carried the melody, sometimes in perfect unison, and at other times in heterophony—meaning the two parts played the same melody, but each introduced its own variations in pitch or rhythm. When a second violin was present, it played harmony.[9] The function of the accordion in these ensembles was to provide a solid rhythmic and harmonic accompaniment.

The use of violins, as common to dance music ensembles as were clarinets in the 1920s, declined gradually in recordings of the 1930s and later. Their demise probably came about as recording ensembles were looking for ways to increase their volume; during the 1930s one sees more and more brass and wind instruments listed on labels. The rare use of violins after 1930 might also have resulted from the violin's old-country or *wiejska* (rural) status. The Polish term *wiejska* appeared on recordings labeled "rural orchestra" (*orkiestra wiejska*) and was used to refer to a wide variety of instrumentations—the only element common to all of them being the inclusion of a violin. Although the term *wiejska* may have been used initially to sell recordings to immigrants of rural background, at some point it seems to have acquired a stigma and come to denote something old-fashioned, because the word disappeared from the labels by 1935.[10]

The inclusion of accordion and piano in the three- and four-piece ensembles of the early 1930s, although more common than in ensembles of the 1920s, was not regular, and would seem to have been optional, as the rhythmic-harmonic functions of these instruments could be carried out by either string bass or the combination of tuba and trap set. By 1936, however, the tuba had gone the way of the dodo bird (at least in the case of Polish-American recordings, a fact not shared by German polka style recordings), and the double bass and traps were regularly joined by either accordion or piano. To this increasingly standardized array of instruments, ensembles of the early 1940s added the sustained tones of the Hammond organ.

Brass instruments were introduced into Polish-American recording ensembles as early as 1916. The cornet, alternating with violin and clarinet, provided the main melodic line, while the trombone played harmony. Neither of these brass instruments survived into the 1940s—the cornet lost out in favor to the trumpet. The trombone's disappearance is more mysterious, as it was not replaced by another brass instrument. Its function seems gradually to have been taken over by the accordion. Bands generally used only one trumpet or cornet until the late 1930s. But in 1938 and 1939, perhaps under the influence of then-popular mariachi music, the orchestras of both Walter Grabek and Edmund Terlikowski introduced a second trumpet part into their arrangements.

---

[9] William Noll (1986:245, 697) noted the addition of a second violin part in nineteenth-century Polish instrumental ensembles that provided double-stopped harmony and rhythmic accompaniment to the first violin part.

[10] For a thorough discussion of *wiejska* style and its influence on Polish immigrant polka styles in the United States, see Janice Kleeman (1982).

Stylistically speaking, early Polish-American dance bands cultivated an assimilative stance toward mainstream American popular music styles—mariachi music is only one of many examples. The popularity of the saxophone among Polish musicians they themselves attributed to the bands of Count Basie and Cab Calloway. The vibraharp used in a 1935 recording of Bernie Witkowski's Orchestra (Victor Vi-V-16341) certainly demonstrates the popular influence of Lionel Hampton.

Polish-American use of specific instruments that were popularized by nationally known musicians demonstrates a tendency among ethnic musicians to borrow from the mainstream. But a much more pervasive influence of the mainstream upon ethnic ensembles can be detected in ensemble size and structure. In the early 1930s, as the old rural (*wiejska*) style appeared less and less on recordings, the sound of the big bands loomed larger and larger on the Polish-American horizon. The big-band sound grew to be an ideal upon which the bands in the eastern United States (and then in Detroit) would attempt to pattern themselves for the next twenty years. The following chapter on Detroit-based bands looks at the musicians' careers, repertories, and their eastern and Chicago styles of playing as they worked out a balance between the mainstream and the local Polish.

7

We'll Have a Little Swing with that Polka

Dance Bands from the 1920s to the 1950s

In the late 1950s, one Polish-American radio musician was able to make a career for himself in Detroit by capitalizing on the multi-ethnic environment of the city. Piotr Aniołek and his orchestra assumed a number of different names and guises under which they performed the repertory of various heritage/cultural groups. As Piotr Aniołek, he and his band played Polish music. Under the name of Mountain Pete, Aniołek directed what was then known as a Hillbilly ensemble. Pedro and his Caballeros provided a program of Mexican music, while Peter Angel (the translation of Aniołek's name into English) and his Orchestra performed big band dance tunes. Aniołek's career points up, admittedly in an exaggerated way, the interactive aspect of ethnic culture in urban Detroit. Polish-American dance bands there, since at least the 1930s, have demonstrated an assimilative attitude toward other-ethnic, pervasively mainstream-American, musical styles, integrating aspects of these styles and repertories into their own recorded and live performances. Polish-American musical ensembles, like other Polonian organizations, have revealed the effects of their continuous interaction with various local ethnic groups and the mass-mediated mainstream in their musical presentations and productions.

In the 1920s and 30s, Polish weddings and local taverns provided abundant professional opportunity for the Polish-American musician. On Friday and Saturday nights the old Detroit Polonia bars and halls pulsed with the sounds of high-pitched violins, wailing clarinets, and the sustained chords and fluid counterpoint of the squeezebox. In the way the musicians' work centered in the Polonia, their repertory emphasized a core of Polish-American dance genres: the polonaise, mazur, mazurka, krakowiak, polka, waltz, oberek, sztajerek, and schottische (exx. 7.1-7.6). The genres that constituted the Polish-American repertory were not all of Polish derivation. The polka, as noted in the previous chapter, is generally conceded to have been a Czech innovation, and the schottische has been dubbed a German polka. Despite the emphasis on Polish-American genres and in-community events, Polish-American dance band musicians who were working in the pre-war years recalled the strong influence that outside musical styles and repertories exerted even then on their musical style.

EXAMPLES 7.1-7.6

All follow strain form (each section of music is played, and then repeated once).
They can be found throughout the repertory either texted or purely instrumental.

(Examples 7.2 and 7.3 are excerpts from Sajewski, *Album Tańców Polskich*, no. 3, for first violin, 1924.
The remainder are excerpts from Vitak-Elsnic Polish Dance Orchestra Collection,
no. 4, for first violin, 1927.)

Example 7.1. The **mazurka**, like the waltz, is a dance in $\frac{3}{4}$. It makes regular use of a dotted rhythm, and emphasizes the second beat of the measure.

Czarina — Louis Ganne

Example 7.2. The sister of the mazurka, the **mazur** is a bit lighter and is usually notated in $\frac{3}{8}$.

Na Bok z Drogi — K. Namysłowski

Example 7.3. The **oberek** is also in a lively $\frac{3}{8}$, and its lilting quality emanates from internal contrasts. It typically shifts emphases, from the first beat of one measure to the second beat of the following measure. The dotted rhythm of one measure typically gives way to a straight rhythm in the next.

Example 7.4. Dances in duple time, usually notated as $\frac{2}{4}$, include the schottische, the polka, and the krakowiak. The **krakowiak** features unexpected accents on the second eighth-note beats of measures.

Example 7.5. The **sztajerek** like the oberek plays with contrasts, juxtaposing triplets and dotted eighth-sixteenth patterns.

Example 7.6. The **polka** like the schottische is rhythmically straightforward, and exhibits a strict march tempo. An exception to this is a type of polka subtitled **goralska** (from the Polish highlands, or in the character of dances from the Tatra Mountains in southern Poland). A polka of this type may feature three-measure phrases, make regular use of grace notes, and juxtapose patterns of two eighth notes with triplet figures.

Radio and recordings, local dances, and touring bands made the music of Artie Shaw, Benny Goodman, Jack Teagarden, Count Basie, Hollywood's singing cowboy Gene Autrey, and the Slovenian accordionist Frankie Yankovic the music also of Detroit's Polish-Americans. Polish-American musicians themselves attribute their use of a "close weave harmony" (or, close parallel harmonization) to Ernie Felice, the jazz accordionist, and credit an Italian American, Charlie Magnante, along with Dick Contino, for the popularization of the concertina and button box in Detroit's downriver area (southwest of the city proper). Members of the Polonia attending a local dance would expect to hear a small sampling of such mainstream innovations as the rumba and fox trot during an evening of obereks, kujawiaks, and polkas. In response to their audience's expectations Polonian musicians developed a non-Polish dance tune repertory. This body of tunes served the musicians in performances at community picnics and taverns, and availed them further opportunity to move beyond strictly Polish-American circles and to perform music at non-Polish events.

While Polish-American dance band musicians in Detroit were by their own estimates playing to audiences ninety-six percent Polish-American in the 1920s and 30s, by 1940 their performance circuit had extended to Eagles', Elks', and yacht clubs, the local YMCA, and dances at the Naval Air Station in Grosse Isle. These non-Polish playing venues were located between Grosse Pointe and Monroe, Michigan, spanning a geographical area of approximately forty-five miles, from the coast of Lake St. Clair south along the Detroit River to Lake Erie. These engagements, referred to by the musicians as "English" gigs, often provided a source of steady, secondary employment for Polish-Americans.

Polish Americans coined the term "English gig" to refer to an event where English was the primary language of the audience. But the term carried musical connotations as well. "English" audiences as a whole—no matter each individual's ethnic background—could not be expected to respond positively to a song sung in Polish (or Czech, or German, or Italian for that matter). Musicians catered to the "English" or "American" (or, what I have referred to as "mainstream") audience at such events. Walker Connor, a political analyst well known for his insightful writings on the subject of ethnonationalism, described the United States as an Immigrant State—a highly diverse population in terms of its ancestry. He noted that the "officially endorsed" archetype of that population is the *American*—not an ethnically defined individual, but an "ethnically neutral" one (Connor 1994, 79). I would extend his observation as it might apply to the Polish-American musician working in the 1930s—a musician for whom the musical mainstream in America was ethnically neutral. By this I do not mean to suggest that popular music of the 30s cannot be traced to any one ethnic group. The African-American roots of jazz are an established fact. And Broadway is clearly indebted musically to East European Jewish musical influence. But I am suggesting that when a clarinet or trumpet player from the old Polonia stepped outside of his neighborhood and played with a swing band, providing an evening of foxtrots for an English-speaking audience, he understood that he was taking part in something non-Polish, something generically American.

An example of the Polish-American musician's participation in long-standing "English" employment is provided by Ted (Thaddeus) Wienclaw (1922-97), one of a family of musicians who played regularly at a bar known as the Blue Ribbon on Livernois and Fort in Detroit beginning in the late 1940s. The Blue Ribbon, like other establishments of that era which sought to cater to a number of different clienteles, offered a polka matinee from 4:30 until 8:30 in the evening, followed by another segment featuring fox trots. Wienclaw, who played weekly at Polish-American dances, worked coterminously for almost thirty years with a group whose repertory consisted mostly of fox trots.[1] (The group, led by Hank Mielnik, was known to English audiences as Mel Henry and the Esquires.[2])

Crossover in the Polish-American repertory and the musicians' ever-widening performance circuit were not unique to Detroit. Charles Keil and Janice Kleeman described similar situations among eastern musicians as early as the 1920s. Kleeman in particular devoted much research to the musical members of the Witkowski family (see Keil 1992 and Kleeman 1982). Leon Witkowski (1868-1923) was a Polish musician born in Poznan, who, after emigrating, settled in Brooklyn. He led two professional orchestras: one, the Polish Orkiestra Witkowskiego, and the other, a forty-five piece ensemble at Luna Park, Coney Island.[3] Leon's nephew, Bernie Witkowski Jr. (also known as Bernie Wyte) eventually inherited the Polish orchestra, but also led a "society band" that played in New York hotels for thirty years (Keil 1991, 20). Keil has contributed to our knowledge of crossover bands also through his interviews with a Bridgeport, Connecticut musician, Ed Krolikowski. Krolikowski, born in Bridgeport, moved with his parents to Poland at the age of ten and studied classical violin in Warsaw. He later returned to the United States an accomplished musician. His life story reads like that of many an American band musician of the 20s and 30s—a story of continual musical adaptation and adjustment as he became adept in a number of popular styles while playing in hotels in the South, moving picture theaters in New Orleans, on Broadway, and finally on radio and recordings (ibid., 27-31). What makes his story intriguing to the study of music and ethnicity is the diversity of musicians with whom he performed and the number of various ethnic communities his band served:

> You see, there were no other bands in those nationalities, so we played the Slovakian neighborhood a lot, the Ukainian, Russian, Jewish, too. We played a lot of Jewish weddings. . . . We'd honor requests for Greek, Syrian, Irish, Italian, German, Hungarian, or any other type of music [ibid., 30].

---

[1] Ted Wienclaw interview, 19 December 1989.

[2] Syl Wienclaw interview, 8 January 2003.

[3] Kleeman 1982, 122. It would be interesting to learn whether the Coney Island group comprised the same members as the Witkowski Orchestra. I would imagine that it did, given the Polish-American musician's propensity for wearing a variety of musical hats.

Krolikowski's evident pride in his ability to serve such a wide-ranging clientele is echoed in the stories of Detroit's musicians.

In discussing their musical histories with me, the musicians typically placed emphasis first on their roles as dance band musicians and only secondly as Polish-American music specialists, thus indicating the significance of the English engagements to their careers. They spoke of having toured with numerous big band orchestras as far west as Colorado and California in their early years, before marriage and family made it more important for them to remain at a steady job. Ted Koltowicz, one of the Detroit community's veteran musicians, recalled playing in a non-Polish dance band accompanying such popular performers as Dick Haymes and Betty Hutton while stationed at Fort Sheridan in Illinois in 1944. Later, when performing on WSPD television in Toledo, Ohio, his band, the Sparks of Fire, accompanied "English" guest artists who were playing at the Commodore Perry, a nightclub in close proximity to the television station.

Ultimately, the musicians' fluent conversance with the English—in particular, big band— repertory informed their stylistic performance of Polish-American music. In the late 1920s and early 30s, Polish-American musicians in the eastern United States developed a style of playing polkas and obereks that was influenced by contemporary big-band arrangements, and incorporated, for example, the mariachi style of trumpets playing in parallel thirds, and the newly introduced vibraphone.

The eastern, big-band-influenced style of playing Polish dance music was exemplified for Detroiters by the music of Frank Wojnarowski and his eastern-based dance orchestra. Wojnarowski's recordings of polkas exhibit standard eastern-style orchestral arrangements— featuring string and brass sections which function as separate homophonic units, contrasting each other in patterns of call-and-response, or providing harmonic support for the melodic line. Drums, piano and plucked strings provide underlying rhythmic patterns. The drumming patterns in particular are simple, with little variation throughout, the steady fast pace of the dance tunes (typically ♩ = 134) incessantly driven by a regular drum-cymbal pattern.

Beyond elements of orchestration and instrumentation, Wojnarowski's dance band borrowed details of technique from the big band: horns were muted, vocal sections were presented by a solo voice over subdued, close, sustained harmonies in the brass, and the ends of phrases were filled in by either brass or piano. Wojnarowski's recorded performances are cleanly articulated and show the director's attention to precise ensemble work; the trumpets play in legato unison, uniformly articulating the ends of phrases in parallel thirds.[4] Wojnarowski's music, along with that of other eastern orchestras—the bands of Bernie Witkowski and Al Sojka—were familiar to Detroiters through radio, recordings, and live gigs.

Detroit's Polish dance bands constituted a broad spectrum of size and volume, from the large groups of musicians on whose style eastern imprint was easily heard, to the small local groups that played at an eastern tempo but could not compare with the eastern bands

---

[4] Wojnarowski's "Finger Dance Polka" exhibits standard eastern-style tempo, form, and orchestration.

in size. Detroit produced a small number of local dance bands that imitated eastern style. Those orchestras that approached the size of an eastern dance orchestra—and this means by broadest definition, had six or more musicians, but usually between eight and twenty-two—were considered *potential* producers of eastern sound. Next to size, the most distinctive feature of eastern style was, and still is, tempo; eastern tempo is generally acknowledged to be quicker than that of Michigan, which in turn is quicker than that of Chicago. As the veteran orchestra leader and accordionist Ted Koltowicz stated (interview, 30 April 1990),

> This has been told to me by people from Chicago and from the east . . . at that time, they used to call it the Michigan style. We were not Chicago or eastern. We were right in the middle for quite a while there: Gene Szal [Szalankiewicz] with the Michigan Polka Tels, myself, Johnny [Sadrack] (well, Johnny tended toward the eastern style), and Clare [Witkowski] started [eastern], but he went to our side.

Koltowicz's careful categorization of bands with respect to tempo is in keeping with the musicians' usual method of distinguishing among ensembles. Beyond classifying Detroit bands as American/English, eastern, or Michigan style, musicians emphasize that every dance band also had a personal style, readily identifiable and distinct from the others. Koltowicz explained:

> If you would take Johnny [Sadrack], myself, Clare . . . Stanley Adamus, I'm talking about the bands, the big bands. . . . If you would take all these bands and let's say we'd go to Ford Auditorium and put us on the big stage, set up our bands right across, each one of us would play the same polka and you'd catch us just like that. You'd know which band it was. Because we each had our distinctive sound. The instrumentations were different. The song was the same, but it was just the way it was arranged. Each one of us had a distinctive sound.[5]

The variety of styles present in Detroit in the 1940s and 50s can be demonstrated with a look at eastern-style recordings produced by dance bands of that era, such as those made by Johnny Sadrack (d. 1989).[6] Sadrack maintained a loyal audience, one which he was able to expand during the latter fifteen years of his life through a radio broadcast known as the

---

[5] Ibid.

[6] In this comparison of Detroit styles it would be useful to know where Peter Uryga fit in. His name appears in the Spottswood listing as Peter Uryga and his Motor City Orchestra. He recorded thirteen sides for Victor on 2 June 1939 in Chicago and sixteen sides for Decca in Chicago—eight on 17 June 1940 and eight on 26 November 1941. I have been unable to locate these recordings that comprise together sixteen polkas, one kujawiak, seven waltzes, two obereks, one tango, one mazurka, and one unlabeled.

"Continental Matinee." His work with his ensemble became best known, however, through live performances. Musicians and polka fans with whom I spoke unanimously referred to Sadrack as the Detroit Polonia's foremost proponent of American big-band sound.

Sadrack's "Bachelor's Polka" (ex. 7.7, transcription no. 1) was transcribed from a cassette that is one of three recorded by Sadrack's wife and was sold at Hamtramck bookstores in the early 1990s. Because it was recorded on non-professional equipment, it carries a good deal of recording noise; however, it affords some opportunity for listening to details of orchestration and tempo. Tempos for all polkas recorded on the three cassettes hold consistently between ♩ = 128 and ♩ =136, and thus are in keeping with eastern tempo. Sadrack's orchestra displays greater variation among sections than is audible in Wojnarowski's recordings. He followed a pattern that grows increasingly dense and varied, playing rapidly with a consistently uniform enunciation. A simple chording harmony can be heard throughout this polka by piano and bass, and is reinforced by what may be a trombone. A rhythmically functioning stringed instrument, most probably a banjo, strums an even pattern of four eighth notes to the measure. The piano plays a simple bass note and triad alternation. The contrapuntal flights in the clarinet effect a light ornamentation that contrasts the rather dense harmonic base. Each of the four-measure phrases presents its first two measures as an arpeggiated antecedent by trumpet answered by two measures of clarinets in parallel thirds. The pre-planned ornamentation that is executed in clean ensemble places Sadrack's style in direct contrast to an older *wiejska* or rural style that at times exhibited heterophony. Sadrack's arrangements display a tempo and orchestration clearly based in eastern tradition. They are evidence also of a more personalized aesthetic that relied on a wide variety of counterpoint and density-producing bellow shaking to further vary recurrent melodic sections already differentiated through modulation. (Bellow-shaking refers to an alternating push-pull motion of the accordion bellows over a single chord, creating a fat, shimmering sound.)

Clare Witkowski's recordings demonstrate, as Ted Koltowicz noted, a style firmly rooted in eastern traditions, but leaning toward a slower tempo. Witkowski's "Kochanka Polka," for instance, like "Bachelor's Polka," moves at a tempo of ♩ = 128, but this tempo is not, for his orchestra, the slower end of a range (ex. 7.8, transcription no. 2). Witkowski's melodic lines are supported by piano, bass, and drums. The drums are steady with little variation, as is common in eastern style, and the piano displays a simple bass note and alternating chord pattern. Here again, parallel thirds are present in the melody. Witkowski's arrangement shows off the technical prowess of his musicians in true eastern tradition, with clean doubling, performance at the upper end of the range, and double and triple tonguing by trumpet.

Most interesting is Witkowski's great variety of sectional arrangement that is achieved through different means than those employed by Sadrack. In "Kochanka" Witkowski successively lowers the solo section by an octave with the presentation of each strain. Section A that begins after a four-measure introduction by clarinet and trumpet, is played by two clarinets in parallel motion at the upper end of the register. This repeated eight-measure section is immediately followed by one featuring two trumpets in parallel thirds playing an octave beneath where the clarinets sounded. Finally, the third section is presented by solo accordion, taking the listener down two octaves below the trumpet part, all of which is followed by an A′ section orchestrated again in the upper range of two clarinets.

In the instrumental "Uncle Polka," as recorded by Ted Koltowicz and His Sparks of Fire, only three different melodies are presented, with little or no melodic variation in the recurring sections (ex. 7.9, transcription no. 3). Characteristic use of parallel melodic lines is heard in section A, voiced by the combined forces of trumpet, sax, and clarinet. Section B spotlights Koltowicz's own instrument, accordion. The accordion, which provides a dense texture with customary bellow shaking in sections A and C, is not present in section B, and thus sets up its sparse texture in contrast to the surrounding sections. As compensation for the loss in density in the middle section, the drum that was rather flat-sounding, and struck four beats to the measure in section A, changes to a softer, more lively snare beat in section B. Of note in this recording is the varied drumming with every repetition of the B section. Section C presents the call-and-response between winds and brass that is typical to eastern style and can be heard in the Sadrack and Witkowski recordings as well. Of significance also to musicians who differentiate style primarily in terms of orchestration and tempo is Ted Koltowicz's choice of tempo, consistently slower than other eastern-influenced bands.

Much of the commentary musicians shared with me concerning pre-1960s polka style focused on big-band sound—fast-paced polkas performed with tight rhythmic precision by alternating sections of brass and winds. Nevertheless, there were a large number of dance bands operating in Detroit that did not fit the eastern mold, most basically in terms of size. Additionally, there is recorded evidence of even another stylistic aesthetic at work in the area's Polish-American dance bands, audible in the arrangements of the Polonia Orchestra, led by Walter Rodgers in Detroit. Rodgers, born in Jersey City, New Jersey, is a classically trained violinist who was one of the organizers and concertmaster of the Hamtramck Philharmonic Orchestra. The liner notes on the orchestra's album state that "Mr. Rodgers played and attended the usual Polish social functions, where he participated in native Polish dances and gained the remarkable sense of authenticity which he invests in his Polonia Orchestra music." "Sense of authenticity" in this comment may refer to Rodger's choice of tempos as well as arrangements. Tempos of the seven polkas on the album average ♩ = 124. They are slower than eastern style, but still faster than the Michigan style. Koltowicz described the sound of the Polonia Orchestra as one resembling an older Polish style of music that could be heard in Polish-American orchestras in the late 1920s. The Polonia Orchestra consisted of accordion, trombone, trumpet, clarinet, saxophone, three violins, piano, upright string bass, and drums. A recording of the "*Trzymajmy Się* Polka" ("Let's hold together") by Frank Kurzawa reveals an arrangement that differs markedly from the previously discussed eastern-style arrangements (ex. 7.10, transcription no. 4). First, there is an emphasis on stringed instruments—the trumpet is only subsidiary. Second, Kurzawa and Rodgers show a preference for unison or octave presentations of the melody instead of parallel harmonies. And third, they introduce heterophony into the melodic line—where the trombone lags slightly behind the clarinet, or where the violins sound the melody slightly ahead of the sax.[7] Heterophony has no place in the eastern style, which places high value on instruments enunciating their parts in strict unison timing.

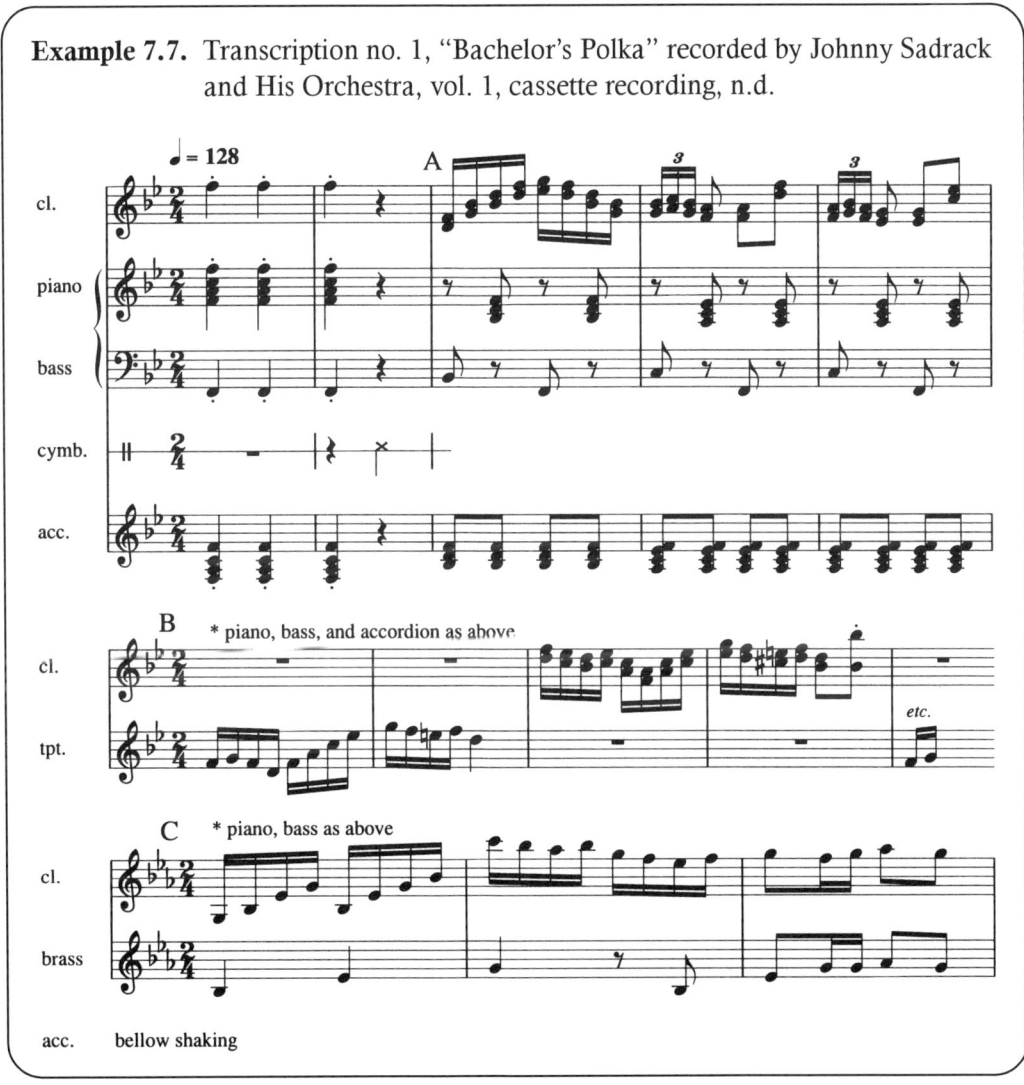

Example 7.7. Transcription no. 1, "Bachelor's Polka" recorded by Johnny Sadrack and His Orchestra, vol. 1, cassette recording, n.d.

---

[7] Kurzawa was born in Poland in 1896, immigrated to the United States in 1913, and settled in Detroit. He was a classically trained violinist and played violin in the Polonia Orchestra. Earlier, he had formed his own orchestra, and Koltowicz recalled that Kurzawa's orchestra was extremely popular in the 1930s, drawing crowds of one thousand to performances (personal communication, 13 August 1992). A composer, Kurzawa wrote both classical and dance music compositions.

Example 7.8. Transcription no. 2, "Kochanka" recorded by Clare Witkowski and His Orchestra, *Music of a Polish Wedding* (Dyno LP 5005), n.d.

Example 7.9. Transcription no. 3, "Uncle" recorded by Ted Koltowicz and the Sparks of Fire. Greater Detroit Musicians Association (IRM LP 505), ca. 1970.

Dance Bands from the 1920s to the 1950s

Example 7.9.—*Continued*

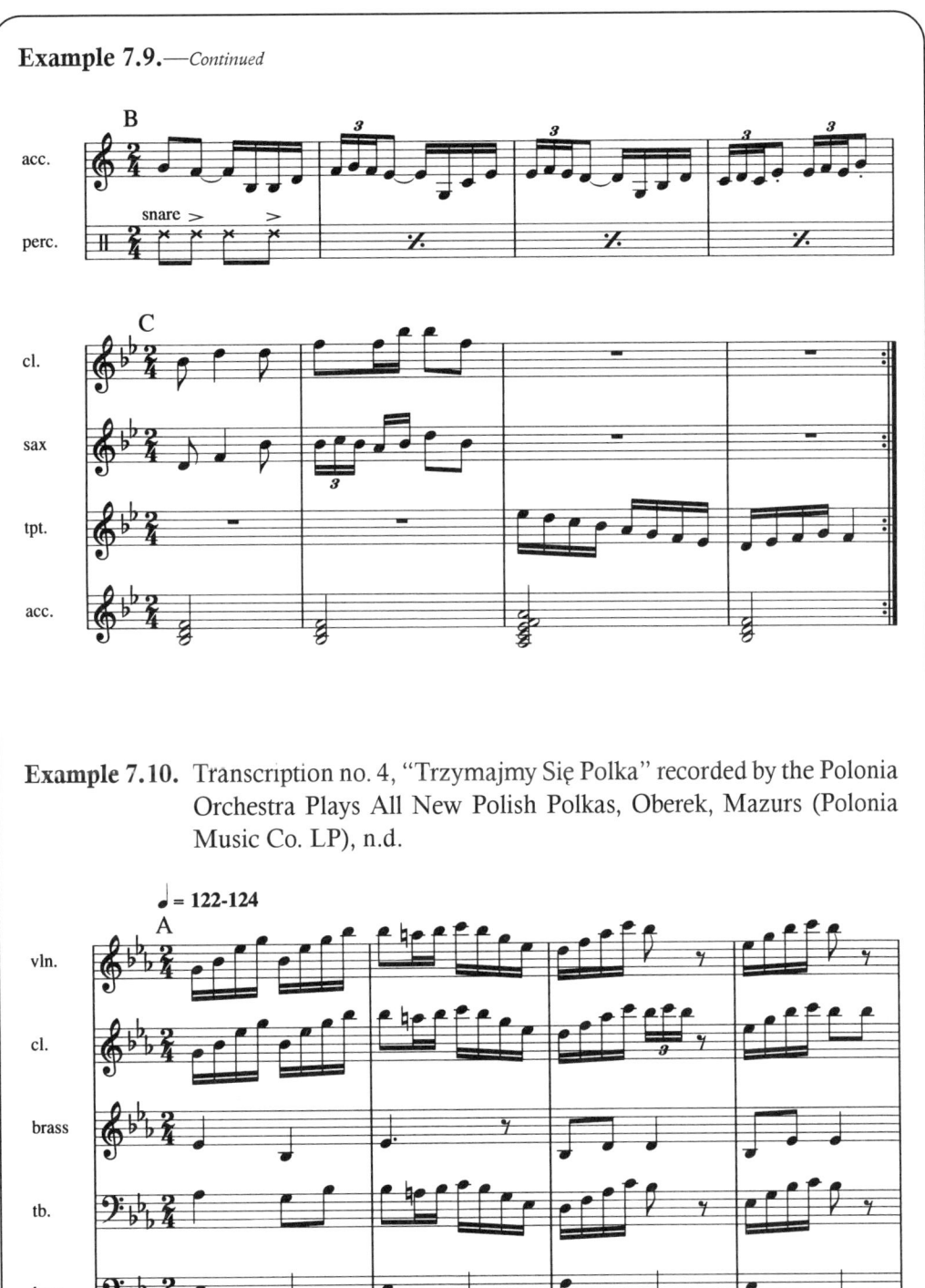

Example 7.10. Transcription no. 4, "Trzymajmy Się Polka" recorded by the Polonia Orchestra Plays All New Polish Polkas, Oberek, Mazurs (Polonia Music Co. LP), n.d.

Continued

Example 7.10.—*Continued*

Eastern style and big band sound constituted only a small portion of the spectrum of Polish-American dance bands working in Detroit. Playing next door or down the street from the big bands were a larger but indeterminable number of smaller bands. These lacked the musical forces necessary to actually imitate eastern sound—as one musician remarked, "We would have imitated eastern sound if we could." In order to sound, for instance, like Wojnarowski's orchestra, an ensemble required eight, nine, or ten musicians. A large ensemble was not feasible for many bands; two musicians recalled that their attempts at maintaining a nine-piece band from 1935 until 1937 proved unsuccessful because many of the individuals who hired the band for a wedding or bar gig could not afford to pay more than three musicians. At that time, three musicians were asking two dollars each for a five-hour bar gig. A three-piece band in the late 20s and early 30s was comprised of a concertina or button box, drums, and a violin. (After the mid-1930s, the button box was replaced by a piano accordion, and the violin had decreased in popularity to the extent that by 1937, the typical three-piece band consisted of accordion, sax/clarinet, and drums. When other instruments were added to the basic trio, they most usually included a trumpet, banjo, string bass or, less often, a guitar.) Frank Wienclaw (b. 1919), who has played in three- and four-piece combos in Detroit since the late 1920s explained:

> He [Wojnarowski] had at least five gold records. So you know when he wrote a tune and it was on the juke box, and [the patrons] would say "Would you play it?" you couldn't hardly copy the style. They had the advantage of having more musicians. We'd play his tunes. In our days, in playing music, we heard a tune, we played a tune, and everybody recognized it [interview, 19 December 1989].

An analysis of the styles of small bands in Detroit is made difficult by a scarcity of recordings, but we can gain some clue about the sound of these earlier ensembles from comments offered by the musicians themselves. We know for instance that smaller bands did not use amplifiers. Musicians laughingly recounted the days when the accordionist "had to stretch like hell" in order to be heard. Frank Wienclaw's brother Syl (b. 1929), who has played in small combos since the early 1940s, noted that prior to the 1950s, the older generation of musicians declined to use amplifiers, maintaining that they were unnecessary. By 1950, however, the playing venues extended to include large community picnics, and "practically all musicians" at that time acknowledged their need for amplification (interview, 27 July 1992).

Repertory for the smaller bands does not seem to have been localized. Generally, local bands played the popular tunes of the day, but arranged them for the musical resources at hand. Victor Greene, an ethnicity historian, noted that for ethnic-group musicians in particular, commercially printed dance music was scarce.

> The Czech, German, Italian, and other ethnic bandsmen had to resort to non-commercial sources, especially for sheet music, because the music they needed was little known to non-ethnic Americans [sic] and thus generally could not be obtained from American music publishers . . . [Greene 1992, 47].

Nevertheless, Polish musicians could rely on two companies for printed music: the arrangements by the smaller bands, like those of the larger ensembles, were based on principles of orchestration demonstrated by the Sajewski and Vitak-Elsnic part books. The founder of the latter, Louis Vitak, grew up in Akron, Ohio, and established a music store there as early as 1895. He moved to Chicago in 1902 where he accepted his nephew Joseph P. Elsnic into the firm as a business partner. Together, they became steeped in composing and publishing music for the Czech-American community. In the early 1920s the firm broadened its Czech-only format to include the music of Polish, German, and Lithuanian immigrants. In fact, between 1923 and 1930 the company published at least nine collections of Polish music alone (ibid., 49-55).

The publisher Władysław Sajewski appears in the *Catalogue of Copyright Entries* for the first time in 1911.[8] During that year, he secured the copyright on fourteen tunes, including polkas, marches, and a mazurka. He did not, however, begin his business career in the music field. Rather, he opened a general store on Chicago's north side in 1897 and began to specialize in music sales only in 1910. Sajewski and his associate Frank Przybylski, a bandleader and arranger, played an important role in the dissemination of repertory and the early recording of Polish folk songs. Sajewski's role in the recruitment of recording musicians was described by his son Alvin:

> We were always interested in folksong records. The company would tell us to find somebody and they would record them. Then you would have to find somebody, and then be able to sell the records. So naturally we were always on the lookout. People would come in and ask for a song they knew on a record. They might sing it, and we would find somebody to write it down. Mr. Przybylski was a capable man. He knew how to arrange these things. We would then find an artist who would be able to sing the song in that type of way that the people wanted—not a concert singer, but a person with an ordinary voice. Often people would come into the store and would sing a song just in that way that you wanted. Then we would have to get Mr. Przybylski or somebody to accompany him [Spottswood 1990, 135-42].

---

[8] Louis Vitak's name appears in the *Catalogue of Copyright Entries* as early as 1910 when he acquired copyright on a piece titled "Laendler" by Nicolai von Wilm.

The Sajewski and Vitak-Elsnic series have provided Detroit musicians with the bulk of their traditional dance tune repertory. They constitute collections of a variety of dance genres: polkas, obereks, obertas, waltzes, kujawiaks, mazurs, mazurkas, schottisches, and sztajereks. First published at least as early as the 1920s, well-thumbed copies of both publications were still in use in 2002. So familiar are Detroiters with both these editions that they refer to a well-known dance tune by its publisher and number in the book, rather than by its name. Both the Vitak-Elsnic and the Sajewski offered notated music for a wide variety of band and orchestra instruments. The 1929 Sajewski series, for example, provided part books for first violin or C melody sax, second violin, flute, clarinet in A, B♭ tenor sax, E♭ alto sax, B♭ soprano sax or B♭ clarinet, first and second cornet in A, tenor banjo, cello, trombone, bass, drums, piano accompaniment, and concertina. Other arrangements were also available in 1929—for instance, there is another collection for first and second violin, viola, cello, bass, flute, clarinet, first and second cornet, trombone, drums, and piano. A 1943 Sajewski publication is arranged for piano, first and second cornet, trombone, first violin, clarinet, and bass. Though the many arrangements of tunes differ in some aspects of instrumentation, the guiding ideas behind the arrangements do not reveal much change over the years. The violin invariably plays the melody, which may be shared by clarinet, or doubled at the octave or unison by flute or cello. The cello more often, however, outlines the supporting harmony, emphasizing the strong beats of the measures, and is accompanied on the off-beats by flute. In certain arrangements, cello and trombone are given the melodic line, or the cello alone may play melody accompanied by sustained pitches in the trombone part. The piano in every case is strictly a chording instrument. The variety of arrangements produced by Detroit's many and varied ensembles must have comprised a beautiful spectrum of sound.

The difference between musicians who played with big bands and those who played in smaller groups can be explained as one of early orientation. Participation in a particular size and scope of ensemble does not seem to have been related to a musician's age, ability to read and write music, or opportunity for early music lessons, because all of these factors appeared to be equal among the various musicians with whom I spoke.

Ted Koltowicz was a bandleader noted by others of his generation to have consistently maintained a large ensemble throughout his career. Koltowicz (1927-2002) was introduced to the accordion by his father, who bought him his first twelve-bass instrument—the accordion was offered at that time along with forty free lessons by the Wurlitzer Company. After completing his first forty weeks of instruction, Ted began working with a private teacher, Al Prinz, who also taught violin, piano, and guitar. Not only did Prinz provide Koltowicz with musical instruction, but he invited the ten-year-old to join a band in which he himself played. This ensemble, directed by Bill Zielenak, never played with less than five or six pieces—trumpet, accordion, two clarinets, string bass, and drums. So Koltowicz's earliest professional experience was with a large orchestra. He himself later formed a three-piece combo that he almost immediately expanded to a five-piece. Drafted in 1944, when Koltowicz returned home in

1946 he formed a six-piece band—a band that he would soon expand at his own expense to seven pieces in order to pass an audition for a stint on local television.

In contrast to Koltowicz's early experience with ensembles of six or more pieces, the Wienclaw brothers, Ted, Frank, and Syl, learned their craft working with three- and four-piece combos. The practical considerations of earning an extra income, and such personal goals as the attainment of an eastern sound, as well as an enjoyment of the work itself were forces that further directed the musicians through their careers.

For many of the musicians in Detroit, playing with a band was a family tradition: the influence exerted by the Wienclaw's father was central to their early experience with music. The senior Wienclaw had evidently had dreams of forming a family band, because he started one of his sons on drums, another on clarinet, and a third on violin. His motivation was probably as much rooted in practical concerns as it was initiated by his own enjoyment of music. As Ted Wienclaw recalled (interview, 19 December 1989),

> [playing in a dance band] was a good livelihood . . . the Depression years [our dad] worked for the McCord Corporation. Some weeks he didn't work at all, some weeks he worked one or two days. So two of us brought that combined income home, you know. Sometimes it was thirty-six or forty dollars in a week.

Musicians often started playing professionally at an early age, and the learning of technique and repertory often took place on the job. Syl Wienclaw was twelve when an accordionist called him to play the drums at a wedding, his first professional gig. (Although his father had intended him to learn the clarinet, Syl had practiced secretly on his brother's drums.)

> I was twelve. I was really little. We wound up at the Marine Hall for a wedding. A Polish wedding. And I remember it very well because there was not heat in the building, the boiler broke [laughs]. And I could see the cooks coming out with these big bowls of hot chicken soup, couldn't even see it for the steam. I figured, Hey, we wouldn't stay there very long. I sat in my coat, had my gloves on and started playing. And Tomy (Mr. Tomaszewski) [the band's accordionist and a local parish organist] was in the background. . . . He's saying [stamping his foot] "That one down a little bit, watch my foot. That's the tempo." And all night long he's prodding me. And first thing you know, he didn't say anything. I was just playing waltzes, polkas, all that stuff, shaking from the heat. Anyway, we made the job through. That day a girl named Dorothy Rzeppa came up to me and said, "I need a drummer. I'm forming an orchestra. Would you like to work with us?" I said, "Sure, why not?" Twelve years old and we swung right into action pretty quick. We played for weddings, picnics, and dances [ibid.].

Fig. 7.1. From left: Bill Schwartz, Syl, Ted, and Frank Wienclaw working through a new arrangement at the piano
Courtesy of Syl Wienclaw

Dance Bands from the 1920s to the 1950s

The Detroit public schools and private teachers provided band musicians with instruction by which they learned the technical side of their instrument. Private lessons were offered by people known as music professors, music educators in the schools, and local church organists who were supplementing their own incomes through teaching and band work. Instead of specializing in the teaching of one particular instrument, music professors usually played an array of instruments and taught the fundamentals of note reading to their students. Ernest Jensen (a violinist) was one such music teacher at a Detroit area school who emphasized the music of Mozart, not American dance music. Other professors used the Sajewski or Vitak-Elsnic publications as their instruction books. Observation and hours spent listening to other musicians in the neighborhood also played a role in a young musician's acquisition of technique and repertory. Koltowicz recalled (interview, 30 April 1990):

> It all started when I was about six or seven years old when my godfather taught me how to play harmonica. So there on in, I always liked music. Whenever we went to a wedding, my mother never had to look for me far, because I was on the bandstand watching the musicians, listening to the music. In those days, the music went to two, three o'clock. There was no limit on it.

The ability to read and write music allowed the musicians to transcribe the most recently composed, popular, eastern style arrangements from recordings for use in their own bands. Frank Wienclaw described a typical transcription session (interview, 19 December 1989):

> When Wojnarowski came out with those records of his, you couldn't buy the sheet music. And the jobs that we played, [the audience] wanted to hear all of those. In our group, I was the one that wrote it all out. Of course, I was lucky, got a piano. [We'd let the record play a bit] then I'd stop and write it.

Other musicians made use of the published part books, rearranging the music to fit the band's resources.

Work opportunities for dance bands were abundant in Detroit; as one musician remarked, there was a bar on every corner, and every corner bar had a band. Bar work, however, could not compete in financial reward with a Polish wedding. A Polish-American wedding could provide musicians with at least two days of work. The gig usually began on the morning of the marriage ceremony, when a few hired musicians customarily gathered outside the home of the bride. There they played on the front porch, leading musicians to refer to this part of their job as *na porciu* (on the porch) music. Polish-American women who were interviewed by Wayne State University students in Detroit in the 1960s recalled that this section of wedding music consisted of "sad songs," the lyrics of which described the story of a young girl taking leave of her mother to go to the house of the groom. One woman remarked, however, that "[the musicians] played funny things, too, with jokes in them." Most accounts concur that at this point also a religious song such as *Serdeczna Matko* (Sweet Mother Mary) was sung.[9] Traditionally, in Polish villages, at the conclusion of the *na porciu* music, the bridal party rode to the church in wagons. They were accompanied on their way by musicians. This tradition, continued by Polish immigrants in the United States who walked to church with musical accompaniment, gradually died out as immigrants increasingly purchased automobiles.

The wedding reception began immediately following the marriage ceremony, and took place in either a church hall or at the bride's home. At this early reception, only family and close friends were present, as the other guests were not expected until the late afternoon. The reception breakfast was a rather filling meal of pork chops, sauerkraut, sausage, and strong drinks. The band was hired to play during this meal and afterwards for dancing, pausing for at least two hours in the afternoon while the bridal party posed for photographs, and resuming their accompaniment at perhaps five o'clock in the afternoon. To the afternoon reception, a larger crowd of possibly up to three hundred guests was invited. Again, a heavy meal of pork, chicken, city chicken, stuffed cabbage rolls, sausage, potatoes, bread, salad, dessert, and liquor was served. Dancing and drinking continued into the night, and at midnight another meal was served. At that time also, a ritual known as *oczepiny* occurred in which the bride's veil was ceremoniously removed, and the head cook or an older woman in the community sang a traditional song. Various accounts name such disparate musical traditions for the accompaniment of this ceremony as the traditional Polish "Twelve Angels," and the American standard "Let Me Call You Sweetheart."

Afterward, dancing continued, frequently into the early hours of the morning, at which time the dance band would disperse. The following day, close friends and family continued the wedding celebration, referred to as the *poprawiny*, at which food and drink left over from the previous night, was consumed. Usually the band was called upon to accompany dancing at this gathering also.

From the musician's point of view, the wedding was an opportunity for earning extra income. Though band members were engaged at a rate of seven or eight dollars for an evening's work, they could expect to take home fifteen or twenty dollars in tips. The traditional wedding celebration afforded a few occasions for earning tips, the most assured occurring as the guests arrived at the evening reception. As each guest or couple entered the hall, the band interrupted whatever dance tune they may have been playing, and would begin to play a Grand March, a Polish polonaise. The playing of this polonaise signaled to the bride and groom that another guest had entered the hall. (This same march would have been played, start to finish, when the bridal party first arrived. Afterward, it would not be rendered fully again, but would be

---

[9] Holmes, "Polish Wedding Customs in Wyandotte," item 1962 (14), p. 5, in WSU Folklore Archives, Polish and Polish-American Folklore Collections.

played long enough that the new arrivals could be greeted by the newlyweds and pass in front of the band.) This pattern of interruptions continued for one or two hours until all guests had arrived,

> decreasing in frequency as the night wore on. Every time some family came in, whatever number you were playing, you stopped right there, at the beginning, every few minutes. Then it tapered off. The latecomers would be business people mostly. They'd close shop maybe nine o'clock and arrive late.[10]

As each guest arrived and was greeted, they promenaded in front of the bandstand, and as they passed before the musicians, they would drop twenty-five or fifty cents into the bell of the saxophone or f holes of the violin or string bass. (One musician was known to have outfitted his string bass with a small door on the back through which he retrieved his tips at the end of the playing session.)

Tipping was expected behavior of all guests. Though musicians agree that it would have been inappropriate to reprimand a guest publicly who had not tipped them, one saxophonist recalled playing with an accordionist who would not allow a non-tipper to go unnoticed— he would follow the person around the room, continuing to play his accordion until he received a tip. In the same way this musician once tried to force a larger tip from a prominent local businessman who had dropped a penny into the bell of the sax. The accordionist retrieved the penny from the bell and

> He stuck it on his forehead, followed [the businessman] back into the bar [playing his accordion all the while]. It really embarrassed the guy cause he dropped a penny in my horn. Pretty soon the guy took his wallet out and took out a dollar bill and showed everybody "Here!" Then he put it in the horn.[11]

The tipping procedure could also be used by guests to their own advantage to make an impression on the community, and to exercise some influence over the band's choice of songs:

> If a guy dropped a dollar, you remembered him. If he came up and *whispered* a request, he got it. Not that we didn't play for anybody else. I just mean, there was a little more effort. You mentioned them by name and tried to remember what kind of a tune they liked.[12]

---

[10] Ted Wienclaw interview, 19 December 1989.

[11] Frank Wienclaw interview, 19 December 1989.

[12] Ibid.

Guests continued to enter into the evening. Although the band was hired to play until two o'clock in the morning, the crowd was usually willing at that point to continue celebrating. "People are in a jovial mood, we'd pass the hat around. They'd want you to play 'til three o'clock. We'd play 'til four."[13] Thus the wedding day for the musicians usually lasted eighteen hours. They took regular fifteen-minute breaks between forty-five minute sets, with an hour and twenty minutes off for the evening meal. During the afternoon, the musicians spelled each other—one could leave the hall for as much as an hour as long as the other two continued playing. This was not the case during the evening. The bride's family would not tolerate the temporary absence of individual band members during the night when the greatest number of guests would be present.[14]

A well played wedding meant additional work for the band. They were their own best advertisement, and were often hired on the basis of their performance for a future wedding or even weekly work at a neighborhood tavern.

Studies conducted in the eastern United States reveal traditions that were similar to those in Detroit and suggest that the wedding ceremony was remarkably uniform among Polish immigrant communities across the Midwestern and eastern regions of the United States. Deborah Silverman, who researched Polish-American folklore in western New York, for example, described the procession from the bride's home to the church and the unveiling of the bride in a way that is strikingly similar to descriptions of the correlative events in the Wayne State University archives. The band's responsibilities—beginning the morning of the marriage ceremony and lasting through the *poprawiny* of the next day—and even the band's financial gains (Silverman reports $14 earned in 1920) are similar between the two regions. Likewise, both Polish- and English-texted songs "Let Me Call You Sweetheart" and *Serdeczna Matko* figured as significantly in the rituals in Buffalo as they did in Detroit. Yet a third source of information concerning the Polish wedding, Susan Davis (1978), who conducted her studies in Utica, New York in the mid-1970s, corroborates the findings of folklorists in Buffalo and Detroit. She adds to the discussion two other parties that were traditionally accompanied by musicians. The first, an engagement party (*zareczyny*), required a three- or four-piece combo to provide dance music. The second was a bridal shower that took place one month prior to the wedding. Women comprised the guest list at this party with the one exception of the bride-to-be's godfather who accompanied the godmother. This last gathering consisted of a meal followed by a dance. None of Davis's findings regarding pre-wedding parties have been reported in the Detroit-based studies, but it is certainly conceivable that these too may have been celebrated in Detroit and in Buffalo as well.

* * * *

---

[13] Frank, Ted, and Syl Wienclaw interview, 19 December 1989.

[14] Syl Wienclaw interview, 27 July 1992.

The involvement of the Polish-American dance band musicians in two realms, Polish and non-Polish has been a constant in their musical work and has challenged them to maintain a multi-faceted repertory. On the one hand, they have provided the Polish-American community with the entertainment and traditional pieces it holds to be distinctly its own. On the other, they have been involved in non-ethnic performances, influenced by mainstream as well as other-ethnic traditions, and ultimately have acted as performers of mainstream popular American music *within* the Polonia.

Many Polish-Americans from the old neighborhoods in the Detroit area can recall listening to a Polish radio program, *Father Justyn's Rosary Hour*. They claim that as children they could walk down the neighborhood streets in the summer and not miss a word of the program—such was its popularity. It could be heard blaring out of the open windows of every house on the street.[15] The variety of programs listened to by Polish-Americans, however, also included those musical shows produced by other-heritage groups. As one musician remarked, "Every Sunday morning at ten o'clock my dad would put the radio on and we'd listen to the Mexican Marimba Típica Band, and I remember the announcer's name was Alois Havrilla."

The issue of cultural interchange among ethnic groups and mainstream American society is one that is dealt with at length by the historian Victor Greene (1992). In writing *A Passion for Polka: Old-Time Ethnic Music in America*, Greene's ultimate goal was to define the relationship between popular music and ethnicity. He sought to present, in his own words, "the full story of how ethnic music became part of the country's 'Hit Parade'" (1992, 14). Greene referred to the period under discussion (beginning in the 1920s), in fact, as the "Crossover Age"—an era when immigration laws had reduced the number of newcomers to America and the children of immigrants did not share their parents' strong emotional ties to the old country. He noted that second-generation dance bands, questing after financial gain, broadened their playing venues to include "English" gigs and expanded their repertory to include mainstream music. On radio, "regional musical aggregations [were] eager for substantial material success. From the beginning they sought broad multigroup appeal by playing pieces from several group traditions" (ibid., 12). Recording companies recognized their opportunity also, and during a period that otherwise exhibited extreme nativistic tendencies, they poured resources into the business of ethnic records (ibid., 88).

---

[15] This radio show began humbly enough in 1926 as a five-minute segment delivered by the Franciscan priest Fr. Justin (born in Pennsylvania as Michael Figas, 1886-1959). The five-minute religious message, originally an addendum to the Polish Variety Program broadcast out of Buffalo, New York, garnered such a mass following that within a year sponsors decided to award Fr. Justin his own hour-long program. Delivered in Polish, it consisted of a twenty-five minute talk on spirituality, and a thirty-minute segment during which listeners could call in and ask for advice. The callers spoke in either Polish or English and were answered by the priest accordingly. The sections of spoken message and conversation were interspersed with choral selections sung by visiting and local choirs. Fr. Justin's popularity spread across the country—the original single station broadcast encompassed fifty stations by 1954. The format of the *Rosary Hour* continued well beyond Fr. Justin's death, and was still being aired in 2002 in the United States and Canada (Burzynski 1997).

The complexities of the Crossover Age would seem to defy my description just three paragraphs earlier of the dance bands' involvement in *two* realms, Polish and non-Polish. Certainly the term "non-Polish" encompasses an enormous breadth of ethnic (Slovenian, German, Czech, Italian) and mainstream styles and genres. "Polish" itself encompasses repertory composed in the old and new countries—the pieces composed in the United States vulnerable to the so-called ethnically neutral and other-ethnic influences. Notwithstanding these complexities, however, I cannot ignore the singular emotional and psychological position of the ethnic minority—the dichotomy of us versus them. One can analyze quite fruitfully all of the ways in which the ethnic group influences the mainstream, and one can look at the ponderous influence of the mainstream on the ethnic group. But then one must eventually return to the notion of national identity—the perception of shared ancestry by which members of an ethnic community differentiate themselves from surrounding society.

Despite their integration into the musical life of the larger Detroit community, Polish-American musicians maintained boundaries by which they defined themselves as a distinct group. They retained their differentiated status by singing Polish texts and performing to largely Polish-American crowds at weddings, picnics, and taverns. A repertory consisting largely of polkas, obereks, and waltzes distinguished the Polish-American dance band from those performing at general citywide or military-base dances.

Dance bands also retained a distinct ethnic identity through their membership—or, at least through the conceptualization of that membership. Although exclusively Polish-heritage membership has *never* been the rule in dance bands, the majority of musicians I interviewed drew attention to the non-Polish members in their dance bands, verbally differentiating them *as though* their presence constituted an exception to the norm. Such verbal differentiations included the naming of a person followed by an ethnic label, such as "He was a teacher named Vargas. A Mexican." Or they involved some measure of surprised explanation, such as "We had a dago in the band that sounded just like the rest of us." Musical boundaries were verbally maintained among musicians of the 1930s and 40s as a matter of course. One musician explained "Italians have Italian [music], and Germans have German. We always played in our own group." Thus, by means of purely musical and textual distinctions and repertory, and the actual, or more often, verbalized distinctions of group membership, the Polish-American bands retained a degree of ethnic identity.

While the musicians then maintained certain tangible limits surrounding Polish dance music, they did not limit themselves to this same circumscribed musical context. To do so would have placed restrictions on their marketability as performers of popular music and would have cost them such work as the thirty-some years Ted Wienclaw played with a non-Polish dance band. While not all musicians could count as many roles in their musical repertory as Piotr Aniołek, they did acquire dual roles, as local musicians in the Polonia and as musicians in the larger Detroit community.

Despite the borrowing from mainstream American dance music, Polish-American dance bands produced recordings that sounded decidedly non-mainstream—if not because of the inclusion of a Polish text, then by virtue of the spotlighted genres: polkas and obereks.[16] In the final analysis, it would seem that the musicians of this generation, for all of their nods in the direction of mass-marketed music in the United States, preferred to continue making music their community would recognize as its own. Musicians of the following generations—those who began their professional careers in the late 1950s—would face a similar dilemma. They would have to forge a path among newly emerging rock and country music styles.

---

[16] I had the opportunity in the early 1990s to interview by phone one of the central figures involved in the recording of eastern style polkas in the late 1940s and 50s, Walt Dana (Daniłowski). Dana clearly looked upon eastern-style polkas as Polish and not American music. Born in Poland in 1902 and trained in classical composition, Dana founded and directed the Chór Dana (Dana Chorus) in Warsaw that toured the United States and Europe. In 1940, Dana left Poland and began working on Polish radio in New York and Detroit, where he observed "These Polish Americans didn't care much for popular music. They like folk music—polkas and obereks." Dana acted upon his observation by founding the Dana Recording Company in New York in 1946 (personal communication, 31 July 1990). He is responsible for recording the best-known Polish dance orchestras in the country—the eastern-style, big-band influenced ensembles of Frank Wojnarowski and Gene Wisniewski.

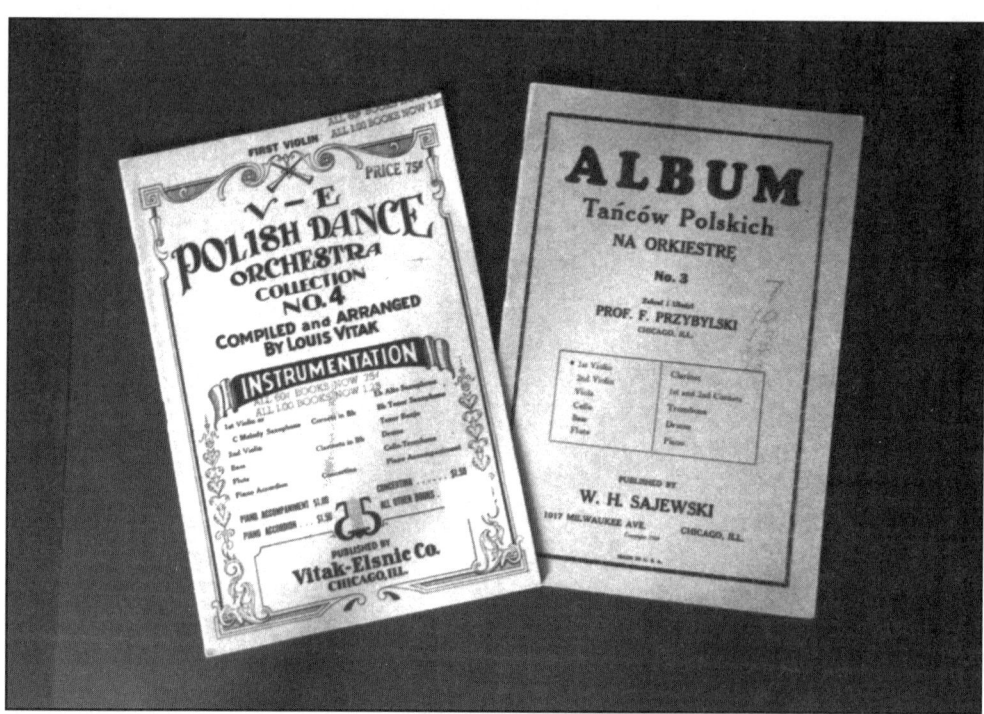

Fig. 8.1. Part Books of Polish dance band music, published in Chicago

8

So What'll It Be? (Rock, Country, or Polish?)

Dance Bands since the 1950s

In the late 1950s, Polish-American dance music underwent an enormous stylistic shift that ultimately effected a change in Detroit styles, from one oriented in the traditions of the eastern United States to one that originated in Chicago. This stylistic shift, along with interrelated changes in the demographics and politics of ethnicity, would have a profound effect on the sounds and contexts of a newly established polka industry over the next thirty years.

At the time that rock and roll emerged to challenge and eventually take the place of older popular styles in the American mainstream, a louder, looser, slower style of polka music from Chicago arose to prevail to some extent over the eastern, big band sound. Musicians in Chicago became the leaders of a new Polish-American sound known as "honky"—an improvisatory rendering of Polish folk tunes, borne of the interaction between four, five, or a half dozen musicians. Within the next decade, honky would spawn a second, louder, energetic style known as "push."

The drummer and singer "Li'l" Wally Jagiello (b. 1930) is credited with the principal innovations and successful dissemination of the earlier honky style. Raised in a Polish neighborhood in Chicago, Jagiello grew up listening to the local bands of Eddie Zima and Steve Adamczyk. He was attracted to the bandleaders' use of the concertina, an instrument disdained by the then popular eastern style bands—its crunchy tone was distinctly rural.[1] But Jagiello was impressed not only by Adamczyk's and Zima's instrumentation, but also with the bands' slow tempos, and their simple renditions of the old Polish folk melodies; in Adamczyk's music, Jagiello heard the beginnings of a stylistic alternative to the eastern sound. Janice Kleeman (1982, 139), in her study of early polka bands noted that

> Although [Adamczyk's] lead instruments played in concert with each other, in what polka musicians call "tight harmony," there was a looseness

---

[1] Siwiec conversation, 29 July 1992.

about Adamczyk's relaxed tempo and relatively simple lead parts which was distinctly different from the big band polka sound.

Jagiello built further upon the Chicago idiosyncrasies. He played without written music, and his renditions usually included a sung text (ibid., 143). In addition, he further slowed the tempo of dance music in Chicago to ♩ = 112. (Zima's tempo of ♩ = 126 was already slower than that of the eastern bands ♩ = 128-136). He released the clarinet part from its strict doubling of the melody at the third, and provided it with opportunities to improvise a counterpoint to the melodic line. Finally, Jagiello increased the density of the snare drum part.

With regard to formal structure, the term honky denotes a usually texted polka with instrumental interludes between vocal sections. Typically, melodic lines are not as ornamented in Chicago as in the eastern style, but display slight variations in repetitions. Honky style, as it is represented by the early recordings of Li'l Wally, features two melody instruments, often two trumpets or trumpet and concertina, or clarinet and trumpet together with a second clarinet playing a third below or improvising a counterpoint around the melodic line.[2] Ed Siwiec, a clarinet player in Detroit who has recorded honky style polkas, described the decorative and improvisatory role of the clarinet in that style. He remarked that the clarinet "decorates the melody within the chord structure, playing counter-melodies and rhythmic licks . . . creating emotion and movement by complementing the arrangement."[3]

Siwiec's reference to emotion in his description of the musical function of the clarinet is in keeping with musicians' general understanding of honky style. The term honky carries connotations of an emotional approach to music making; musicians speak of the style as being loose and exuberant and heartfelt. As Siwiec described it, "The term honky means good old-fashioned polka music—from the heart. It's what you feel. Honky usually denotes simple rhythm, simple chords. . . . It's simpler, more downhome."[4]

Honky repertory, like that of eastern style, borrows tunes from the vast repertory of Polish folk songs. One Detroit-based musician who has toured with Li'l Wally remarked that the bandleader travels with a small tape recorder. He collects folksongs from older members of his polka audience and later arranges these tunes for his band. Unlike eastern style, honky typically retains the asymmetric phrasing of the old folk songs. These songs, when arranged for use on the dance floor, sometimes cause problems for those who are dancing. I attended a polka awards banquet one evening in Detroit where a Chicago-style band performed an asymmetrically phrased tune entitled "Pretty Girl Polka." The floor was filled with practiced dancers, all who were jerked to a bewildered pause with every recurrence of the odd-numbered measures. The honky musicians' loyalty to older phrase

---

[2] Concertina here refers to a squeeze box, the notes of which are produced by the depression of a series of keys on both the left and right hand sides of the instrument.

[3] Siwiec interview, 12 September 1989.

[4] Ibid.

structures in their performance of folk tunes beautifully symbolizes and characterizes their respect for early Polish immigrant culture.

As an innovator, and perhaps as significantly as a promoter, Li'l Wally Jagiello played a central role in the early standardization and dissemination of the Chicago-derived style. But he was not the only one working on new musical developments. A second Chicago musician, Marion Lush (b. 1931), was instrumental in transforming Jagiello's honky style into the style known as push. Instead of Jagiello's contrapuntal arrangements for clarinet, Lush's sound focused on two trumpets playing in parallel thirds, and relegated the clarinet to a simply optional status. His arrangements that did include clarinet, provided the instrument with the main melodic line, accompanied at the sixth or tenth by trumpet. Drumming patterns on Lush's recordings tended toward an eastern sound with their rather open and unvarying pattern of bass and snare and very little use of cymbal.

The developments of both Jagiello and Lush were given a boost especially in the early 1970s through the ascending fame of a third Chicago musician, Eddie Blazonczyk. Blazonczyk and his band, the Versatones, accepted Lush's two-trumpet lead, but added to it a clarinet that wove in and around the melody line in true honky style. Blazonczyk's recordings in the new push style set the standard toward which the majority of young Detroit-based musicians would aspire.

The term push is used by musicians to refer both to the style of an entire piece or to a section of a tune where "pushing" or "riding" takes place. Despite the various uses of the term, the musical requirements are quite specific. A section of push involves one or usually more of the following elements: bellow shaking on the accordion (the accordion bellows are alternately pushed with four quick shakes—sixteenth notes—and then pulled in four shakes over a single chord creating a pulsating wall of supporting harmony); a continuous sounding of the ride cymbal by the percussionist (referred to as riding); and energetic rhythmic displays by the melody instruments. While it is technically impossible for the concertina to be shaken because it sounds a different note when pushed than when pulled, the concertina player can approximate the sound of the accordion by playing a quickly alternating chromatic pattern. Rarely is pushing heard beneath a vocal line.

During the past thirty years, the term push has come to mean more than a vocal piece containing sections of push. It denotes an entire sound complex that may be described most basically as brassy and cleanly executed, with a more tightly woven ensemble than the traditional honky of Li'l Wally. Push style bands normally consist of two trumpets, saxophone/clarinet, bass guitar (or upright bass), accordion, drums, and, as in honky, a concertina. True to its Chicago roots, the push style that is played in Detroit maintains a slow tempo, is heavily amplified, features much syncopation, and may be either texted or purely instrumental. Of the two Chicago styles, push is more popular in the Detroit area.

Improvisation plays a role in the execution of both Chicago styles, varying in degree from band to band, depending upon band members' abilities and stylistic aims. In certain bands, the leader arranges all parts in writing for members who then read them at rehearsal.

In other bands, players work without written music, and maintain that they never play a tune the same way twice. Improvisation is especially central to good concertina playing and, as one musician noted, even when a concertina player knows how to read music, he is expected to play without written music, improvising fluid, often chromatic contrapuntal lines.[5] In Detroit, a wide variety of styles are categorized as push style. Some follow Lush's simpler drumming patterns and make little use of clarinet, giving most melodic voice to the powerful trumpet duos or sax. Others follow the complex drumming patterns begun by Li'l Wally, adding to them a greater diversity of highly syncopated patterns. The drum set used in push generally includes bass and snare drums, mounted toms and high hat and possibly other cymbals.

Accordion playing, too, varies greatly from band to band depending upon the technical ability of the player and the overall stylistic aims of the group. Some players fulfill only the minimum requirements of the Chicago style by outlining a simple chord, while others can show off a well developed technique, devising complex counterpoints to the melodic line.

Vocals are sung in a relaxed manner. As one musician explained, "We sing like we speak." Vocals do not employ falsetto, and usually do not extend to the upper or lower ends of a singer's range. Texts are delivered syllabically, singing style is smooth, on or slightly below the notated pitch, and there is very little sliding from one pitch to the next. Vocalists generally make no attempts to blur or play with the sounds of the words; the clear enunciation of the English and Polish texts is valued by performers and listeners alike.

A small number of bands in Detroit display a mixture of the styles introduced by Jagiello, Blazonczyk, and Lush. They may feature a brassy trumpet section in parallel harmonies and the syncopated drumming of Blazonczyk as well as an improvisatory contrapuntal clarinet and concertina reminiscent of earlier honky arrangements. Despite variety in style, all of these bands acknowledge that they are patterning themselves after a Chicago sound. Together they constitute the larger fragment of the Polish-American dance band picture in Detroit that includes eastern-big-band-influenced ensembles and three-piece combos as well.

Depending upon the experience and preferences of musicians in Detroit, a particular band will present their dancing audience with more than one style of Polish polkas during an evening's performance. Audiences made up of older polka afficionados appreciate the willingness and ability of young bands to perform honky style successfully. On the other hand, dancers in their twenties and thirties seem to grow quickly impatient with the sparse, open quality of honky sound. I recall one instance vividly in which I was part of a crowd in a bar listening to one of the younger bands play. After listening for the first hour to pieces performed in push style, I requested a song that I knew the band had recorded in honky style. The band played this request and followed it with another honky-style piece. At the close of this second number, the crowd began shouting "We've had enough of that honky, play some push!" The difference in requests made by older and younger polka audiences clearly demonstrate a generational split over stylistic preference.

---

[5] Fudalla interview, 17 April 1990.

The tremendous changes in the *sound* of Polish-American dance music since the 1950s belie a break in the continuing traditions maintained by the musicians and their audience. In truth, there are strong threads of continuity binding the new musical era to the old. The assimilative stance taken by Polish-American musicians—their outlook that allows (even encourages) them to borrow stylistic elements and repertory from outside of the Polish-American dance music tradition—is arguably one the most profound dynamics tying the new generation to those that came before.

Modern Polish-American dance band musicians, like their predecessors, do not act unaware of the shifts in United States popular music. The acceptance of a louder, looser polka style in the late 1950s, in place of a big-band, eastern sound reflected the displacement of big band jazz and dance music by rock and roll in the dominant musical mainstream, and followed the dominant strand of mass media acceptance. In the way eastern style music displayed similarities to its mainstream contemporary, so does the push style reveal the influence of contemporary rock and country western styles. Played by a band typically comprised of brass, wind, bass, accordions, and drums, push style music is heavily amplified. The influence exerted by country music is especially evident in the polka repertory that includes country songs, arranged with a polka beat. (The better known arrangements of this type are those made in the 1970s and 80s by Eddie Blazonczyk.) The adaptation of a country-western repertory by polka musicians has been facilitated by structural features common to both polkas and country-western songs. Both repertories share a formal structure consisting of multiple verses and a recurring refrain. Like the texts of country and western music, polka texts deal largely with the theme of love, and are normally delivered by a main melodic voice and one or two harmonizing voices. Rock music in the top 40, of course, also shares these structural and thematic features. But its crossover into the Polish-American repertory is more rare, largely because of the styles' opposite beat-emphasis structure. While rock emphasizes beats 2 and 4, in polkas the strong beats occur on 1 and 3, precluding an exchange of repertory.

The second important constant that links the newer to the older bands—the primary constant being the assimilative stance toward outside sources—is the repertory itself. Musicians estimate that there are a couple hundred long-established polkas and waltzes that form a core repertory still performed in the 1990s. This is not surprising in a tradition where young musicians acquire their technique by listening to old recordings and learn their craft by playing with experienced performers. Daily polka radio programming features a majority of old favorites. Newly produced albums, usually comprised of a dozen cuts, typically offer at least six pieces from the earlier tradition. The bands offer imaginative rearrangements of the older polkas, as one musician stated, "in order to breathe new life into them."

The great variety of musical types that comprises the repertory of modern-day bands—polkas, obereks, waltzes, standards from the big-band era, country-western music, top-40 pop tunes, and European tangos—has resulted in a specific terminology in use among musicians who carefully label categories of bands. Because the categories that are defined below refer to typical repertories, they do not have direct counterparts in stylistic classifications.

While Polish-American dance fans use the term "polka band" rather loosely to refer to a Polish-American band that plays polkas as well as some country and top-40 selections, most *musicians* reserve that term for the very few bands in the area that specialize in playing polkas, obereks, and waltzes. As one polka musician, Ed Siwiec (interview, 20 September 1989), explained,

> There are polka bands and there are wedding bands. We [polka musicians] can cross over and do their pop and country and do quite a good job at it. They [wedding band musicians] cannot and probably do not care to cross over and *really* play polkas.

The terms "wedding band" or "commercial band" refer to an ensemble, the repertory of which centers on, as Siwiec commented, pop music—the current top 40 hits, and rock and country standards—and consists additionally of a number of the better known traditional polkas and waltzes. The label "wedding band" is derived from the situation at which these groups find the greater portion of their work. Siwiec spoke of the practical demands made upon a polka band in the context of the wedding (ibid.):

> In a wedding situation, we know we have to mix up a variety of music.... We'll play tunes from the '40s. If we see a lot of younger people there, we'll play contemporary music. We try to get away with as many polkas, obereks, and waltzes at a wedding as we can. It depends what the people who hired us want.... It's a little frustrating when you've spent so much of your time listening and learning. We feel we're a high-caliber polka band. Someone comes up to you and says, "Is that all you guys play is polkas?" It's disheartening. Where else can you go? We like all kinds of music, but we specialize in polkas, and we're proud of it. We want to carry the torch on.

This comment reflects the musicians' efforts to balance their roles as ethnic-genre specialists on one hand, and mainstream pop performers on the other—a balance not unlike that achieved by Polish-American dance band musicians in the 1930s and 40s.

In contrast to polka band musicians, are those who approach their role as performers from another angle. They are not dedicated in the same strict sense to Polish polkas, obereks, and waltzes, and thus they do not share the polka band's desire or sense of responsibility to performing these genres. They choose to organize not only their wedding gigs, but their picnics, bar dates and festival performances as well around a repertory based on current mainstream popular music. These musicians form the ensembles referred to as "commercial" or "wedding bands." Not as unified a group as their placement under a single label implies, these musicians vary greatly in the extent of their knowledge of music in general, and polkas in particular. But, certainly, they differ as a whole in their musical emphasis from the polka bands.

The third category of Polish-American dance bands in Detroit is the "continental" band. Continental ensembles specialize in playing European tangos, some rock, waltzes, and just a few polkas. These bands are in the minority in Detroit; only two different ensembles appeared on the various dance event advertisements during the period of my investigation. As with the other two categories—polka bands and wedding bands—the "continental" label refers to a repertory. But the bands categorized in this way differ from each other also with regard to audience and instrumentation. The audience for which the continental bands play differs significantly from that which attends performances by polka and commercial bands. Continental bands are hired to perform at wedding receptions and picnics to which, primarily, recent Polish immigrants have been invited; at these gatherings, the bandleaders make all of their announcements in the Polish language. The audience members demonstrate a preference for the emphasized genres of the band's repertory, dancing when the band plays a tango (a popular genre in Poland), and sitting down to rest or go to the bar for drinks on the rare occasion when a polka is played. It is not unusual at such a dance, that when the band introduces a single polka into a set comprised almost entirely of tangos, the crowded dance floor clears. I recall attending a typical picnic fundraiser in the 1990s sponsored by a cultural organization—the membership of which included a great majority of post-War immigrants. Those of us interested in dancing had gathered on long benches surrounding the dance floor—a temporary wooden structure, at one end of which was a raised bandstand, and at the other, a bar. The majority of the audience and the band members alike were speaking Polish among themselves. But when I approached them in English, they responded in English. I would estimate that only twenty percent of those gathered at the event were members of the old Polonia. The band had been playing mostly instrumental tangos and modern Polish songs (with a rock beat) for approximately a half an hour, when they started a polka. Twenty couples left the dance floor arm in arm, some making their way to the bar, and others to the benches or food tent. Two older couples, members of the old Polonia stayed to dance. Four young Polish women—recent immigrants—also stayed. Laughing at their own attempts, they studied and imitated the dance steps of the Polish-American couples.

In terms of instrumentation, the continental and wedding bands are more akin to each other than either is to the polka band. Unlike the polka bands, the wedding and continental groups do not employ a concertina. Rather, their instrumentation typically consists of piano accordion, drums, tenor and alto saxophone, and trumpet. Finally, unlike most polka bands, continental bands include members from the post-World War II wave of immigration. They, like those musicians who specialize in polkas, refer to the other bands as "commercial," but they use the term specifically to mean a band that is familiar only with "American" tangos, such as "La Paloma" and "Blue Tango."

A small number of Polish polka bands in Detroit further expand upon their repertory by borrowing tunes and arrangements from polka bands outside of their own ethnic group—for example, the Slovenian polka repertory. Beyond the in-genre borrowing that takes place, polka and commercial bands have looked for inspiration to television jingles and the swing era. For example, in 1990, a Detroit-based band known as the Zug Islanders recorded two selections, "The Gilligan's Polka" and the "Masterpiece Polka."[6] The first borrowed its theme from the opening music of a 1960s television situation-comedy (*Gilligan's Island*); the second was a polka version of Jean Joseph Mouret's "Rondeau" from his *Sinfonies de Fanfares* that accompanied the public television feature *Masterpiece Theater*. Another Chicago-style band in Detroit has incorporated tunes from the 1940s and has experimented with the production of a Glenn Miller sound. Still, the influence of big band music on Chicago style is small in comparison to its earlier influence on eastern groups.

Formal musical training among the younger generation of musicians ranges from one or two years of ensemble classes—band or orchestra at the junior or senior high school level—to college degree programs in music. Listening to the younger generation of musicians describe their training, one hears no more about the music professors of the older generation. Instead, one hears of trumpet lessons in the seventh grade and church choir rehearsals. The background of Ed Siwiec, a clarinet player and leader of the former band Prime Drive, illustrates the difference between the older generation of musicians and the younger. An extraordinary musician, Siwiec's ability goes well beyond that of many musicians who earn extra income playing weekend engagements. Nevertheless, his formal training in music is rather typical of his contemporaries. A third-generation Polish American, Siwiec was raised in a Polish parish in the suburb of Dearborn. The Polish National Alliance offered Polish folk dance classes in the area, and his parents enrolled him. Thus, by the time he was a teenager, he had gained experience in stylized folk dance and its musical accompaniment, and he had grown familiar with dance band music through his attendance at church festivals and weddings. His formal musical education began in the school band; he studied the clarinet for three years in grade school and the saxophone for one and a half years in high school. In his junior year, he won a scholarship to attend two weeks of summer music camp at the prestigious Interlochen Fine Arts Academy in northwest Michigan. While Siwiec was honing his musical skills, he was already working in bands. In the ninth grade, in imitation of a friend's older brother, he and his friends put together a small ensemble and began playing wedding engagements.

Siwiec and his first band played from written music; they learned some of their earliest repertory from a set of part books, similar to the Sajewski and Vitak-Elsnic sets published by Ignacy Podgorski.[7] His generation includes some musicians who can read music, and others who do not. So deeply is the traditional repertory ingrained in the minds of the musicians, and so acceptable is the practice of deviating from written arrangements, that those musicians who are able to read music, do not always find it necessary to exercise their reading skills when playing with a band.

---

[6] The Zug Islanders took their name from a small island situated between the Rouge and Detroit Rivers.

[7] Siwiec interview, 12 September 1989.

Despite a modern emphasis on institutionalized instruction, the majority of musicians rely, as did their predecessors, on family and community members for their most essential training. A concertina player in Detroit explained the role his father played in influencing himself and his two brothers to take up the concertina. His father, who played accordion (although only around the house), invited a man he had heard play concertina at a local bar to his home and asked him to play for his three young sons. The concertina player merely demonstrated for them the basic principles of playing the instrument. Each of the brothers practiced, listening to polka recordings and radio, until all could play the improvisatory Chicago honky and push styles.[8] Many musicians began their professional careers playing in bands of their high school peers, or with the band of an older male relative—an uncle or father.

> Listening is central to the learning of techniques and styles. I would learn note for note off the recording. I'd pick out a couple of guys that I thought played very well that I would learn from and I would learn their lick note for note. After a few years went by, I got pretty proficient at playing their licks, and over a period of time I developed my style, which is a combination of things I heard and things that I now wanted to create.[9]

Musicians who spend hours imitating what they hear on recordings are learning the repertory at the same time that they are improving their technical skills. It is not uncommon that a musician who works steadily with one band will be called upon to substitute for a regular member of another band. The substitute's knowledge of the standard repertory is crucial to his personal reputation and so also to his continued employment.

Though so much is learned on the job, rehearsal plays an important role in the formation of a band's sound. Weekly rehearsals, most musicians would agree, are especially necessary to a band that is attempting to integrate new members (the turnover rate of personnel is high), or to one that is preparing for a performance or a recording session. Bands that have experienced a low turnover rate, and have performed together for perhaps ten years, do not rehearse regularly, and may get together only once before every playing engagement. Other bands, that are aggressively seeking engagements and hoping to develop a local following may maintain an intense schedule of weekly rehearsals over a number of years, regardless of how well they know each other's playing styles.

Bands range widely in the extent to which they rely on written music. Some rehearse with and perform from notated music. The bandleader may write out an original arrangement for the band, or he may make use of a published arrangement, altering it to fit the instrumentation of his band. Other bands maintain an almost unchanging repertory, originally

---

[8] Fudalla interview, 17 April 1990.

[9] Siwiec, ibid.

learned from written music, and play much of their material from memory. Much less common in Detroit are bands such as one that had been known as Prime Drive, which placed great emphasis on improvisation and the aural working out of an arrangement. The members of Prime Drive found that writing out charts consumed too much of their time, and they relied instead on tape recorders. The individual who composed a piece or re-arranged an old standard, recorded his musical ideas of tune and harmony on a cassette. He then used whatever skills he possessed of the other instruments in the band to sketch out on tape what he imagined each of the other members would play on their respective instruments. The cassette was then copied and passed among members who would then meet for rehearsal. At rehearsal, the piece would be worked out further, each of the instrumentalists developing their individual parts, taking cues from each other. Ed Siwiec, the leader of Prime Drive, explained the rehearsal of his band as a type of jam session (ibid.):

> Our music is fairly complex, especially when you realize nothing is written down. Each player is a strong, confident player, and when you put six competent musicians together, you almost have to hold them back. But we've developed a real respect for each other and we stay within the realm of what each is capable of, and we work off of each other. If the trumpet player has taken a solo and he comes up with a lick, I say "That's cool. Do that again." And I'll match him [on clarinet].

This method of arranging a piece is uncommon, undoubtedly because it requires pre-rehearsal preparation and also demands of the musicians a great deal of mutual respect for each other's skills.

Some portion of rehearsal time is spent in learning the correct pronunciation of Polish-language texts. Increasingly, vocal polkas have featured English rather than Polish texts. The change in the proportion of English to Polish texts reflects a similar shift in language use among the Detroit Polish-American population as a whole. It may be said generally, that the greater percentage of polka musicians aged forty and younger are second and third generation descendants of the earlier wave of immigration, many of whom do not understand word for word what they are singing when they sing in Polish. In spite of this, Polish-language polkas continue to make up a large portion of the repertory. Albums recorded even in the 1990s typically feature six Polish vocals out of the usual twelve cuts.

Unlike the Polish arts clubs and choral groups that are influenced by members of the post-World War II immigration, the polka bands do not include Polish texts in order to attract the new Polonia. Rather, polka bands continue to sing in Polish for two reasons. First, they do so in order to please an audience that consists largely of dance music afficionados who *do* understand Polish and appreciate the older, traditional repertory. Second, as one composer explained to me, "It makes no sense to translate the texts into English [when re-recording an old tune]. The music sounds better with the Polish words."

Bands committed to singing in Polish learn from listening to recordings. Non-Polish-speaking bands whose members compose new songs in English may ask an older relative to translate the text into Polish verse form, and then learn from that relative the correct pronunciation. At a point in time when many of the younger generation communicate daily in English, the repertory that is heard on radio, recordings, and in live performances includes at least twenty-five percent Polish-language texts—the younger musicians sing in the language of their grandparents.

This seeming anachronism is accompanied by another in the field: women, who constitute at least half of the country's polka fans and are well represented as columnists in the polka press, play a much smaller role in performance than do the men. When one considers the Polish-American woman's participation in the workforce (outside of the home) and her daughters' regular presence in school bands, choirs, and orchestras, her absence in the male dominated dance bands is striking. Angeliki Keil, in her study of polka organizations across the eastern and midwestern states, referred to female polka performers as "rare creatures" (1992, 122). Her observation echoed that of Bob Norgard, a polka columnist, who commented on the lack of female bandleaders in dance bands across the United States.[10] Another regular contributor to the polka press, Gerald Reeves, researched the issue, and then disputed Norgard's comment, publishing his results in the same publication. He culled a list of female bandleaders from record jackets and added to that number the names of bands with which he had become familiar through his work with the United Federation of Polkas. He acknowledged that the list was incomplete, but stated that it contained some fifty-five bands led by women. His list took into account a number of different national polka styles, including Slovenian, Bohemian, and German, as well as Polish, from the states of Colorado, Illinois, Michigan, Ohio, Arkansas, Indiana, Wisconsin, Texas, and Minnesota. Though Reeves had intended to disprove Norgard's statement, his findings support rather than negate Norgard's initial assumption. When it is considered that in Michigan alone at least forty different bands play regularly, Reeves's fifty-five bands, some of which had already retired at the time of his writing, can be only a small proportion of a tally from all of the states listed in his article. Keil (ibid., 122) further corroborated Norgard's observation, even as she began to analyze the role of women as performers:

> Few women are members of polka bands, and they generally portray feminine familial roles on stage: wife, sister, daughter. The Langner Sisters are a good example: prim and proper little-sister types, their singing is defined by smoothness at the expense of expressive force. They are decorative, there to draw the residual interest of the audience.... The Langner Sisters, despite their talents, have nowhere to go.

---

[10] *Polka News*, 8 August 1990.

Along with the Langners, Keil named three more exceptions: the female bandleader Concertina Patti from Milwaukee and the Buffalo-based, nationally known mother-daughter team of Wanda and Stephanie (Pietrzak).[11] Male musicians in Detroit who enjoy Wanda and Stephanie's performances concur that they are "good, but not excellent," musicians—a novelty act that endears the audience to them by the sheer power of their personalities. In Michigan the number of dance bands directed by women in the 1990s was still relatively small. I know of only three in southern Michigan, two of which are in Detroit. Female membership (not leadership) in bands is more frequent, where one finds teams of husbands and wives or entire families performing together.[12]

Male musicians with whom I discussed the lack of women in the bands responded variously, explaining that they would not feel comfortable with a woman in their group, or that a woman's presence might cause tension between the men. While their opinions regarding female membership naturally limit the number of women in otherwise male bands, they do not explain fully the lack of all-female bands. In comparison to the women I interviewed in the choral society who seemed quite comfortable discussing gender roles within their organization (chapter 5), few women band members were willing to reflect aloud on this issue. In answer to my questions, one woman briefly offered that there were more women involved in the 1990s than in the 60s and 70s, an era she described as one in which women did not cross certain invisible lines. She explained that there would always be some, however, who were more assertive, and who would in fact ignore those boundaries. Seven women were performing regularly in Detroit in the 1990s. Two had retired before the year 2000. In a culture where women typically go outside the home to work, the *concept* of the traditional family in which men are assigned a more public, leading role is still highly and unapologetically valued. Female musicians in dance bands were as rare in 2002 as they were when Dorothy Rzeppa, the young woman mentioned in the previous chapter, invited the then-twelve-year-old Syl Wienclaw to join her band. The Polish-American dance hall milieu remains a place where men provide the music, and women and men together promote that music and dance to its accompaniment.

Modern dance bands have persisted working in the direction set down for them by their predecessors; they continue to mark their musical distinctiveness from surrounding cultural groups through their use of the Polish language and their maintenance of a traditional repertory. They identify with a circumscribed community by performing in contexts at which Polish-Americans make up the majority of the audience: Polish ethnic festivals, Catholic Masses in Polish churches, weddings at which either the bride or groom is of Polish descent, Polish church fundraisers, and neighborhood bars. Like the musicians who played in the 1930s,

---

[11] Keil, 122-24. For a rare book-length study of a female bandleader, see the 1986 thesis by Mary Spalding on the Irene Olszewski Orchestra.

[12] Examples from the 1980s were Chris, Jack and Music (husband and wife), and Big Daddy Lackowski and his La Di Das (a family band).

members of modern dance bands exhibit an assimilative stance toward contemporary popular music arrangements and instrumentation.

But the demographics of the old neighborhoods have changed. Band musicians, like the members of the choral groups discussed in chapter 3, may travel ten or fifteen miles in order to rehearse or perform together. The sound of the music itself has changed—the strong tendency within the bands to assimilate surrounding influences has resulted in a new, dense, amplified style of polka music. Finally, there is a general feeling among dance band musicians and dance music promoters that their audience has dwindled. They sense in the younger generation a turning away from specifically Polish-American dance music and a movement toward the highly visible, energetically marketed rock and country music styles. The musicians' and promoters' response to this apparent phenomenon has wrought what is perhaps the biggest change in Polish-American dance music—that is, the establishment of a politically active dance music *industry*.

Fig. 9.1. Senate Café, Hamtramck. Once the venue of remote polka-radio broadcasts and live bands Friday and Saturday nights

9

United We Stand

The Establishment of a Polka Industry

It was not until the late 1960s that a national polka industry emerged. A formal, pan-ethnic, politically and commercially oriented organization of musicians and promoters, the industry focused upon a single dance genre—the polka. By 2000, it comprised fan clubs, conventions, journal publications, radio programs, and sites on the internet. Its continual expansion since the 1960s grew out of the aspirations of its promoters who wished to compete with national, mainstream rock and country music. But its birth came about as a response to concurrent trends in Euro-American dance music and demographic changes in the old immigrant neighborhoods. The phenomenon of a pan-ethnic *polka* industry was the ethnic musicians' answer to a diminishing repertory and a dispersed population.

The pre-1960, diverse Polish-American repertory that included polkas, kujawiaks, obereks, waltzes, and krakowiaks among other genres, dwindled over the next two decades so that by 1980 it consisted mainly of polkas and waltzes, some modern polka bands not knowing how to play an oberek. To illustrate: I attended a wedding reception at which a woman in her eighties requested the band of musicians (all of whom were in their twenties) to play an oberek. The bandleader agreed to her request and proceeded to play a waltz instead. The oberek in $\frac{3}{8}$ time has characteristic rhythmic patterns, and is not interchangeable with the slower waltz played in $\frac{3}{4}$ time. The woman who had made the request realized immediately the exchange that had occurred, but she merely shrugged her shoulders and smiled, recognizing the limitations of the youthful band performing that evening. The market for the less-often performed genres has naturally shrunk, as fewer and fewer members of the audience recognize them or request their performance.

While the number of genres dwindled, the old performance venues began to atrophy. The centers of Polish-American activity described by veteran dance band musicians of the 1940s and 50s in many cases no longer exist, or no longer service a primarily Polish-American clientele. In the late 1980s, for example, one of the polka taverns in Hamtramck, a scene of remote radio polka broadcasts and venue of weekly late night-early morning jam sessions, changed hands; the new management devoted Friday nights to country-western music, leaving only Saturday nights for polkas. The atrophy is not surprising when one considers that the once-largely Polish neighborhoods have changed. Members of the old Polonia have increasingly relocated to the suburbs, and other ethnic groups have settled into the old downtown areas. Hamtramck, for example, had a population seventy percent Polish in 1950 (Wood 1955, 16). But by 1990 Census figures for that city indicated that of a total population of 18,372, only 7,174 people (34%) claimed "Polish" as their ancestry. Meanwhile, the same census revealed that a large Polish contingent constituted almost thirteen percent of the northern suburb of Sterling Heights. The number of those in Hamtramck who reported Polish as the language spoken in the home in 1990 was only 3,892. Other languages reportedly spoken in Hamtramck homes in 1990 were English, German, Yiddish, Greek, Indic, Italian, French, Spanish, Russian, Arabic, Tagalog, Chinese, and Korean.[1]

Significantly though, in spite of the dispersal of the old Polonia, modern day musicians are working as often as the older generation did. Some play at least three nights a week during the heavy dance season from May through September. But now, instead of finding the greater portion of their work at a neighborhood bar, they play increasingly at large festivals, termed "polka festivals," where thousands of musicians and dancers might gather for a weekend of jam sessions, dancing, and socializing. Such festivals (like the annual Seven Springs Music Festival held in Champion, Ohio) *are not specific to any one ethnic group* or any one style of music; rather the focal point around which every one of these festivals is developed is the polka. This distinction is vital because it points up the importance of the genre itself, an importance that would seem to minimize the issue of ethnic background.

The polka is prominent in the dance repertory of many different nationality groups in the United States, but each group has developed its own style of performing the genre and its own body of polka melodies. Victor Greene's 1992 *A Passion for Polka* demonstrates clearly the polka's importance to the history of several ethnic groups: Scandinavian, Polish, German, Czech, and Slovenian. Charles Keil, in *Polka Happiness* (1992), noted the great diversity of polka styles and grouped them into three "ethnic-geographic streams": Chicano and Papago-Pima of America's Southwest; German, Czech, and Bohemian in the West and Midwest; and Polish and Slovenian in the Midwest and Eastern United States (Keil 1992, 14). A very detailed differentiation among the various styles of the Midwest was offered by the Wisconsin folklorists Richard March and James Leary, who identified Slovenian, Bohemian (or Czech), Dutchman (or German), and Polish streams. Beyond these four they noted extraregional styles, such as Mexican, that have influenced the Midwest, and styles that are represented

---

[1] From "Summary Tape File 3A" of the *1990 Census of Population and Housing*. In 1990 Detroit single-ancestry Polish Americans numbered 31,119 out of 1,027,974 (approximately 3%), and in Chicago 169,753 out of a total population of 2,783,726 (a little more than 6%).

by a relatively smaller following and fewer bands, such as the Finnish polka style.[2] March and Leary characterized the four midwest styles with regard to their primarily urban or rural constituency, instrumentation, and orchestration, including characteristic bass and rhythm patterns. I have briefly summarized the characteristics discussed by Leary and March for Slovenian, German, and Czech styles in the following paragraphs.

Slovenian: This is an urban style that is most clearly represented by the recordings of Frankie Yankovic of Cleveland. The core of the instrumentation is an accordion and banjo.[3] The banjo is used rhythmically, strummed on all four beats of a $\frac{2}{4}$ measure. Extra rhythm instruments may include piano, bass, or drums. A second accordion may be introduced to handle melodic riffs or improvised counterpoint. March (a Slovenian-style accordionist himself) noted also that Slovenian style has been "receptive to outside cultural influences, often incorporating a jazz-style walking bass, wailing sax and two- or four-bar drum breaks" (March 1988, 5).

Bohemian: Also referred to as Czech, this style is primarily rural and is represented by the music of Romy Gosz (1911-66). It features a core of two trumpets, two reeds, tuba, drum, and chording piano. The band is characteristically arranged in rows, members seated behind box-style music stands, playing entirely from written arrangements. Bands vary in quantity of contrapuntal arrangements and in use of vocals.

German: This style, primarily rural, is represented by the music of "Whoopee" John Wilfahrt. It is sometimes referred to as "Dutchman" style after the name of another representative band, Harold Loeffelmacher and His Six Fat Dutchmen. Both German and Bohemian styles are sometimes labeled "old-time" and their repertory includes polkas, waltzes, laendlers, schottisches, and two-steps. Though this style usually incorporates two trumpets and a reed, these are only additions to a minimum core of concertina, tuba, and drums. (The concertina is less dissonant than that used in Polish-style bands.) The tuba bounces along a lively bass line (to which a banjo may be added on the off beats). Percussion includes staccato strokes on a cymbal and frequent use of woodblock and cowbell. Although Leary has noted some eclecticism in both this style and the Czech in those bands trying to survive in an urban setting, March maintains that German style has been the least resistant to change of all four midwest styles since the 1920s.

---

[2] March 1988, 4. Leary and March provide discographies of well-known players and bands representative of each of the four major styles as well as a list of bands that performed in those traditions in and around Wisconsin in the 1980s. See March 1989, and Leary 1988, "Czech- and German-American 'Polka' Music" 101 (July-September 1988), and in *The Folklife of the Upper Midwest*, "Music of Midwest Polka Bands Comes in Four Ethnic Flavors" (summer 1988).

[3] In the 1940s and 50s Slovenian bands used an Alpine diatonic button box. This instrument was replaced variously by a chromatic button box, piano accordion, or cordovox (an electronic accordion). Since a button box revival in the 1970s, some bands have gone back to using the original diatonic boxes.

As March noted, all varieties and combinations of these four (Polish included) can be found in the Midwest. And, while the nomenclature may say something about stylistic origin, region of the United States, and language of sung texts, it is not a clear-cut indication of the nationality of those playing the music. Many examples can be found, for instance, of musicians of German background playing Polish style, and others of Polish background playing Slovenian style. Angeliki Keil (1992), in fact, has documented the dominance of Slovenian style bands in the mostly Polish and German city of Milwaukee. Nevertheless, the stylistic categories and labels are used by the musicians themselves as a shortcut way to refer to the style of a particular band under discussion. The extent to which bands travel and hear one another's styles has made them aware to varying degrees of the other midwest styles. Their awareness has been greatly enhanced with the advent of the polka festival.

The reference to the large music festivals as "polka festivals" reveals a significant phenomenon that has taken place gradually during the last forty or so years: the rise of a pan-ethnic industry that concentrates on the promotion and preservation of the polka band. This industry comprises a loosely associated array of recording companies, radio programs, newspapers, cable television shows, and national and local clubs.

Polka musicians, promoters and fans have supported a number of polka news publications since the late 1950s. In 1989 the United Federation of Polkas counted thirty-nine Polish journals published in the United States, including some of the better known titles, *The Texas Polka News*, *J.R.D.*, *The Entertainment Bits*, *UPB* (United Polka Boosters Magazine), *Polka Files*, and *The Polka News*.[4] A great number of such publications are produced and disseminated only locally (copies are available through subscriptions or, more rarely, can be picked up at a dance), and they vary greatly in their longevity. *Polka Files* was one of the lesser known, but short-lived, high-quality newspapers. Published by Jeff Veverka, it was a monthly paper, averaging ten pages per publication. It included record reviews, local (Sublette, Illinois) club and lounge listings, English translations of Polish lyrics, and news columns. It was really only intended for a small readership in Illinois, meant to inform a small polka music audience about events and personalities in its own neighborhood. For news concerning musicians and promoters beyond the boundaries of Sublette, readers could turn to sources that were more national in scope.

Probably the best known such source is *The Polka News*, founded by Carl Rohwetter in 1970. Published in St. Charles, Michigan, this semi-monthly polka journal serves over four thousand subscribers. The contents of the journal pertain to polkas throughout the United States—band listings in the classifieds include advertisements from an average of twenty-five states in this country as far-flung as Alaska, Connecticut, and Florida, as well as from Ontario, Canada. The largest number of listings reflects the newspaper's midwest orientation: Illinois (with 8), Indiana (6), Michigan (40), Ohio (25), and Wisconsin (10). In addition to band listings, the paper contains photographs accompanying historical sketches of performers

---

[4] Reeves, *Polka News*, 22 November 1989.

and bands, descriptions of recent dance events and picnics, as well as news about marriages, births, band and family reunions, and obituaries. Its editorials provide *The Polka News* reader with a political platform from which various issues of concern to performers, promoters and fans are discussed. (I will return to these issues in chapter 10.)

Polka pages on the internet, in contrast, are apolitical; heavily illustrated, they tend toward a newsy, let's-get-acquainted approach. The term "polka" typed into a search engine results in a multitude of links—web pages devoted to individual bands, single performers, clubs, and promoters. The pages of the Chicagoan Eddie Blazonczyk typify those dedicated to individual bands; they provide a personal profile of Blazonczyk himself, the band's schedule, a newsletter, photographs of the band, and advertisements for recordings. Some sites allow the computer user to listen to excerpts from current compact disc recordings; others advertise videos.

The type of format favored by internet promoters follows the pattern set by *The Polka News*. *Nancy's Place for Polkas*, for instance, is subtitled "the internet's most comprehensive polka site." The page has numerous links to a variety of industry sites; one might spend as much time there as one would reading a newspaper. *Nancy's Place* consists of biographies of various musicians, band histories, advertisements for tours and upcoming festivals, band schedules, notice of radio and television broadcasts, a chat room, and even a store. The paper publications and the internet serve the ethnic dancing community with contact information, and provide a conceptual framework for enjoying the music. In so doing, they maintain a sense of community among dancers, musicians, and promoters.

Recordings and radio provide a major portion of the data that is analyzed and reviewed by journalist and internet readers and writers. In 1990 (November 22), Bob Norgard, a columnist for *The Polka News*, compiled a list of recording companies and distributors of polka music. His list, which omitted smaller firms (such as Zug Records of Detroit), named ninety-three companies in the United States and Ontario, Canada. Following the lucrative lead of Columbia and Victor, and the great variety of their ethnic labels of the 1920s and 30s, these record companies do not limit themselves to any one ethnic minority. Rather, they sell all styles of midwest polkas and categorize them in terms of national background. Typically, companies send out an advertisement of available recordings under such labels as "Polish," "Serbo Croatian," and "German." These recordings, in turn, are purchased and promoted over the airwaves.

In 1989 approximately two hundred commercial FM and AM stations in the United States offered polka music programming. Four of those stations—WNZK, WCAR, WSMA, and WMIC—provided polka music for Detroit-area listeners. Each of these offered between three and twelve hours weekly, for a total of approximately thirty hours. Promoters monitored scheduling so that there was little or no overlap among the various broadcasts in a listening area.

Fluctuating greatly in scheduling and personnel, radio is at best a rather unsteady forum for polka promotion. But it is nevertheless a forum by which bands may advertise their latest work, and fans and musicians alike can listen to vintage as well as modern dance music.

During the period of my investigation, the character of the daily programs in the Detroit listening area varied with the disc jockeys. While one disc jockey planned the entire show in advance, another accepted off-the-air requests. One disc jockey remarked to me that because the title of his program did not specifically indicate a "Polish music" format, he played only seventy or eighty percent Polish music selections, and devoted the remainder of the hour to music recorded by Louis Armstrong, Glenn Miller, and a mixture of non-Polish polka styles. His musical choices were influenced by what he referred to as an "ethnically diverse audience," that drew the support of both German and Slovenian advertisers. He based his selection of programming on the six to ten phone calls and five or six letters he received daily at the station, and followed also his own agenda, which was to broaden his listeners' interests and to educate the younger crowd in a variety of polka styles. Another disc jockey who had been working on radio for five years at the time of our interview, emphasized that the requests made by her listening audience were most influential in her decisions regarding the selections she would play. She kept abreast of the latest music by attending local dances and questioning patrons as to their musical preferences.

Despite the different personal agendas and styles of broadcasting of the individual disc jockeys, all of the polka radio shows in Detroit present a majority of polkas, obereks, and waltzes, along with fewer samples of country, big band, and Cajun music selections. The polkas cover a wide range of styles, but because they broadcast to a primarily Polish-American population, the deejays showcase Polish push and honky styles. Programs are broadcast in English, flavored with Polish phrases. Two thirds of every program are usually given over to polkas, one sixth to waltzes and obereks, and the remainder to a mix of country, big band, and novelty or humorous songs. This last category is in English, while the polkas and waltzes and obereks are sung in Polish or English, or are purely instrumental. Of all the branches of the polka industry, radio is most apt to favor one ethnic group over another. This is because polka radio is largely a local effort and cannot vie with the powerful stations' country, rock or syndicated talk shows. Deejays must stay in touch with their audiences' tastes and preferences. Moreover, they are responsible to attract and maintain advertisers. Ethnic radio, comprised of small locally-run programs, is one of the most informative indicators of the ethnic makeup of an area.

In contrast to local radio, the polka press and the recording companies are more concerned with promoting the polka genre than with catering to any one ethnic group. In this concern, they are joined by another branch of the polka industry—a system of national, regional, and local clubs that provides centralized organization to what would otherwise be a widely dispersed field of ensembles and ensemble styles. Angeliki Keil researched the history of the International Polka Association (IPA), one of the largest polka organizations in the country. She demonstrated that the roots of the IPA, established in 1968, are to be found in an organization founded ten years earlier, the Radio-TV Polka Club of America. The club comprised a group of musicians, radio personalities, and bar owners. It printed *The Polka Guide* that Keil referred to as "an efficient means of bringing together polka professionals

The Establishment of a Polka Industry

and their public" (Keil 1992, 79). She also noted that it was a publication heavily biased toward Polish venues in Chicago, the city in which the Radio-TV Club began. Nevertheless, *The Polka Guide* generated news for an ethnic community that had dispersed throughout the metropolitan area, and it began building a sense of national community among polka dancers and musicians. This sense of the national polka scene, heightened through the efforts of the Radio-TV Club, was enhanced also by touring bands. The business of touring bands, not unknown in either Chicago or Detroit prior to this, picked up momentum in the 1950s and 60s. Keil related the story of one promoter, Ed Zimmerly, who began inviting outside bands to Chicago in 1951. He would typically bring in big names such as the Connecticut Twins to perform with Chicagoans like Marion Lush (ibid., 83). Other promoters followed in the wake of Zimmerly's success.

> The notions of a big polka party, professional networking, and an international cultural organization coalesced: a major step was taken toward the establishment of the IPA. The 1964 schedule of the "International Polka Convention, presented by *The Polka Guide* and the Radio-TV Club, representing the Polka Music Industry," is the prototype of IPA convention souvenir programs [ibid., 84].

A great success, the International Polka Convention moved around in the following years, shifting its headquarters among various Polish-American communities, from a suburb of Buffalo in 1965 to Detroit in 1966, and back to Buffalo in 1967. Finally, in 1968 the Convention gave impetus to the incorporation of the IPA. In 1969 the International Polka Association began staging annual summer polka festivals. In 1990, the festival stretched out over four days; musicians, dancers, disc jockeys, and polka promoters congregated for nightly dances, polka pool parties, awards banquets, beauty pageants, jam sessions, and a polka Mass. The Association hired sixteen or so bands to handle all of the music during the four-day weekend.

The IPA in the Midwest, and its counterparts such as the United States Polka Association (USPA) that was founded in Connecticut, serve the industry in a couple of ways. First, because their leadership consists of officially elected boards, they lend a formalized appearance to the industry. The IPA's charter indicates that it was founded in Chicago in 1986 in order "to promote, maintain, and advocate public interest in polka entertainment; to advocate the mutual interests and create greater cooperation among its members . . . and to encourage and pursue the study of Polish music dancing and traditional folklore" (ibid., 86). *The Polka News* (24 January 1990, 7) stated the aims of the IPA a little differently, noting that the purpose of the organization was to give polka music

> proper recognition of its artists and leaders of the industry. This was further necessitated because of the refusal and failure to recognize the merit of polka music by the established news media and the various music-entertainment associations.

The IPA attempted to generate national recognition of the polka industry with the establishment in 1969 of a Polka Music Hall of Fame and Museum. The Hall of Fame, located in Chicago, serves to honor those people in the polka field who contributed to the advancement of polka music. Angeliki Keil (1992, 87) has described its establishment as "part of the IPA's struggle against the belittlement of polka music from both outside and inside the ethnic community."

Second, in addition to formalizing the polka industry, the clubs tend to influence polka band styles toward standardization. Clubs such as the IPA and the United States Polka Association hold annual award conventions at which they reward excellence in such categories as: favorite band, song, album, male vocalist, female vocalist. Hence the clubs are official arbiters of polka style.

The clubs derive their power through rather large memberships. Polka Music Clubs United, based in Cleveland, in 1990 counted over seventy-five thousand individual and organizational members.[5] The United States Polka Association, which has moved its headquarters from the East to Cleveland, claimed over five hundred members. These clubs in turn include as members a number of smaller organizations in the industry, such as the statewide associations. The Michigan Polka Hall of Fame, for instance, is an affiliate of the International Polka Association. It was created to award those musicians and promoters in Michigan who contributed greatly to the industry, but did not achieve national status. Finally, at the base of the pyramid, the grassroots support of the entire club structure, are the clubs that are the most locally integrated of all the industry's associations: the polka boosters. Organized within city centers or suburbs, the boosters are polka fans who support local bands and raise the funds necessary to bring nationally known performers into their own cities and towns. One can easily spot the boosters at picnics and church festivals around Detroit. They wear fancy uniforms, often in the red and white of the Polish flag. Typically, men wear white trousers and red shirts, while women often dress either in pants and blouse, or blouse and short skirt. For some, costumes include white shoes or knee-high boots, and the blouses and shirts, often decorated with sequins or embroidery, usually sport the booster's logo. The boosters support of the bands consists of a lot of behind-the-scenes work. They arrange band dates, choose performance sites, and advertise events through posters, announcements in church newspapers, and phone calls to radio programs. On the day of the actual event, boosters spend their time on the dance floor. Among them are to be found the best fancy dancers, performing intricate steps and turns with their partners.

One major aim of all polka promoters, at every level of organization, has been to unify the industry, and thus gain a more powerful voice in mass mediated music in the United States. To this end, polka promoters campaigned in the late 1980s in *The Polka News* for a nationally networked radio show.[6] The industry's efforts at gaining a place in the musical

---

[5] Polka Music Clubs United was founded by Carl Rohwetter, who also established *The Polka News*.

[6] On 27 October 1990, Florida-based promoters ran their first national polka radio broadcast over a dozen stations in Pennsylvania, Michigan, Florida, Wisconsin, Minnesota, Wyoming, Kansas, and Utah with future broadcasts planned for Illinois. *Polka News*, 12 December 1990.

mainstream met with great success in 1985 when a polka category was included in the National Grammy Awards for the first time. Its inclusion therein was interpreted a victory by industry promoters. Through strong organization, the industry has been able to lobby for a place on the roster of nationally recognized popular music.

The formal organization of a polka industry coincided with a new awareness of European-heritage ethnicity in the 1960s. Not only did it expand the playing field for Polish-American dance bands, but it provided music makers and promoters a forum from which they could define and contest their place among American popular music styles. Their arguments in favor of polka music are sometimes phrased in terms of a shared European ethnicity, and involve issues of identity. They form the basis for discussion in the following chapter.

10

I'm Not with Him

Music and Identity

In the preceding chapters I have been concerned primarily with musical styles and repertories produced by Polish-American music makers as they seek a balance between their American and Polish communities. In this last chapter, I am shifting my focus to self-representation and the Polish-American identity, especially with regard to the polka, and particularly as discussed in printed material—scholarly and popular. The polka has acquired various meanings both within and outside of the ethnic group. Academics have examined its role in the ethnic community and described it as a sort of dividing line, one that separates upper-crust Polish America from the riffraff. In the polka press the dance has been invoked both as a positive influence on American family life, and as a symbol of the struggle of a European ethnic minority against a powerful anti-European music media.

Scholars who note divisions in the Polish ethnic community (either class-based divisions, or divisions between the old and new polonias) are wont also to note that these divisions find expression in aspects of culture—especially music. Eugene Obidinski, for example, wrote an article pointing out distinctions within the ethnic group according to period of immigration. He introduced his discussion of division within the Polonia with a description and analysis of a conversation he had overheard among faculty and students at Alliance College, a Polish-American institution. The students and teachers, he noted, concurred that an affinity for Polish food, use of an Americanized Polish language, and enjoyment of polka music were not sufficient criteria by which an American might justifiably describe himself as Polish. They believed rather that self-definition as a Polish-American should be the privilege of those who know Polish history and culture, and speak a high form of the Polish language. Obidinski explained the difference between what the ascription "Polish American" means and what, according to the discussants he was quoting, it *should mean* in terms of the sociologist Emile Durkheim's categories of the sacred and the profane:

> In the present discussion, culture is defined as a "way of life" in a rather complete sense, including non-material elements (language and beliefs); material elements (objects and artifacts); and symbolic aspects (flags, rituals, etc.). Any culture includes the "refined" products of human relations—fine music; "great" literature; the "arts" in various forms and "sciences" . . . as well as the commonplace, vulgar, pragmatic aspects of daily existence [Obidinski 1975, 6].

He further explained the sacred (refined) and profane (commonplace) aspects of Polish immigrant culture as products of two separate waves of immigration, divided chronologically by the Second World War, and he classified the polka as a profane element produced by members of the old Polonia.

The analysis proposed by Obidinski, in which the community's cultural division into two sub-groups corresponds to two periods of immigration, finds some support in the performing ensembles of Detroit. A comparison of leadership in the city's polka bands with that of the three secular choirs reveals that the driving force behind the former are descendants of the earlier wave of immigrants, and that the latter are, for the most part, directed by post-World War II immigrants. Moreover, the membership of the polka bands has been formed entirely of members of the old Polonia.

The situation in Detroit, however, also presents exceptions to the analysis. For example, the choir of which I became a member and later interim director, consisted of a membership ninety percent of which was derived from the old Polonia, and included at least one person who had played with a polka band. One can as easily find contradictions to the two-immigration analysis at the national level; the Polish Singers' Alliance of America—a national, umbrella organization for Polish American choral groups is, after all, an organization that was established by nineteenth-century immigrants. Furthermore, Leon Blaszczyk, in his history of the Polish Singers' Alliance of America, noted the mixture of old and new Polonias in the Alliance membership that included "blue collar workers, white collar workers, businessmen, industrialists, professionals, teachers, scholars, and artists of first, second, third, and even fourth generation Polish Americans."[1]

The researcher Charles Emmons, whose work in the Chicago Polonia resulted in a lengthy sociological study, admitted to his readers that he had based many of his initial hypotheses upon the two-immigration analysis, but then uncovered many exceptions to this analysis during the course of his study. He offered as an exemplary exception a description of a post-World War II immigrant and media personality who

> expressed the opinion in a high-level committee meeting of Polonia leaders that the reason there were so many Polish jokes was that they

---

[1] Blaszczyk, "The Polish Singers' Movement in America," *Polish American Studies* 38 (1981): 58.

Music and Identity

> were true. He said that Polonia must police itself, discouraging low, unsophisticated behavior.
>
> When I talked with him earlier he said that he resents having to approve of all Polish things, especially polka parties and picnics. When I mentioned that he seemed to favor Continental Polish culture, he said, "Is there any other kind?" [Emmons 1971, 94].

But, Emmons went on to remark, this same media personality had hosted a radio show devoted to polka music almost a decade prior to his interviewing him. The former polka disc jockey defended his past employment to Emmons, explaining that *his* polka program had "featured an excellent accordion player who has accompanied famous singers and who now travels to state fairs. The show also had a well rehearsed band and dancers" (ibid., 95).

Isolated examples of repertory also contradict the analysis that rests solely on a two-immigration chronological division. Choirs share with the dance bands a traditional Polish repertory of obereks, kujawiaks, krakowiaks, and waltzes. Each ensemble type features an arrangement of folk song particular to its own style—the choir presents folk songs in four-part harmony, in a fashion similar to what can be heard on recordings of the former Polish State ensemble Mazowsze. Li'l Wally Jagiello arranges folk songs for his Chicago-style polka band. In 1990 a group of polka musicians who were partially sponsored by a grant from the New York State Council of the Arts recorded an entire album of Polish folk tunes, all derived from the extensive ethnographies compiled by Oskar Kolberg (*Kolberg Sampler*).

These exceptions do not negate the general idea behind the two-immigration analysis, but do challenge its rigidity and its way of viewing culture as a collection of elements unambiguously situated on a single scale of values. I would like to depart from these analyses, and release the polka from its thus far traditional placement at one end of a single scale of values, and demonstrate instead the dance's significance for community musical and ideological structures. So strongly is the polka linked to such structures, and so universally familiar are these structures to the members of the ethnic group, that Polish-Americans will distance themselves verbally from the polka merely in order to define their position or status within the ethnic group. For example, at one point during my investigation, I interviewed a husband and wife, both descendants of the earlier wave of immigration and both actively involved in the Polish arts clubs of Detroit. The woman readily admitted that she enjoyed polka music and listened to it on the radio on her daily drive home from work. Her husband, however, said that though he did not dislike polkas and listened to them with his wife, he did not want to be stereotyped by me as a typical Polish-American descendant of Polish peasants who listens to polkas. He wished to distance himself from the negative characterization of the genre.

The polka's negative connotations are known and reinforced outside of the ethnic group as well, and can cause Polish-Americans to dissociate from the genre when they are living or working beyond the boundaries of the ethnic community. As an example, a young polka musician described to me the seemingly contradictory behavior of his Polish-American coworker. On weekends, while playing polka engagements, the musician regularly noted the presence of his work acquaintance, "out on the dance floor making a fool of himself." When both men were back at work on Monday morning, however, the musician would hear the other mocking polka musicians and audiences. Like the Polish arts club members, the young worker, though he enjoyed dancing polkas, realized a disadvantage in admitting his association with the genre while among his coworkers.

From what does the polka derive its lowbrow status? The polka, when part of a dance band repertory, has a couple of strikes against it, one being its origin and the other its failure to measure up aesthetically within a traditional Western European value system. One evening I attended a rehearsal of one of the choral groups in Detroit. After being introduced to the group, I explained that I was interested in researching Polish-American music, and would be studying choral groups, music societies, folk dance ensembles, and polka bands. During a rehearsal break, a choir member who had emigrated from Poland following the Second World War took me aside and advised me against researching the polka, as it is not Polish. She urged me instead to concentrate on Polish regional music styles and music by Polish composers.

The sociologist Charles Emmons noted that the polka is regarded by the post-World War II immigrants as a product of a less sophisticated, earlier immigrant culture:

> The most recent immigrants especially are likely to point out that Old Polonians are not really Polish anymore. But ironically, although they have lost their Polishness they have not lost their peasant status, we are told; they're all peasants just like their peasant ancestors who immigrated in the great wave from the 1880s through the 1920s. New immigrants find parallels between working-class south-side-of-Chicago culture and Polish peasant culture and contrast it with the life styles and sophistication of present-day urban Poland. . . . One first generation student, for example, told me that all these peasants seem to be interested in is television, football, and WLS, a Chicago rock radio station. A much more frequent music-cultural association is made between the old Polish community and polkas. "Polkas are a cheap way of being Polish" [Emmons, 68-69].

Emmons's last statement is similar to one that I heard made by a Detroit church musician and descendant of the second wave who, frustrated by his congregation's seeming indifference to art music, ascribed their preference to their peasant background.

Not only did the polka not originate in Poland, it has little relevance in the lives of Poles there (see chapter 8). The genre is heard only infrequently in Poland; one is much more likely to hear a tango than a polka on Polish radio. Evidence of the relative insignificance of the polka as a popular music style for new immigrants is the success of a European-style discotheque that opened in Hamtramck in 1990. It catered to an all-Polish clientele in their twenties and thirties, and featured only current European rock recordings.

The comment made by the choir member to me when I began my research also speaks to an aesthetic judgment that is based upon the sacred cultural values of the dominant society. In a system of aesthetics and music styles rooted in Western European art music traditions, the polka does not meet the legitimizing requirements of good music. An illustration of the polka's lack in this regard can be found in a collection of letters of Jan Kreutz, a news reporter who immigrated to the United States in the 1940s and worked on Detroit Polish radio for approximately twenty years. In a letter that Kreutz had composed in response to a woman who was prominent in the city's Polish-American arts clubs, he defended his choice of musical programming. She had evidently made the statement regarding a new Polish program, that "at last, good Polish music comes to Detroit." He responded with the claim that he had already brought good music to Detroit, and that he had devoted "only a minimal part" of his program to polkas, the rest of his musical selections included examples of Polish classical music and the most recent Polish popular music.[2]

The polka's ignoble ancestry also made it a target of Edward Piszek, the owner of Mrs. Paul's Kitchens. Piszek initiated a half-million dollar advertising campaign in 1972 through which he intended to laud Polish history and to render the polak joke a thing of the past. In a statement that is all the more interesting as it was not part of a discussion on musical styles per se, Piszek asserted "If I thought the polka was the only thing that Poland had contributed in one-thousand years, I too would cry 'Shame!' But let's not forget Chopin."[3] Piszek's interviewer, Michael Durham, further paraphrased Piszek's opinion that the polka, "a vigorous but monotonous musical form . . . contributed to the Poles' low esteem in this country" (ibid., 70). Musicians who emigrated from Poland in the 1970s and 80s and who ascribe to the polka a lowbrow status fault the genre for its similarities to other popular music styles in its harmonic simplicity, repetitious melodies, and especially for its "inane" texts that they charge do not carry political comment.

Church and secular choral music, in comparison, stand up well under the scrutiny of those who fault the polka for its origins and musical simplicity. The choral repertory demonstrates a relative lack of contextual ambiguity and it carries a validity acquired through its integration in other, already legitimized musical styles and genres. Its musical ties to Poland are not questioned. In fact, when a Polish-American chorus is engaged to sing at religious services during the holidays, a particular parish might advertise in advance their participation, billing it as "a true re-creation" of a Polish Christmas or Easter liturgy. The choirs' association with a European and especially Polish heritage allows them to represent the

---

[2] Jan Marian Kreutz letter, 6 June 1972.

[3] Durham, "One-Man Crusade Against the Polish Joke," *Life*, 14 January 1972, 70-71.

Detroit Polonia at official presentations and celebrations of the community's national origins, as well as at receptions honoring visiting religious and government officials from Poland and the United States.

The ethnomusicologist Charles Keil developed a class-based analysis of the evident disparity between ethnic ascription and the disagreements over musical representation among those so ascribed. His 1979 publication argued that Polish-Americans, confronted by the dominant society's stereotypes, reacted varyingly, and that the variance could be explained in terms of class. He noted that the polka is a source of embarrassment to the "relatively small Polish-American middle class [that] quests desperately for higher status, better image and something called heritage." His use of the term "class" revolves most significantly around the issues of upward mobility, and the aspirations of Polish-American professionals to a higher social status. Confronted by a larger Polish-American working class, Keil argued, members of the Polish-American middle class are ". . . from the same rural poverty as everyone else but are now 'upholding their heritage' and lording it over their supposed inferiors" (Keil 1979, 37). He offered a further polarized description of the ethnic group: "Conducting research on the polka the past few years has convinced me that there are two clear and distinct Polish-American communities: the pretending Polonia of the polonaise and the real Polonia of the polka" (ibid.).

Keil did not introduce the factor of two periods of immigration into his argument and he chose not to comment on the impact recent waves of immigration have had on the community's musical life. His aim was to convince academics that the study of Polish-American polka music has been neglected, not for reasons of its insignificance to the lives of that group's members, but because of discriminatory practices caused by "strict class division within the ethnic group and within the University community" (ibid., 43). To this end, his polarized description of the community certainly finds justification. Keil's description of the typical Polish-American polka fan as one who is real, was, in fact, echoed by a Polish-American woman in Detroit, who explained to me that polkas could be heard in the city's "not-so-haughty" bars. And it finds sympathy as well in a published statement made by a nationally known polka bandleader, Frankie Yankovic. Yankovic, a Slovenian-American accordion player, described his role as a polka musician in the following terms: "I like to think of myself as the blue-collar worker's musician. I'm proud of that. After all, this country was built on the blood and sweat and guts of the blue-collar man" (March 1985, 6). Keil's use of class is an especially strong antidote to the two-immigration analysis because it allows the issue of individual motivation and the quest for status to enter into the argument.[4]

---

[4] For a discussion of class-based marketing of music, see McLucas 2001. She (p. 150) remarks that "The importance of an individual's socio-economic class in determining musical taste, creativity, and consumption is probably less now than it was earlier in the century, but it continues to be a factor, if at times, an unseen one, even in current cultural decisions. Paying attention to the history of its development in America, as well as looking for its traces in contemporary culture, can illuminate sides of musical choices that might go otherwise unnoticed."

Another sort of motivation—quite different from one involving social class—impels the polka press to invoke the dance as a symbol in defending the rights of European heritage minorities. Editorials in the *Polka News* have described the polka as the most characteristic music of white European ethnic groups and have set the polka in opposition to rock music. Nick Jablonski, a columnist for the *Polka News*, wrote (27 February 1991):

> Welcome to the European world of Polkas. The last column brought a bevy of responses to the question of "what can be done to increase the public's awareness of polka music?" . . . When taking it upon ourselves to insure the growth and development of European cultural music, all the answers become quite obvious. What's it all going to take? It's very simple—each and everyone of us working together.

Rock, on the other hand, is frequently characterized as the representative music of African-Americans, and the music that is most favored by the United States popular music industry. Although highly visible among European-heritage ethnic groups, the polka is not part of the mainstream recording or performing industry in the United States. This non-mainstream status allows the European ethnic to portray the polka as a sort of musical underdog, or as the stylistic choice *of* the underdogs. By labeling rock music "the music of African-Americans" the European ethnic minority discovers in the music industry an area in which the African-American minority is shown favor by "the establishment."

> Polka music is very popular throughout America with no help from Hollywood movies or network-controlled television which helps to determine what people will follow. . . . Can you agree that rock and roll is not sung in the English language? It is done in an African brogue . . . P.M.C.U. (Polka Music Clubs United) Pres. Steve Holwczak undoubtedly holds Polka as the most modern because it is sung in the most English accent and it is in fact a music of masses of people who choose it all on their own accord without network pressure or brainwashing. An anti-European establishment has never allowed polka music to compete and even so . . . it has millions of followers [ibid., 24 January 1990].

Articles and letters like this one were written in response to what columnists in the *Polka News* viewed as the establishment's public disparagement of the polka. A Coors Beer television commercial, aired in June 1989, depicted a barroom filled with young people who quickly abandoned the bar when one of the patrons played a polka on the jukebox. This commercial angered polka promoters and resulted in published protests, a nationally announced boycott of Coors Beer, and finally, a published report of an official apology made by Coors to Polka Music Clubs United.[5] The Coors apology was acknowledged as a small victory

---

[5] *Polka News*, 14 June 1989, 28 June 1989, 12 July 1989.

for the polka industry, as is made clear in the following letter that appeared in the *Polka News* (12 July 1989):

> The controllers of American airwaves have directed African origin music at young people for many years, but inject enough English pronunciation to call it American music.... It was good solid European power that made them see the error of their ways. Now, when the made in American (*sic*) Polka-Waltz music is compared to the establishment's American music, the discrimination they have been practicing for many years will have to cease, or the *Peoples Airwaves* must become known as *Special Interest Airwaves*.... If it is to be the Peoples Air Waves, there must be some "Human Rights" involved to balance with money and power.

Though this letter is couched in terms of human rights, it may be argued that the type of racist rhetoric used to fight Coors was as much motivated by economic concerns and the desire to maintain and advance the polka within the popular music industry as it was to defend the rights of a European minority. Musicians with whom I spoke in Detroit, though they were not pleased with the Coors commercial, felt that polka promoters had taken unfair advantage of the situation and had overstated the issue of discrimination in order to reap a victim's rewards. Whether the Coors commercial more adversely affected the industry's business or a music community's pride is debatable. The rhetoric employed, however, implied that the media had been guilty of an un-American stance.

The racist slant of the rhetoric used in Coors-related articles can be viewed against a backdrop of history of competition between African-American and white working class minorities in midwest urban areas. Thaddeus Radzilowski, in his 1974 article "The View from a Polish Ghetto: Some Observations on the First One Hundred Years in Detroit" (p. 134), briefly describes confrontations between Polish-Americans and African-Americans as "deeply rooted in economic and political issues." Sociologists have documented competitive housing and working situations in Chicago and Detroit and have noted in particular cases that these situations were often exacerbated by company management to prevent workers' unionization.[6] Such competition between Polish- and African-American (as well as Latino) groups has also marred relationships between parishes within the church. In an article that appeared in the *Polish Daily News* in 1979, a Detroit resident complained that the Detroit Archdiocese supports a Latin American secretariat and a Black Secretariat, but "There is no Polish Secretariat. The Worship Department does not offer workshops on Polish liturgy. American publishers do not offer printed guidelines nor Polish supplements for their missal booklets (as they do for Spanish)."[7] The articles in the *Polka News* demonstrate

---

[6] See also Parot 1972.

[7] Koscielska, "Ethnic Liturgy: Spanish, Black and Polish," *Polish Daily News,* 29 September 1979.

the European-heritage ethnic groups' transposition of allegations of discrimination from the areas of housing, work and institutionalized religion to that of musical style.

Those polka promoters who follow a pro-European or anti-African-American approach have carefully chosen to emphasize only the elements of polka music that are different from competing musical styles—for instance, the polka's past and present associations with second and third generation European immigrants. Silence about certain aspects of polka music—its similarities to rock music in terms of volume level, a simple I-IV-V harmonic structure, instrumentation, and album cover concepts—is as significant as those elements that are voiced.

Many polka musicians, promoters, and fans with whom I had contact spoke not about issues of class, nor immigration analysis, nor racial stereotyping. Instead, they invoked the polka as a style of music that is oriented to and representative of values ideally shared in the old Polonia—family cohesiveness and community solidarity. Functioning in this role, the polka's ascribed meaning is sharply defined through its comparison to rock music. In this comparison, however, rock is not referred to as the music of African-Americans. It is instead criticized as a promoter of drug use, violence, and the division of the family along generational lines. Again, the *Polka News* columnists and writers of letters to the newspaper's editor have made their views available to the general readership:

> Wholesome music—Polkas, Waltzes, etc.—is *bad business* for the big drug traffickers (the bootleggers and the big pharmaceutical companies), who thrive on *sick* minds; obviously, they prosper much better in an atmosphere of hard rock, rock and roll, acid rock, etc.: To that gang showcasing polka music on such as the Grammy Specials would be like dropping a tossed green vegetable salad into a lake of garbage and they just simply don't want that vast difference showcased! [27 March 1991, 5].

A less flamboyant article in the *Polka News* (13 November 1991) suggested to readers that they mail a plea to network television executives, requesting that the polka receive air time. This article, like the excerpt quoted immediately above, presented the polka as family-oriented music:

> The need for getting polka music into mainstream America has never been more evident. With the high incidence of moral decay in so many aspects of society, polka music has been a constant reminder of the values of family, freedom, respect of fellow man, and love of creator.

The theme of family and community unity is reinforced on polka radio broadcasts, in the polka press, and is evident in comments made by polka musicians. In the course of conversation, for instance, when one musician makes reference to another's ability or training, he will often refer also to that other musician's family members. Thus, when a musician refers to the musical capabilities of Paul Fudalla, a concertina player, he will invariably mention that Paul is one of the Fudalla brothers "They can all play concertina." Or an older musician will explain the talent of the accordionist Johnnie Zelasko Jr., stating "Well, his old man's a great accordionist." The handing down of the polka tradition from one generation to the next is an element of the polka industry acknowledged by both musicians and their audiences.

Musicians refer often to the lack of a generation gap among polka fans. As one musician recalled:

> What's so nice about this field is that there's no generation gap. You get into rock and roll, older people aren't really accepting it—all the youngsters and that's it. You get into slower music and the younger people won't accept it. When you get into polka music, everybody gels. . . . A lot of my good friends are probably fifteen years older than me.[8]

Marv Herzog, a well-known performer who has played polkas for forty-five years, made a similar statement: "When you go to polka festivals you have father, mother, grandparents, children and grandchildren all traveling in the same car together, dancing all day long."[9]

Polka disc jockeys reinforce this concept of family unity in polka music by dedicating birthday and wedding anniversary requests over the air. Polka recordings also celebrate the passing of musical traditions from one generation to the next; a 1990 release by the Versa Js entitled *Three Generations of Polkas* features performances of then three-year-old Ryan Ogrodny and his grandfather Henry Jasiewicz on the violin.

Rock is viewed as damaging to this concept of family that is promoted with the polka, and is criticized further as a danger to society. Because no attempt is made to link the polka to any particular minority or national heritage group, its origins are not an issue in this particular argument. Rather, by emphasizing the generational and familial relationships among audience and band members, the genre's promoters can invoke the polka as a symbol of solidarity, and simultaneously to mark its distinction from rock music.

The varying contextual and stylistic distances between polka and rock music leave the comparison of the two open to differing interpretations. That the similarities and differences between the two are of concern to polka musicians and promoters is demonstrated by articles in the polka press in which writers have attempted to delineate and describe boundaries between their music and other popular genres. Thus, for example, in a guest editorial in the *Polka News*, Brian Juntikka described the polka as "truly American" and not ethnic or European. Its popularity, the author indicated, is older than that of rock, and polka lyrics are happy while

---

[8] Habratowski conversation, 20 September 1989.

[9] *Polka News,* 13 June 1990, 13.

> Country-Western music features lyrics dealing with cheating, divorce, death, unemployment, car crashes, train wrecks and other negative aspects of life in general. . . . Rock and Roll on the other hand features lyrics that relate to everything from crooked politicians to love to drugs to sex to violence and in a few cases to Satanism.[10]

Despite their attempts to distinguish polka music from rock, polka musicians have found it necessary to incorporate certain aspects of rock and country music into their styles. During the course of my study, several musicians alluded to the requisite inclusion of top-40 tunes in their repertory. One musician, whose career has spanned fifty years, criticized a band of younger musicians for employing a concertina, as he believed that its old-fashioned sound barred them from playing modern rock numbers at weddings. In published articles that have appeared in the polka press, musicians have argued in favor of borrowing from rock:

> There is someone out in Polkaland who can adapt polka music (the beat and the style) and convert that music to other forms of music that just might click with more people. The music (polka with a new style/form) could get us on MTV . . . if the vast majority of young people today wanted to get involved in polka music the way it is currently being performed, they would have done so long ago. They are in a sense giving [polka musicians] a message . . . the young polka bands/artists are the ones to achieve the change.[11]

A twenty-two year old musician who submitted a letter to this same newspaper, noted that his friends who at one time reacted with "a negative response to polka music," began to change their opinion of the genre after he introduced them to a song by a Toledo-based band that is arranged "with a twist of modern Top 40 music." He concluded, "because of this new innovative arrangement of a traditional song, these people who used to ridicule, now attend dances and festivals to support it!"[12] Another musician, who has played polka music since the 1940s, was quoted in *Detroit Monthly* magazine explaining that a former member of his ensemble "sort of quit us and we sort of let him go—because he couldn't play rock!"[13]

Thus, with regard to rock music, polka musicians are maintaining the stance toward mainstream popular music they have held since at least the 1920s. They acknowledge the importance of the mainstream musical trends to their audience. The challenge for bands at the end of the century is similar to what it was at its outset: while incorporating instrumentation,

---

[10] Ibid., 27 September 1989.

[11] Ibid., 13 February 1991.

[12] Ibid., 28 November 1990.

[13] Bak, "Afterwords," *Detroit Monthly*, March 1990, 112.

advertising, and album concepts from other popular music styles, the Polish-American dance band has attempted to maintain a sound that the ethnic group will receive as its own.

The representations of the polka I have been outlining in this chapter—an indicator of low-brow status, a promoter of family values, an emblem of the working class, and an emblem of European heritage—illustrate a process in which advocates of various agendas select from a composite of the polka's typical elements, ignoring atypical or exceptional elements, and combine those that are necessary to achieve a particular interpretation of the genre. These four representations are not permanently tied to the polka. As with representations of polkas in the past these are likely to change, while the essence of the music will endure. As early as 1853, when the polka was a popular dance in family parlors and salons, a writer for *Putnam's Magazine* invoked the genre as a symbol of American independence, contrasting it with the minuet which was made to symbolize national subservience.

> For after all, what is that awful difference between the minuet and polka? . . . Was not this boasted minuet the offspring of the false etiquette, the ceremonious stiffness which the little, otherwise the grand monarch introduced into his corrupted court? And does it not become all good Republicans to discountenance a royal abomination, adopted by our ancestors while they were British subjects. . . . And so, coming to the polka as the representative of modern ideas on the subject; is woman to be still a plaything, petted and idolized, indulged and tyrannized over as was said before? . . . Shall she not only be debarred from having her say in politics, from giving her views on government, from discussing the rapidity or inertness of the wheels of our administration; but also be deprived of the right to dictate to (*sic*) the music, to choose a rapid polka in place of an inert, tiresome minuet?[14]

The representations of the polka described here are being perpetuated at present to delineate the boundaries of the Polish-American ethnic group and its subgroups, and to distinguish the music of these groups from surrounding or competing styles. In this study I have focused on the strategic process of boundary negotiation, drawing attention to ways in which Polish-American musicians and their audiences have balanced "Polish" and "American" elements in the creation and performance of their music. The polka has been central to this focus, as it reveals most clearly the dynamics of assimilation on the one hand, and the attempts of musicians to maintain musical separation on the other.

The Polish-American community of Detroit shares a common national heritage, but is not in fact uniform in terms of its members' periods of immigration, educational backgrounds, or political affiliations. This non-uniformity is reflected in the variety of musical

---

[14] "Minuet and Polka," *Putnam's Magazine*, December 1853, 647-48.

styles produced by the community, each style made to represent the Polonia to its own members and to the Detroit Metropolitan area. Musicians have shaped and formed their ensembles—their vehicles of group and self-definition—by aligning themselves first with Poland and then the United States. Choices of repertory and use of language—English or Polish—have been significant in this regard. Through public performances, most overtly through repertory and verbal language, each of the Polonia's ensemble types continually renegotiates the boundaries of its own identity, and thus also that of the community. Each realigns itself in terms of national allegiance and political position and resituates itself in the context of parallel popular, folk, and classical styles. All of the ensembles struggle to maintain a balance between their Polish and American elements as they continue to define the place of the Polish-American community and its subgroups in relation to American society.

Bibliography

Books and Journal Articles

Allen, Debra
    2000   "An Unacknowledged Consensus: Polish American Views about the Oder-Niesse [*sic*] Line during the Truman Administration." *Polish American Studies* 57, no. 1:73-83.

Anderson, Benedict
    1991   *Imagined Communities: Reflections on the Origin and Spread of Nationalism*. Rev. ed. New York: Verso.

Barth, Frederick
    1981   *Process and Form in Social Life: Selected Essays of Frederick Barth*. London: Routledge and Kegan Paul.

Blaszczyk, Leon
    1981   "The Polish Singers' Movement in America." *Polish American Studies* 38:50-62.

Blejwas, Stanislaus A.
    1981   "Old and New Polonias: Tensions within an Ethnic Community." *Polish American Studies* 38, no. 2:55-83.
    1999   "'To Sing Out the Future of Our Beloved Fatherland': Choral Nationalism and the Polish Singers Alliance of America, 1889-1939." *Journal of American Ethnic History* 19, no. 1:3-25.

Bodnar, John, Roger Simon, and Michael P. Weber
    1962   *Lives of Their Own: Blacks, Italians, and Poles in Pittsburgh, 1900-1960*. Urbana: University of Illinois Press.

Bohlman, Philip
    1980   "Music in the Culture of German Americans in North Central Wisconsin." Master's thesis, University of Illinois, Urbana.

Brown, T. Alliston
    1964   *A History of the New York Stage from the First Performance in 1732 to 1901.* 3 vols. New York: Dodd, Mead and Co., 1903. Reissue, New York: Benjamin Blom.

Brozek, Andrzej
    1985   *Polish Americans, 1854-1939.* Trans. Wojciech Worsztynowicz. Warsaw: Interpress Publishers.

Budweil, Władysław, and Jozef Kawecki, eds.
    1990   *Spiewnik stulecia Orchard Lake.* Orchard Lake, Mich.: Orchard Lake Schools.

Bukowczyk, John J.
    1980   "The Immigrant 'Community' Re-examined: Political and Economic Tensions in a Brooklyn Polish Settlement, 1888-1894." *Polish American Studies* 37, no. 2:5-16.
    1987   *And My Children Did Not Know Me: A History of the Polish Americans.* Bloomington: Indiana University Press.

Burzynski, Rev. Michael H.
    1997   "Fr. Justin Figas." *The Rosarium: Monthly Newsletter of the Fr. Justin Knights of Columbus, Council* 5670, spring.

Chorosinski, Jan
    1953   *Melodie Taneczne Powisla.* Kraków: Polskie Wydawnictwo Muzyczne.

Chrobot, Leonard F.
    1978   "The New Ethnicity in America: Toward Cultural and Human Resources." *Indiana History Bulletin* 55, no. 5. Reprint, Orchard Lake, Mich.: St. Mary's College, n.d.

Cohen, Abner
    1974   *Two-Dimensional Man: An Essay on the Anthropology of Power and Symbolism in Complex Society.* Berkeley: University of California Press.

Cohen, Anthony P.
    1985   *The Symbolic Construction of Community.* New York: Tavistock Publications.

Connor, Walker
    1994   *Ethnonationalism: The Quest for Understanding.* Princeton: Princeton University Press.

Cooley, Timothy
    1998   "Authentic Troupes and Inauthentic Tropes: Performance Practice in Gorale Music." *Polish Music Journal* 1, no. 1 (1998), http://www.usc.edu/go/polish music/PMJ.

Cowdery, James R.
    2001   "Blurring the Boundaries of Social and Musical Identities: Border Crossings." *The Garland Encyclopedia of World* Music. Vol. 3: *The United States and Canada.* New York: Garland.

Crease, Robert P.
    1989   "In Praise of the Polka." *Atlantic Monthly*, August 1989, 78-83.

Davies, Norman
    1982   *God's Playground: A History of Poland*. 2 vols. New York: Columbia University Press.
    1984   *Heart of Europe: A Short History of Poland*. Oxford: Clarendon Press.

Davis, Susan
    1978a   "Old-Fashioned Polish Weddings in Utica, New York." *New York Folklore* 4 (summer-winter 1978): 89-102.
    1978b   "Utica's Polka Music Tradition." *New York Folklore* 4:103-24.

[Detroit]
    1990   Directory of the Archdiocese of Detroit: Archdiocese of Detroit and Department of Communications.

Durham, Michael
    1972   "One-Man Crusade Against the Polish Joke." *Life*, 14 January 1972, 70-71.

Emmons, Charles F.
    1971   "Economic and Political Leadership in Chicago's Polonia: Some Sources of Ethnic Persistence and Mobility." Ph.D. diss., University of Illinois at Chicago Circle.

Erdely, Stephen
    1964   "Folksinging of the American Hungarians in Cleveland." *Ethnomusicology* 8:14-27.
    1979   "Ethnic Music in America, An Overview." *Yearbook of the International Folk Music Council* 11:114-37.

Fox, Paul
    1970   *The Poles in America*. New York: George H. Doran Co., 1922. Reprint, New York: Arno Press.

Frith, Simon
    1987   "Towards an Aesthetic of Popular Music." In *Music and Society*, ed. Richard Leppert and Susan McClary, 133-49. Cambridge: University of Cambridge Press.

Goranowski, Helen K.
    1951   "An Analysis of 65 Polish Folk Songs with Conclusions Based on this Analysis Concerning the Relation Between Language Rhythms and Music Rhythms; and Concerning the Evolution and Transplantation of these Songs to America." Master's thesis, Wayne State University, Detroit.

Greene, Victor
    1975   *For God and Country*. Madison: State Historical Society of Wisconsin.
    1976   "Polish American Worker to 1930, the 'Hunky' Image in Transition." *Polish Review* 21, no. 3:63-78.

Greene, Victor—*Continued*
    1992   *A Passion for Polka: Old-Time Ethnic Music in America.* Berkeley: University of California Press.

Greenstone, David J.
    1975   "Ethnicity, Class, and Discontent: The Case of Polish Peasant Immigrants." *Ethnicity* 2, no. 1:1-9.

Gronow, Pekka
    1976   "Recording for the 'Foreign' Series." *JEMF Quarterly* 11, no. 41:15-20.

Gross, Feliks
    1976   "Notes on the Ethnic Revolution and the Polish Immigration in the U.S.A." *Polish Review* 21, no. 3:149-76.

Grzelonski, Bogdan
    1976   *Poles in the United States of America 1776-1865.* Trans. Robert Strybel. Warsaw: Interpress Publishers.

Haiman, Mieczysław
    1939   *Polish Past in America, 1608-1865.* Chicago: Polish Roman Catholic Union Archives and Museum.

Hathaway, Richard, ed.
    1978   *Ethnic Newspapers and Periodicals in Michigan: A Checklist.* Michigan Archival Association.

Hoerder, Dirk, ed.
    1986   *Struggle, A Hard Battle: Essays on Working Class Immigrants.* De Kalb: Northern Illinois University Press.

Hyde, Charles K.
    1980   *Detroit: An Industrial History Guide.* Detroit: Detroit Historical Society.

Ireland, Joseph N. (pseudonym, H.N.D.)
    1860   *Fifty Years of a Play-Goer's Journal; or Annals of the New York Stage, from A.D. 1798 to A.D. 1848.* New York: Samuel French.
    1866-67   *Records of the New York Stage from 1750 to 1860.* 2 vols. New York: T. H. Morrell.

Jabusch, Willard F.
    1980   *A Heritage of Hymns: Melodies from Around the World.* Chicago: World Library Publications.

Jaroszynska-Kirchmann, Anna D.
    2000   "The Polish Post-World War II Diaspora: An Agent for a New Millenium." *Polish American Studies* 57, no. 2:45-66.

Kaplan, Max
    1960   *Leisure in America: A Social Inquiry.* New York: John Wiley and Sons.

Books and Journal Articles

Kardas, Jan Kleeman
    1976   "Acculturation of the Folk Music of a Polish-American Community in Lackawanna, New York." Master's thesis, Brown University.

Katzman, David M.
    1973   *Before the Ghetto: Black Detroit in the Nineteenth Century.* Urbana: University of Illinois Press.

Keil, Charles
    1979   "Class and Ethnicity in Polish America." *Journal of Ethnic Studies* 7 (summer 1979): 37-45.
    1982   "Slovenian Style in Milwaukee." *Folk Music and Modern Sound.* Ed. by William Ferris and Mary L. Hart. Jackson: University Press of Mississippi.
    1985   "People's Music Comparatively: Style and Stereotype, Class and Hegemony." *Dialectical Anthropology* 10:119-30.

_____, Angeliki V. Keil, and Dick Blau
    1992   *Polka Happiness.* Philadelphia: Temple University Press.

Kieniewicz, Stefan
    1969   *The Emancipation of the Polish Peasantry.* Chicago: University of Chicago Press.

Kleeman, Janice Ellen
    1982   "The Origins and Stylistic Development of Polish-American Polka Music." Ph.D. diss., University of California, Berkeley.

Kolberg, Oskar
    1960-61   *Dziela Wszystkie.* 66 vols. Wrocław: Polskie Towarzystwo Ludoznawcze.

Korson, George, ed.
    1949   *Pennsylvania Songs and Legends.* Philadelphia: University of Pennsylvania Press.

Kościelska, Regina
    1984   "Polka Mass: Ethnic Liturgy?" *Pastoral Music,* February-March 1984, 27-29.

Kowalik, Jan
    1978   *The Polish Press in America.* San Francisco: R and E Research Associates.

Krzyzanowski, Julian, ed.
    1965   *Słownik Folkloru Polskiego.* Warsaw: Wiedza Powszechna.

Lange, Roderyk
    1974   "On Differences Between the Rural and the Urban: Traditional Polish Peasant Dancing." *Yearbook of the International Folk Music Council* 6:44-51.

Leary, James P.
    1988   "Czech- and German-American 'Polka' Music." *Journal of American Folklore* 101 (July-September 1988): 339-45.

Leggett, John C.
  1968   *Class, Race and Labor: Working Class Consciousness in Detroit*. New York: Oxford University Press.

Levy, Mark
  2000   "Central European Music." *The Garland Encyclopedia of World Music*. Vol. 3: *The United States and Canada*. New York: Garland.

Library of Congress
  1909-14   *Catalogue of Copyright Entries*. Washington: Library of Congress.

Lopata, Helen Znaniecki
  1976   "Polish Immigration to the U.S." *Polish Review* 21, no. 4:85-109.

Lornell, Kip, and Anne K. Rasmussen
  1997   *Musics of Multicultural America: A Study of Twelve Musical Communities*. New York: Schirmer Books.

Loza, Steven J.
  1993   *Barrio Rhythms: Mexican American Music in Los Angeles*. Urbana: University of Illinois Press.

Lutnia Singing Society
  1978   December Newsletter. In the Hamtramck Public Library Clippings File, "Societies, Polish."

Mackun, Stanley
  1964   "The Changing Patterns of Polish Settlement in the Greater Detroit Area: Geographical Study of the Assimilation of an Ethnic Group." Ph.D. diss., University of Michigan.

March, Richard
  1985   "Slovenian Roots Inspire Two American Polka Styles." *Expressions* 1:5-18.
  1988   "Music of Midwest Polka Bands Comes in Four Ethnic Flavors." *Folk Life of the Upper Midwest* 4:4-5, 7.
  1989   "Slovenian- and Polish-American 'Polka' Music." *Journal of American Folklore* 102:81-88.

Mattfeld, Julius
  1962   *Variety Music Cavalcade*. Englewood, N.J.: Prentice-Hall.

McGill, Raymond D., ed.
  1976   *Notable Names in the American Theatre*. Clifton, N.J.: James T. White and Co.

McLucas, Anne Dhu
  2001   "Music and Class in the United States." *The Garland Encyclopedia of World Music*. Vol. 3: *The United States and Canada*. New York: Garland.

Meier, August, and Elliott Rudwick
  1979   *Black Detroit and the Rise of the UAW*. New York: Oxford University Press.

Books and Journal Articles

Migała, Joseph
    1987   *Polish Radio Broadcasting in the United States.* Trans. and abridged by author from his doctoral dissertation at the University of Warsaw. New York: Columbia University Press.

Milostan, Harry
    1977   *Enduring Poles.* Mt. Clemens, Mich.: MASSPAC Publishing Co.

Moore, Gilbert W.
    1978   *Poverty, Class-Consciousness and Racial Conflict: The Social Basis of Trade Union Politics in the UAW-CIO, 1937-55.* Ann Arbor: University Microfilms International.

Mrotek, Ryszard
    1981   "*Dwie emigracje.*" *Polish American Studies* 38, no. 2:54.

Narroll, Raoul
    1964   "On Ethnic Unit Classification." *Current Anthropology* 5:283-312.

Nettl, Bruno, and Ivo Moravcik
    1955   "Czech and Slovak Songs Collected in Detroit." *Midwest Folklore* 5:37-49.

Niles, Christina
    1978   "The Revival of the Latvian Kokle." *Selected Reports* 3, no. 1:211-39.

Noll, William
    1986   "Peasant Music Ensembles in Poland." Ph.D. diss., University of Washington.

Novak, Michael
    1973   *The Rise of the Unmeltable Ethnics.* New York: Macmillan.

Obidinski, Eugene
    1975   "American Polonia: Sacred and Profane Aspects." *Polish American Studies* 32, no. 1:5-18.

Odell, George C. D.
    1931   *Annals of the New York Stage.* New York: Columbia University Press.

Oestreicher, Richard Jules
    1989   *Solidarity and Fragmentation: Working People and Class Consciousness in Detroit, 1875-1900.* Urbana: University of Illinois Press.

Olszyk, Edmund
    1940   *The Polish Press in America.* Milwaukee: Marquette University Press.

Orzell, Laurence
    1978   "A Minority within a Minority: The Polish National Catholic Church, 1896-1907." *Polish American Studies* 36, no. 1:5-32.

Ostafin, Peter
    1949   "The Polish Peasant in Transition: A Study of Group Integration as a Function of Symbioses and Common Definitions." Ph.D. diss., University of Michigan.

Pan Z Wami
    n.d.   Orchard Lake, Mich.: Polish American Liturgical Center.

Parot, Joseph
    1972   "Ethnic Versus Black Metropolis: The Origins of Polish-Black Housing Tensions in Chicago." *Polish American Studies* 29, no. 1:5-33.
    1975   "The Racial Dilemma in Chicago's Polish Neighborhood, 1920-1970." *Polish American Studies* 32, no. 2:27-37.
    1981   *Polish Catholics in Chicago, 1850-1920: A Religious History*. De Kalb: Northern Illinois University Press.

Pawlowska, Harriet, ed.
    1961   *Merrily We Sing: 105 Polish Folksongs, with an Analysis by Grace Engel*. Detroit: Wayne State University Press.

Peña, Manuel
    1985   *The Texas-Mexican Conjunto: History of a Working-Class Music*. Austin: University of Texas Press.

Piękoszewski, Jan
    1981   *Problemy Polonii Amerykanskiej*. Warsaw: Instytut Wydawniczy Pax.

Polenberg, Richard
    1979   *One Nation Divisible: Class, Race, and Ethnicity in the United States Since 1938*. New York: Viking Press.

Polish American Congress
    1948   *1944-1948: Selected Documents*. Chicago: Polish American Congress.

Polish American Historical Association
    1991   Newsletter, 47 (April 1991): 2.

Porter, James
    1987   "Introduction: The Traditional Music of Europeans in America." *Selected Reports in Ethnomusicology* 3, no. 1:1-23.

Przybylski, Frank, ed.
    1924   *Album tańców Polskich na orkiestre*, no. 3. Chicago: W. H. Sajewski.

Radzialowski, Thaddeus
    1974   "The View from the Polish Ghetto: Some Observations on the First One Hundred Years in Detroit." *Ethnicity* 1:125-50.
    1976   "The Competition for Jobs and Racial Stereotypes: Poles and Blacks in Chicago." *Polish American Studies* 33:5-18.

Rankin, Lois
    1939   "Detroit Nationality Groups." *Michigan History Magazine* 23:129-206.

Books and Journal Articles

Remigia, Sister M., O.S.F.
    1945   "The Polish Immigrant in Detroit to 1914." *Polish American Studies* 2, no. 1:4-12.

Renkiewicz, Frank
    1973   *The Poles in America, 1608-1972*. Dobbs Ferry, N.Y.: Oceana Publications.

Rojek, Chris
    1985   *Capitalism and Leisure Theory*. New York: Tavistock Publications.

Royce, Anya, ed.
    1982   *Ethnic Identity*. Bloomington: Indiana University Press.

Rust, Brian, ed.
    1975   *The American Dance Band Discography, 1917-1942*. 2 vols. New Rochelle, N.Y.: Arlington House.

_____, and Allen G. Debus, eds.
    1973   *The Complete Entertainment Discography from Mid-1890s to 1942*. New Rochelle, N.Y.: Arlington House.

Savaglio, Paula
    1996   "Polka Bands and Choral Groups: The Musical Self-Representation of Polish Americans in Detroit." *Ethnomusicology* 40, no. 1:35-47.
    1997   "Big-Band, Slovenian-American, Rock and Country Music: Cross-Cultural Influences in the Detroit Polonia." *Polish American Studies* 54, no. 2:23-44.

Schünemann, Georg
    1923   *Das Lied der deutschen Kolinisten in Russland*. Munich: Drei Masken Verlag.

Serafino, Frank
    1983   *West of Warsaw*. Hamtramck, Mich.: Avenue Publishing Co.

Siedlecki, Jan, ed.
    1901   *Spiewniczek zawierający pieśni kościelne z melodyami dla użytku wiernych*. Kraków: Gebethner i Wolff.

Silverman, Deborah Anders
    2000   *Polish-American Folklore*. Urbana: University of Illinois Press.

Skendzel, Eduard Adam
    1979   *The Kolasinski Story*. Grand Rapids, Mich.: Littleshield Press.

Slobin, Mark
    1982   *Tenement Songs*. Urbana: University of Illinois Press.
    1984   "Klezmer Music: An American Ethnic Genre." *Yearbook for Traditional Music* 16:34-41.

Spalding, Mary
    1986   "The Irene Olszewski Orchestra: A Connecticut Band." Master's thesis, Wesleyan University.

Spottswood, Richard, ed.
- 1977 "Karol Stoch and Recorded Polish Folk Music from the Podhale Region." *JEMF Quarterly* 13, no. 48:196-204.
- 1982 *Ethnic Recordings in America: A Neglected Heritage*. Washington: Library of Congress, American Folklife Center.
- 1990 *Ethnic Music on Records: A Discography of Ethnic Recordings Produced in the United States, 1893 to 1942*. 7 vols. Urbana: University of Illinois Press.

Stanczyk, Benjamin C., ed.
- 1955 *Poles in Michigan*. Detroit: Poles in Michigan Association.

Symanski, Raymond S.
- 1930 "'Polacks' or 'Poles.'" *Polonian Review*, May 1930, 13.

Thomas, William I., and Florian Znaniecki
- 1958 *The Polish Peasant in Europe and America*. 5 vols. Vols. 1-2, Chicago: University of Chicago Press; vols. 3-5, Boston: Badger Press, 1918-20. Reprint, in 2 vols., Boston: Gorham Press.

Trochimczyk, Maya, ed.
- 2000 "Constructing an 'Authentic' Folk Music of the Polish Tatras." In *After Chopin: Essays in Polish Music*, 243-62. Los Angeles: Friends of Polish Music.

Ubriaco, Robert
- 1994 "Bread and Butter Politics or Foreign Policy Concerns? Class Versus Ethnicity in the Midwestern Polish American Community During the 1946 Congressional Elections." *Polish American Studies* 51, no. 2:5-32.

Vitak, Louis, compiler
- 1927 *V-E Polish Dance Orchestra Collection*, no. 4. Chicago: Vitak-Elsnic Co.

Walser, Robert
- 1992 "The Polka Mass: Music of Postmodern Ethnicity." *American Music* 10, no. 2:183-202.

Waraksa, Henryk KS, and Władysław Budweil
- 1967 *Parafialny Śpiewnik Polonii*. Cincinnati: Ralph Jusko.

[Warsaw]
- n.d. *Wiedza o Polsce*. 5 vols. Warsaw.

Welk, Lawrence, with Bernice McGeehan
- 1971 *Wunnerful, Wunnerful: The Autobiography of Lawrence Welk*. New Jersey: Prentice-Hall.

Wolfe, Charles K.
- 2001 "Two Views of Music, Race, Ethnicity, and Nationhood: Country and Western." *The Garland Encyclopedia of World Music*. Vol. 3: *The United States and Canada*. New York: Garland.

Wood, Arthur Evans
 1955 *Hamtramck Then and Now: A Sociological Study of a Polish-American Community.* New Haven: College and University Press.

Wrazen, Louise
 1991 "Traditional Musical Performance Among Gorale in Canada." *Ethnomusicology* 35, no. 2:172-94.

Wrobel, Paul
 1979 *Our Way.* South Bend: University of Notre Dame Press.

Wylie, Jeanie
 1989 *Poletown: Community Betrayed.* Urbana: University of Illinois Press.

Wytrwal, Joseph A.
 1971 "The Changing Role of the Polish American Congress." *Ethnic Groups in the City.* Ed. Otto Feinstein. Lexington, Mass.: D. C. Heath and Co.

Zuk, Marian, ed.
 1985 *Śpiewnik nowych pieśni kościelnych i piosenek religijnich.* Olsztyn: Warminskie Wydawnictwo Diecezjalne.

Articles in Newspapers and Magazines

"America's Original Party Music." *The Polka News,* 27 September 1989, p. 2.
"Back to the Future, 'A Kolberg Sampler.'" *Polka Files,* August 1990, p. 4.
Bak, Richard. "After Words." *Detroit Monthly* (March 1990): 112.
Billboard Magazine, 11 July 1936, p. 13; 20 May-30 December 1939; 6 January 1940, p. 10; 7 June, 14 June, 27 September 1941 (supplement); 1 January 1944; 6 January, p. 6; 13 January, pp. 5, 12, 14; 4 August 1945, pp. 8, 12; 7 December 1946; 10 January, September 1948; 1 January, 14 May 1949.
"Campaign for Polkas." *The Polka News,* 13 November 1991.
Chicago Tribune, 14 May 1989, p. 11.
"Choir Salutes Solidarity." *Polish Daily News* [?] In the scrapbook of the Polonaise Chorale.
"The Connection." *The Polka News,* 27 February 1991, p. 6.
"Discovering a New Pride in Ethnicity." *The Polish World,* 10 January 1991, p. 11.
"Ethnic Liturgy: Spanish, Black and Polish." *Polish Daily News,* 22 September 1979.
"Glosy Poloneza brzmialy jak dzwony." *Dziennik Polski,* 4 July 1986, p. 11.
"A Goal of Public Broadcasting." *The Polka News,* 8 May 1981, p. 3.
Goldberg, Michael. "Biz Blasts New LP Charts." *Rolling Stone* (11-25 July 1991): 17, 19.
"Grammy Nominees." *The Polka News,* 24 January 1990, p. 1.

"Guido Deiro's Own Story of 'Sharpshooters March.'" *The Polka News*, 24 May 1989, p. 5.
The Hamtramck Citizen, 16 February 1950; 22 March 1951; 22 October 1953; 2 September, 15 March, April 1954; 9 and 30 September 1956; 11 November 1965; "Anniversary Edition," 1972.
Illustrated London News, 23 March 1844, p. 184; 6 April 1844, p. 224; 13 April 1844, p. 234.
"Jak na dyskoteke—to do Hamtramck!" *Swiat Polski*, 27 September 1991, p. 15.
Knickerbocker 24, no. 1 (July 1844): 101.
"Kościol matki boskiej Częstochowskiej—Polska misja pastoralna." *Polish Daily News*, 27 June 1990, p. 13.
"Letters to the Editor." *The Polish World*, 26 April 1991, p. 10.
"A Lively World's Last Days." *Life*, 25 April 1955, pp. 137-45.
"Minuet and Polka." *Putnam's Magazine* (December 1853): 644-49.
"My Name is Cocaine." *Polka News*, 26 July 1989.
"National Polka Month." *Polka News*, 10 January 1990, p. 3.
"Newsy Names." *Polish Daily News*, 25 March 1966.
"On the Eve of ACPC's Convention." *Polish-American Journal*, August 1989, p. 2.
"Oodles Admire Oom-pa-pa." *The Polka News*, 13 June 1990, p. 13.
"Poles Subjected to College Bias, Dean Complains." *Detroit News*, 1 October 1975.
"Polish American Cultural Clubs Set Pace for Polonia." *The Polish World*, 9 August 1991, p. 7.
"'Polish Echoes' Debuts on Airwaves." *Polish Daily News*, 27 June 1990, p. 5.
"Polish Expatriates Torn by Two Dreams." *The New York Times*, 22 August 1989, p. 4.
"Polish Singers in Birthday Concert." *Detroit News*, 16 November 1958.
"Polka Bashing." *The Polka News*, 10 October 1990, p. 6.
"Polka Mass is Lauded: An Open Reply to Regina Kościelska." *Polish Daily News*, 15 November 1975.
"Polka Mass: Worship with a Toe-tapping Beat." *Polka World*, 15 September 1974, p. 19.
"Polka Music Radio National Network." *The Polka News*, 8 August 1990, p. 1.
The Polka News. (Editorials and brief notices), 13 March 1981, p. 3; 14 June, p. 1; 28 June, p. 1; 12 and 26 July; 9 and 23 August; 13 September, pp. 2, 23; 20 December 1989; 24 January, p. 2; 14 and 20 November; 12 December 1990; 13 and 27 February; 27 March; 10 April 1991, p. 1.
"Polkatime America Network Radio." *The Polka News*, 12 December 1990.
"Polonaise Chorale's Ladies Chorus Wins Top Honors." *Polish Daily News*, 31 May 1986.
"Polski Swing." *The Polka News*, 14 February 1990, p. 6.
"'Polskie rozmaitości' WNZK, 690 AM." *Dziennik Polski*, 20 June 1990, p. 1.
"President Moskal Speaks to Polonia." *The Polish World*, 8 March 1991.
"Promote Pride to Combat the Hurt of the Polish Joke." *Polish Daily News*, 25 April 1990.
"Put Aside the Tuba: These Folks Insist Polka Has Panache." *Wall Street Journal*, 28 June 1989, pp. 1, 9.
"Recording Companies and Distributors as of 10/15/90." *The Polka News*, 14 November 1990, p. 2.
"Senator Apologizes to Poles for Calling Them Polacks." *Detroit Free Press*, 10 August 1971.
"Seventy-five Years of Music Lessons." *Polish Daily News*, 20 June 1990, p. 3.
"Solidarity Supported in Chicago." *The Milwaukee Journal*, 4 June 1989, sec. A: pp. 1, 8.
Tech Center News (General Motors), 26/7, 22 October 2001: 1A and 4A.
"United Federation of Polkas." *The Polka News*, 22 November 1989, p. 3; 27 June 1990, p. 20; 13 February 1991.

Variety, 3 May-17 May 1939; 7 May, p. 64; 28 May 1941, p. 87.
"White Eagle's Journal." *The Polka News*, 27 February; 10 April, p. 18; 23 October 1991.
"Why Not?" *The Polka News*, 28 February 1990, p. 12.
"Wladyslaw Budweil is 'Mr. Polish Music.'" *The Polish World*, 10 January 1992.

Programs, Program Supplements
"Fifty Year Anniversary Concert of the Hamtramck Philharmonic Orchestra." 26 November 1972. In Hamtramck Public Library Clippings File, Music.
"Forty-Second International Convention, Polish Singers' Alliance of America, One Hundredth Anniversary Year." Booklet. 25-28 May 1989.
Frankenmuth, Michigan. "Summer Music Fest." August 1990.
"History of Club Filarets." Printed for the Club's Fiftieth Anniversary Grand Ball. 20 April 1985.
"A Polish Celebration: The Macomb Symphony Orchestra." 12 October 1990.
"Polonaise Chorale: Fifth Inaugural Ball." 3 October 1987.
"The Polonaise Chorale Sings Polish Christmas Carols." 1987.
"A Salute to Poland: The Warren Symphony Orchestra." 11 April 1976.

Internet Sources

Polish Singers Alliance of America Districts and Choruses. http://www.ivandv.com/psaa/ChorusList.htm, 1999.
Polka Broadcasts. http://www.polkas.com/radiotv.htm
The Polka News Band Listings. http://www.galaxymall.com/music/polka/bands.html

Discography

Ampol Aires: *Lucky Seven*, Ampol LP5014; *Hit Again*, Ampol LP 5015; *One More Time*, Ampol LP 5031.
Brunon Kryger and his Dance Orchestra. 78 rpm. H1185-A and H1185-B.
Chris and Music. *Music Ambrosia*. Cassette M-1990.
Clare Witkowski and His Orchestra. *Music of a Polish Wedding*. Dyno LP 5005.
The Dynasticks: *Take Another Look*, Ampol LP 5029, Ampol Records, 1740 W. 47th St. Chicago, IL 60609 (1981); *Back on Track*, WRP LP 20100, World Renowned Sounds, Inc., P.O. Box 91906, Cleveland, OH 44101 (1989).
The Dynatones: *Chapter Seven*, WAM LP4050; *Polkas for Children*, Polish Community Center of Buffalo, Inc., 1987.

Echa Ojczyzny. Cassette Polskie Nagranie MUZA CK-005 (SX0204).
Ed Krolikowki and his Orchestra. 78 rpm. Columbia 12194F.
Eddie Zima and His Orchestra. *A Dance Date with Eddie Zima.* LPD598-2.
Frank Wojnarowski and his Orchestra. 78 rpm. DANA 2029-A and 2029-B.
Frankie Yankovic. *Frankie Yankovic Featuring the Great Johnny Pecon.* LP Polka City 378, Polka City, 7625 Bush Lake Rd., Edina, MN 55435.
Greater Detroit Musicians Association. LP 505.
Grupy Szamotulska. *Poznań.* Cassette by CEPELIA, ethnographic museum funding, Poland, 1979.
Jan Stern, vocalist. 78 rpm. 65000 and Col E359.
Jimmy Sturr and his Orchestra. *The Big Band Polka Sound.* Star Records LP 502.
Johnny Prytko. *Long Island Sound Polka.* Rex Records LP 730.
Johnny Sadrack and his Orchestra. Three Cassettes, vol. 1-3. Available 1990 at http://www.polartcenter.com.
Jozef Kallini, tenor and Chor I Orkiestra Polonia. 78 rpm. Polonia 172-A, 172-B.
Lenny Gomulka and the Chicago Push. *From the Polka Capital.* Bel-Aire LP 4064.
Leon Witkowski Orchestra. 78 rpm. 77489-A, 77489-B.
"Li'l" Wally Jagiello: *Wesole piosenki, malego Wladzia,* Jay-Jay LP 1008; *All Big Hits,* Jay-Jay LP 5005, JayJay Record Co., P.O. Box 4155, Normandy Branch, Miami Beach, FL 33141.
Lutnia Singing Society. *The Pride and Spirit of Poland.* LSS1-2.
Makowska Orkiestra. *Polska Zabawa.* Chicago Polkas LP 4101.
Marion Lush. *Beer, Beer, Beer.* Dyno LP 1633.
Mark Ksiazek's Zug Islanders. *Do It!* Zug LP 19891.
Marshall Lackowski. *Polkas for Lovers.* Sound LP 1066.
Paul Drabczyk and his HiFives. *Detroit Goes Polka. Muzyka z Detroit.* Micro MMLP A-101.
Polonaise Chorale. *Christmas Concert.* Cassette, 1985.
Polonia Orchestra. *Plays All New Polish Polkas, Obereks, Mazurs.* LP Polonia Music Company.
Recordings of Ukrainian and Polish Popular Music Made in the United States. New World LP 283.
Six Fat Dutchmen. *Ten Fat Hits.* SPC-3083. Re-release of Dot Records by Pickwick, Pickwick International, Inc., Long Island 1, NY.
The Sounds. *Polka Night Life.* WAM LP W4042, WAM Records, 1441 Oakridge Dr., Ambridge, PA.
Toledo Polkamotion. *Polkas in Motion by TPM.* LeMans LPC 114.
Twenty-five Famous Polka Hits! Twenty-five Great Polka Artists! Vol. 1. IPA, 1969.
Walt Solek and his Orchestra. 78 rpm. H 1194-A and H 1194-B.

Index

Adamczyk, Steve, 107-08
American Council of Polish Cultural Clubs, 39-40, 46
American Polish Cultural Center, 41-42, 51
Art of Poland Associates, 40
Autrey, Gene, 85

Barth, Frederic, 4-6, 12
Basie, Count, 85
Battle of Grunwald, 51, 65
Beer Barrel Polka, 74-76
bilingualism, 41-42, 50-51, 65, 116-17, 126
Billboard, 74-77
Bismarck, Otto von, 14
Blaszczyk, Leon, 132
Blau, Dick, 8
Blazonczyk, Eddie, 109-11, 125
Blejwas, Stanislaus, 8
Bohlman, Philip, 7
Borgess, Caspar, 18-19
Bowery, 74
Budweil, Władysław, 48, 63
Bush, George, 6

Chicago style dance music, 107ff.
Chopin, Frederic, 39, 135
Chopin Singing Society, 43, 51
choral rehearsals, 50ff., 62-63
choral repertory, 52ff., 62, 133, 135
Christmas carols (*koledy*), 40, 50, 59-60, 65
Club Filarets, 46-47, 60, 63, 65
Cohen, Abner, 5

Cohen, Anthony, 6
Concertina Patty, 118
Contino, Dick, 85
Coors Beer, 137-38
country-western music, 111, 126, 141
cultural exchange (Poland and U.S.), 44

Dana (Daniłowski), Walter, 105
Davies, Norman, 21-22
Davis, Susan, 102
Dembinski, Bolesław, 43, 52
Detroit
    churches, 15-19, 25ff., 48
    inter-ethnic relations, 17-20, 38
Detroit Historical Museum, 40
Detroit Symphony Orchestra, 65-66
Dvořák, Antonín, 74

Eastern style dance music, 107-08, 111
Emmons, Charles, 23, 132-34
ethnicity
    ascription by others, 5ff., 13, 42, 131ff.
    dual national loyalties, 48-49
    self-identification, 4ff., 17, 29ff., 42, 48ff., 51, 81ff., 131ff.

Father Justyn's Rosary Hour, 103
Felice, Ernie, 85
Friends of Polish Art, 40-41
Fudalla, Paul, 140

gender roles, 10, 46-47, 58-59, 61, 117-18
General Motors, 6, 40

Goodman, Benny, 85
Gorale, 10
Goranowski, Helen, 7-8
Grabowski, Frank, 43
Great Poland Singing Association, 43, 52
Greene, Victor, 8, 95-96, 103, 122

Halka, 58-59
Hamtramck, 5, 9
    population, 5-6, 122
Hamtramck Accordiana Band, 42
Hamtramck Historical Commission, 40
Hamtramck Municipal Band, 43
Hamtramck Philharmonic Orchestra, 41, 43
Herzog, Marv, 140
honky style dance music, 107-08, 110, 126

immigration
    Austrian (Galicia), 15
    post-World War II, 21-24, 132ff.
    pre-World War II, 14ff., 22-24, 132ff.
    Prussian (Poznania), 14
    Russian (Congress Kingdom), 15
International Polka Association, 126-28
International Polka Convention, 127
Ireland, Joseph, 72, 74

Jagiello, "Li'l Wally," 107-10, 133
Jewish Historical Society of Michigan, 40
Jullien, Louis, 71-72

Katzman, David, 17-18
Kawecki, Bolesław, 58, 60
Keil, Angeliki, 8, 117-18, 124, 126-28
Keil, Charles, 8, 86, 122, 136
Kleeman, Janice, 8, 79, 86, 107
Knickerbocker, 72
Kolasinski, Dominic, 18-19
Koltowicz, Ted, 87-88, 90, 92-93, 97, 99
Kosciuszko Foundation, 44, 48
Krolikowski, Ed, 86-87
Kubinski, Richard, 67
Kulturkampf, 14-15, 43
Kurzawa, Frank, 90-91

labor, 13, 19-20
Langner Sisters, 117-18
Laur folk song and dance ensemble, 43
Leary, James, 122-23
Lira, 43
Lush, Marion, 109-10, 127
Lutnia Singing Society, 46-47, 57ff.

Mackun, Stanley, 17-18
Magnante, Charlie, 85
Mallek, Antoni, 43
March, Richard, 122-24
mariachi music, 79-80, 87
Martha Washington Theater, 43
Mazowsze, 133
Memories of Poland, 66-68
Mexican Marimba Típica Band, 103
Michigan Polka Hall of Fame, 128
Monisuzko, Stanisław, 39-40, 52, 58, 65
multi-ethnic dance bands, 81, 85-89, 100, 103-05, 122

Narroll, Raoul, 4-5
Niblo's Garden, 74
Norgard, Bob, 117, 125
Nowak, Stanley, 13

Obidinski, Eugene, 131-32
Ostafin, Peter, 8

Panuknik, Andrzej, 66
partitioned Poland, 14
Pawlowska, Harriet, 7-8
Peña, Manuel, 7
Penderecki, Krzysztof, 39
Perkovich, Frank, 26-28
Piszek, Edward, 135
Podgorski (Ignacy) publications, 114
Poletown, 6
Polish American Academic Association, 40
Polish American Congress, 5, 40, 49
Polish American Historical Association, 40
Polish Daily (Dziennik Polski), 10
Polish folk dance ensembles, 40, 114
Polish Heritage Society, 40
Polish hymns, 31-38

Index

Polish National Alliance, 5, 16, 39-40, 47, 114
Polish newspapers, 16-17
Polish Roman Catholic Union, 16, 39-40
Polish Singers' Alliance of America, 5, 40, 43ff., 55, 58, 60, 132
    international conventions, 44, 63-65
Polish wedding music, 99-102
Polish Women's Alliance, 40
polka
    class-based analysis, 132ff.
    ethnic-regional styles, 122-25
    nineteenth century, 71ff.
polka band/dance band
    gigs/playing venues, 95, 97-102, 121-22
    instrumentation, 77-80, 87ff., 108ff., 113, 123
    labeling of, 111-13
    musicians' training, 114-16
    repertory, 81ff., 111-15, 121-22, 126, 133-34, 141
polka boosters, 128
Polka Files, 124
Polka Guide, 126-27
polka industry, 121ff.
polka internet, 125
Polka-mania, 74
polka Mass, 25-28, 38
Polka Music Clubs United, 128, 137
Polka Music Hall of Fame, 128
Polka News, 124-25, 127-28, 137-40
polka press, 117, 124-26, 131
Polonaise Chorale, 46-47
Polonia Orchestra, 90-91, 93-94
Poole, Valter, 66
Prinz, Al, 97
Przybylski, Frank, 96
push style dance music, 107-09, 126
Putnam's Magazine, 72, 142

Rachmaninoff, Sergei, 74
radio, 17, 103, 111, 122, 125-26, 128, 134, 138, 141
Radio-TV Polka Club of America, 126-27
recordings
    choral, 47-48
    companies, 77, 125
    foreign language series, 76-79, 125
    polka, 76-80, 111, 116, 125-26, 129, 133, 141
Reeves, Gerald, 117

rock music, 107, 111, 126, 133-34, 137, 139-41
Rodgers, Walter, 90-91
Rohwetter, Carl, 124, 128
Rozmarek, Charles, 49

Sadrack, Johnnie, 88-89, 91
Sajewski publications, 96-97, 99, 114
Shapiro and Bernstein publishers, 74
Shaw, Artie, 85
Siarkowski, Bronisław, 47-48, 52, 66
Siarkowska-Depa, Ewa, 48-49
Silverman, Deborah, 102
Siwiec, Ed, 108, 112-14, 116
Sojka, Al, 87
Solidarity (Trade union), 21-22, 49
Spalding, Mary, 118
Spiewnik, 31
Spottswood, Richard, 10, 76-80
Stokowski, Leopold, 66
Strauss, Richard, 74
Szalankiewicz, Gene, 88
Szymanowska, Maria, 39

Teagarden, Jack, 85
Thomas, William I., 8

United Auto Workers, 13
United Federation of Polkas, 117, 124
United States Polka Association, 127-28

Vitak-Elsnic publications, 96-97, 99, 114

Walser, Robert, 26
Wanda and Stephanie (Pietrzak), 118
Wawel folk dance ensemble, 66
Wayne State University Folklore Archives, 10, 99
Welk, Lawrence, 71, 75-76
Wiejska, 79
Wienclaw, Frank, 95, 98-99
Wienclaw, Syl, 95, 98, 118
Wienclaw, Ted, 86, 98
Witkowski, Bernie, 86-87
Witkowski, Leon, 86
Witkowski (White), Clare, 88-90, 92

Wojnarowski, Frank, 87, 95, 99
Wood, Arthur Evans, 8
Wrobel, Paul, 8

Yankovic, Frank, 85, 136

Zelasko, John, 140
Zielenak, Bill, 97
Zima, Eddie, 107-08
Zimmerly, Ed, 127
Znaniecki, Florian, 8